1945 HOURS: A SPECIAL TIME

"The minutes crept by, but still John Murphy did not fire the signal shot. He glanced at his watch . . . 1944 hours. There was a coincidence about that next minute. What difference would one more minute make? It was January 30, 1945 . . . 1945 hours was indeed a special time.

"At exactly 1945 hours, Lieutenant John Murphy raised his M1 rifle, aimed it at an open window in the nearest enemy barrack, and squeezed the trigger. In the next few seconds, complete pandemonium engulfed the area. Volleys of rifle, BAR, carbine, and Tommygun fire erupted along the dirt road at the rear of the stockade. The bamboo box at the top of the guard tower splintered into large pieces that flew wildly into the air. Five men rushed the fences with wire cutters. The raid on Cabanatuan had begun . . ."

—from HOUR OF REDEMPTION

"An absorbing story, well documented with maps, diagrams, and photos. . . . With remarkable attention to detail, the author describes as fully and accurately as possible the training, organization, uniforms, and equipment."

—*Soldier of Fortune*

"Accurate . . . exciting and touching . . . uses a novelist's approach, rich descriptions of the participants' individual characters, foot soldiers' lingo, and local colors."

—*Lemer Skyline Newspapers*, Chicago

Jim Babb 2014

HOUR OF REDEMPTION

The Heroic WWII Saga
of America's
Most Daring POW Rescue

FORREST BRYANT JOHNSON

WARNER BOOKS

An AOL Time Warner Company

Copyright © 1978, 2002 by Forrest Bryant Johnson
All rights reserved.

Warner Books, Inc., 1271 Avenue of the Americas, New York, NY 10020
Visit our Web site at www.twbookmark.com.

 An AOL Time Warner Company

Printed in the United States of America

First Warner Books Printing: September 2002

10 9 8 7 6 5 4 3 2 1

Library of Congress Cataloging-in-Publication Data

Johnson, F. B.
    Hour of redemption : the heroic WWII saga of America's most daring POW rescue / Forrest Bryant Johnson.
        p. cm.
    Originally published: Hour of redemption : the Ranger raid on Cabanatuan. New York : Manor Books, c1978.
    Includes bibliographical references.
    ISBN 0-446-67937-2
    1. World War, 1939–1945—Campaigns—Philippines—Luzon.   2. World War, 1939–1945—Prisoners and prisons, Japanese.   I. Title.

D767.4 .J64 2002
940.54'25—dc21

2002069131

Text design: Stanley S. Drate/Folio Graphics Co. Inc.
Maps by Sharon Wenda
Cover design by Tom McKeveny
Cover photo: U.S. Army

In 1976, a former Filipino guerrilla commander, Major Juan Pajota, came to America to file for citizenship in the country whose Constitution he had once sworn to defend. He qualified through participation in World War II as a member of the U.S. Army, but citizenship for Filipino veterans had been blocked in federal court. Late in 1977 the case was resolved in favor of the veterans. Major Pajota died a few days before he could see his lifelong dream to become an American fulfilled. To Major Pajota and the other Allied soldiers who risked their lives during the raid on Japanese POW camp Cabanatuan, this book is most gratefully dedicated.

Acknowledgments

I felt very comfortable under the protective wing of my agent, Agnes Birnbaum. She is a professional warrior in her field. Her wonderful sense of humor and compassionate understanding can lift the spirits of any author. Thank you.

My thanks also go to the talented people at Warner Books for breathing new life into this project. I am especially grateful to my editor, Dan Ambrosio, who was quick to grasp the significance of events in the story and guided me with very creative ideas.

HOUR OF
REDEMPTION

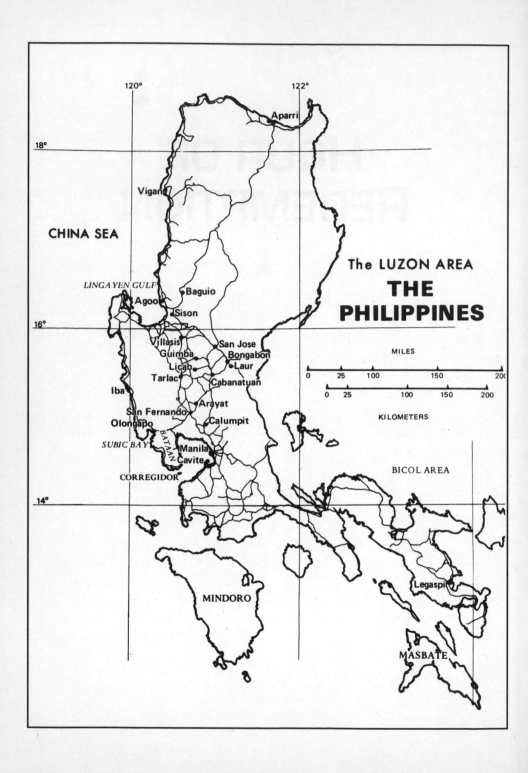

The LUZON AREA
THE PHILIPPINES

CHINA SEA

120°
122°
18°
16°
14°

Aparri

Vigan

LINGAYEN GULF
Agoo
Baguio
Sison
Villasis
Guimba
Licab
Tarlac
San Jose
Bongabon
Laur
Cabanatuan
Iba
Arayat
San Fernando
Calumpit
Olongapo
SUBIC BAY
BATAAN
Manila
Cavite
CORREGIDOR

BICOL AREA

Legaspi

MINDORO

MASBATE

MILES
0   25   100   150   200

0   25   100   150   200
KILOMETERS

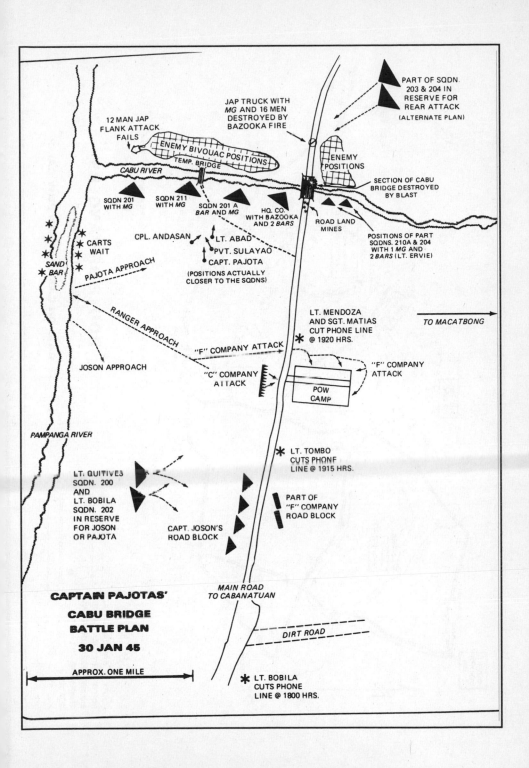

PART OF SQDN. 203 & 204 IN RESERVE FOR REAR ATTACK (ALTERNATE PLAN)

JAP TRUCK WITH MG AND 16 MEN DESTROYED BY BAZOOKA FIRE

12 MAN JAP FLANK ATTACK FAILS

ENEMY BIVOUAC POSITIONS

ENEMY POSITIONS

TEMP. BRIDGE

CABU RIVER

SECTION OF CABU BRIDGE DESTROYED BY BLAST

SQDN 201 WITH MG

SQDN 211 WITH MG

SQDN 201 A BAR AND MG

HQ. CO. WITH BAZOOKA AND 2 BARS

ROAD LAND MINES

POSITIONS OF PART SQDNS. 210A & 204 WITH 1 MG AND 2 BARS (LT. ERVIE)

CARTS WAIT

CPL. ANDASAN

LT. ABAD

PVT. SULAYAO

CAPT. PAJOTA

(POSITIONS ACTUALLY CLOSER TO THE SQDNS)

SAND BAR

PAJOTA APPROACH

RANGER APPROACH

LT. MENDOZA AND SGT. MATIAS CUT PHONE LINE @ 1920 HRS.

TO MACATBONG

JOSON APPROACH

"F" COMPANY ATTACK

"C" COMPANY ATTACK

"F" COMPANY ATTACK

POW CAMP

PAMPANGA RIVER

LT. TOMBO CUTS PHONE LINE @ 1915 HRS.

LT. QUITIVES SQDN. 200 AND LT. BOBILA SQDN. 202 IN RESERVE FOR JOSON OR PAJOTA

PART OF "F" COMPANY ROAD BLOCK

CAPT. JOSON'S ROAD BLOCK

CAPTAIN PAJOTAS'

CABU BRIDGE

BATTLE PLAN

30 JAN 45

MAIN ROAD TO CABANATUAN

DIRT ROAD

APPROX. ONE MILE

LT. BOBILA CUTS PHONE LINE @ 1800 HRS.

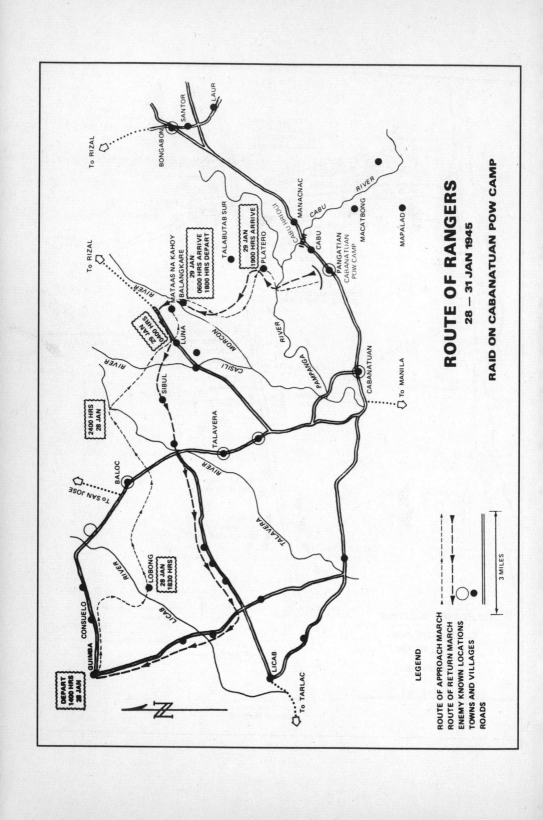

ROUTE OF RANGERS
28 — 31 JAN 1945

RAID ON CABANATUAN POW CAMP

LEGEND

ROUTE OF APPROACH MARCH
ROUTE OF RETURN MARCH
ENEMY KNOWN LOCATIONS
TOWNS AND VILLAGES
ROADS

3 MILES

DEPART
1400 HRS
28 JAN

2400 HRS
28 JAN

28 JAN
0400 HRS

LOBONG
28 JAN
1830 HRS

29 JAN
0600 HRS ARRIVE
1800 HRS DEPART

29 JAN
1900 HRS ARRIVE

To RIZAL
SANTOR
LAUR
BONGABON

MANACNAC
CABU RIVER
CABU
CABU BRIDGE
PANGATIAN
CARANATUAN
POW CAMP
MACATBONG
MAPALAD

TALABUTAB SUR
PLATERO
MATAAS NA KAHOY
BALANGKARE
LUNA
MORCON
PAMPANGA
CASILI
CABANATUAN
To MANILA

To RIZAL
RIVER
SIBUL
TALAVERA
RIVER
TALAVERA

BALOC
To SAN JOSE
RIVER

GUIMBA
CONSUELO
RIVER
LICAB
LICAB
To TARLAC

N

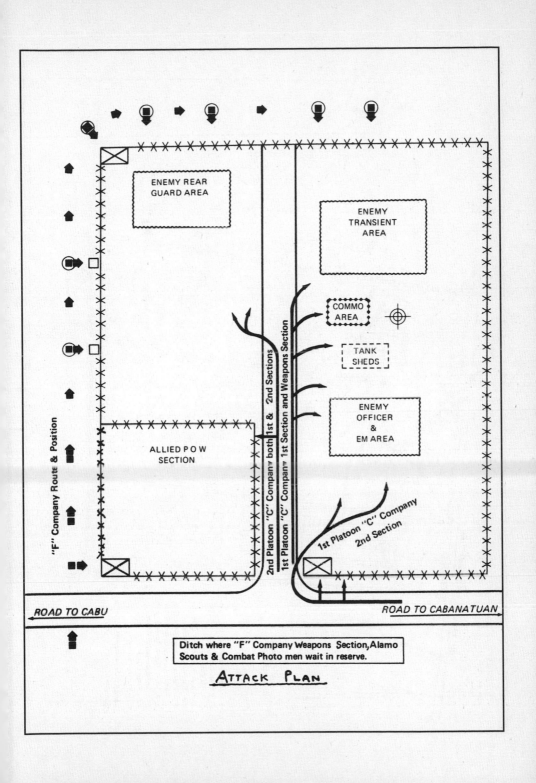

ENEMY REAR
GUARD AREA

ENEMY
TRANSIENT
AREA

COMMO
AREA

TANK
SHEDS

ENEMY
OFFICER
&
EM AREA

ALLIED P O W
SECTION

"F" Company Route & Position

2nd Platoon "C" Company both 1st & 2nd Sections

1st Platoon "C" Company 1st Section and Weapons Section

1st Platoon "C" Company
2nd Section

ROAD TO CABU

ROAD TO CABANATUAN

Ditch where "F" Company Weapons Section, Alamo
Scouts & Combat Photo men wait in reserve.

ATTACK PLAN

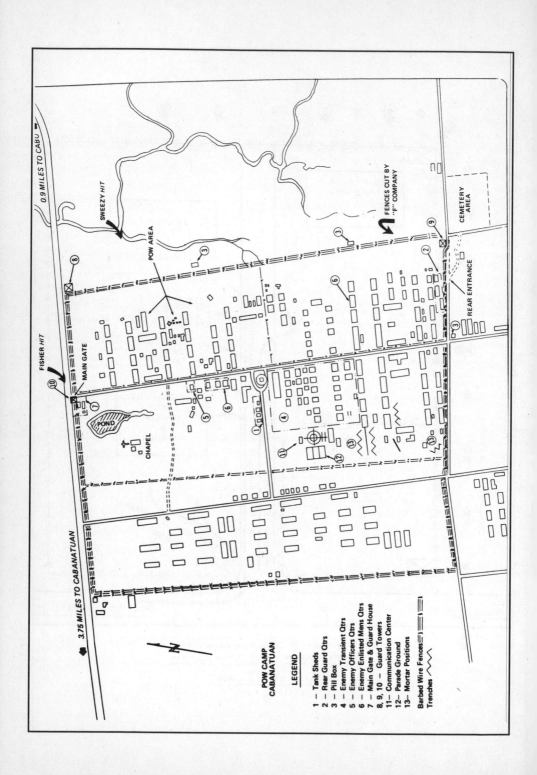

PROLOGUE

My men and I were the victims of shortsightedness at home, of blind trust in the respectability of scheming aggressors. The price of our unpreparedness for World War II was staggering to the imagination.

—General Jonathan M. Wainwright, 1946

BATAAN, THE PHILIPPINES
(April 1942)

Corporal Leonard Hicks of the 12th Quartermaster Transportation Company sweated profusely in the late afternoon sun near the end of the first long column of prisoners forming along the sandy gravel road outside Mariveles. He had heard the rumor that there were a few American generals at the front of his column, but that was a good mile up the road, near the foot of a hill.

On each side of Hicks's column, at about every ten paces, Japanese soldiers stood with bayoneted rifles at the ready. A small way down the road, another group of prisoners was being shoved into forming a second column.

About a hundred yards ahead of Corporal Hicks, several Japanese armed with bamboo poles began to knock the helmets from the heads of those POWs who still had such protection from the sun. After a while, the men with the poles lost interest in the game and moved down the line jabbing at the faces and stomachs of their helpless captives.

In two hours, each POW had been searched more than once for anything of possible value—fountain pens, combs, lighters, matches, rings.

A soldier next to Hicks was shivering from malaria and whispered that if the enemy planned for them to walk up the hill, he would never see the top.

"You'll make it, buddy," Hicks assured him. "You'll make it if I have to carry you!"

The long line finally began to move. Hicks and his fellow prisoner approached the hill that wound its way some 900 feet from the Mariveles beach.

They had climbed about halfway up when the other soldier stumbled, staggered, and fell. Before Hicks could reach for him, a Japanese officer rushed over to the sick man. A samurai sword flashed through the hot air, landing with a dull muffled sound on the fallen American's neck. The body spurted blood at the trunk, jerked once, and the head rolled over with eyes open, frozen in a lifeless stare at the clear sky.

Hicks gasped. He doubled forward, vomit surging from his belly, but was pushed on by the men behind him.

As the center of the first column began to walk farther up the steep hill, a sharp report from a pistol startled Sergeant Abie Abraham shuffling along, mumbling the Twenty-third Psalm under his breath.

The short, muscular Syrian-American was no ordinary soldier. He was an experienced jungle fighter, having served his country in Panama long before receiving orders of assignment in the Philippines. A professional boxer and boxing coach for his unit, Abraham knew the value of being in top physical shape for a march in tropical climates. But like most of the other POWs, he had not eaten for days. Now that the Japanese had taken the Americans' canteens, Abraham knew the frightening truth: Without precious water, the captives had almost no chance of surviving whatever journey the Japanese had in mind.

In a while, Abraham's group mounted the crest of the hill and started down the other side, moving toward Cabcaben. They could see the result of the pistol shots heard earlier. Bodies of prisoners littered the gullies on both sides of the road.

Two men a few yards ahead of Abraham could take no more. They bolted from the road, stumbling down a ravine in a desperate dash for freedom.

An Imperial Army guard quickly raised his rifle and fired.

One escapee pitched forward to the ground. The other turned, arms raised in surrender, and proceeded to climb back to the column. Abraham saw the silly smile on the American's face, like that of a mischievous child caught in a naughty act.

The guard returned the smile, slowly cranking the bolt of his rifle. He took his time for careful aim and squeezed the trigger.

With a scream, the POW dropped his arms and grabbed for his right shoulder. Another guard rushed up and rammed his bayonet through the American's back, withdrawing the blade with a quick jerk only to jab again at the quivering form on the ground.

It was twilight by the time the exhausted prisoners reached Lamao, but there was no indication that they would be allowed to rest. Nor had they been given any water or food during the fifteen-mile trek. With the rough road now running close to Manila Bay, the cool breeze blowing across the waters was a refreshing relief.

No one had been allowed to leave the march. Those with the worst cases of dysentery were in such weakened condition that they began to fall to their knees. Jerked upright by their comrades, these sick men had to be dragged from this point on. Those who couldn't find comrades to help staggered from the road and collapsed nearly unconscious.

In Limay, a distance of several more miles, the Japanese gave out rice balls and salt until their supplies ran out. They also began to separate the American troops from the Filipinos. Rumors ran rampant about the sick soldiers who had fallen out along the last several miles. The rumors were soon confirmed by the spastic sounds of rifle and pistol fire. The Japanese "clean-up squad" was finishing its job.

After a fifteen-minute rest, the POWs were ordered to march again, leaving behind those too exhausted to get to their feet. Groaning and weeping, the terrified men started to crawl along the road in an effort to catch up with their comrades. In a few minutes, bayonets and smashing rifle butts brought an end to their suffering.

All through the night, the prisoners marched on, passing through silent barrios. By dawn, the columns neared Orion. They had marched for twenty-three miles, most of them without water.

A mile south of Orion, another rest was called. But neither food nor medical attention was given. After thirty minutes, they were on the move again.

Suddenly, excited guards began to trot up and down alongside the column, forcing the weary men closer together with bayonets. Private George Dravo, dragging a buddy through four inches of powdery gray road dust, puzzled over the strange look on the guards' faces. As Dravo drew his tall body straighter to peer over the heads of men in front of him, he saw why the Japanese were so worried.

Along both sides of the road, hundreds—perhaps thousands—of Filipinos had gathered. They stood silently as if in prayer, hands lifted, fingers in the familiar "V" sign. By the time Dravo's section was halfway into Orion, shouts sprang from the civilians:

"Victory, Joe! Victory, Joe!"

Private Dravo turned his head to watch the Filipinos, noticing that most of the brown dirty faces of the men, women, and children were streaked with tears. Old women, holding rosaries, murmured prayers while counting the beads.

"God bless America!" Dravo heard one of the Filipinos shout.

"God bless the Filipinos!" Sergeant Abraham called back.

Bottles filled with water sailed through the air, tossed by the chanting crowd into the desperate hands of the POWs. This was followed by a barrage of rice cakes, bananas, papayas, and clothes.

The guards fired a volley of shots. A small girl, standing close to Dravo, toppled in front of him, a red hole at her temple.

In the melee that followed, as guards fired at random, some of the Filipino prisoners quickly slipped on the clothing that had been tossed to them and leaped into the retreating crowd. Within minutes the civilians and the few fortunate Filipino soldiers disappeared among the nipa houses.

In the meanwhile, the second column of POWs formed in the road near Mariveles had been forced to stand in the sun for hours while frustrated guards attempted to count them, then gave up and proceeded to search for bounty. First Lieutenant Merle Mc-Neal Musselman, M.D., stood silent while a guard patted his body with both hands, breathing a sigh of relief when the Japanese finally gave up, moving to another officer in front of the physician.

In the next moment, the guard jerked something from the shirt pocket of the POW and shouted to another guard as he waved the item above his head. Dr. Musselman could see that the treasure was a comb.

The guilty officer was abruptly pulled from the line, trying to explain that he had purchased the comb in Manila, that it wasn't a souvenir from a dead Japanese soldier. His efforts were fruitless. Both guards fired almost simultaneously from the hip; the man fell backward into a ditch.

Musselman closed his eyes, trying to swallow. The column began to move slowly down the road.

As the men reached the top of the hill, they could see corpses, now covered with blue-black flies, lying everywhere. By the time they reached Limay in late afternoon, Musselman's group began to stumble across headless bodies scattered about the road—POWs killed from the column ahead of his.

Beautiful land of love, O land of light,
In thine embrace 'tis rapture to lie.
But, it is glory ever, when thou art wronged
For us, thy sons to suffer and die.

—Jose Palma, The Philippine National Anthem
(from the original English translation)

Some 10,000 years ago, a little more than 7,000 islands developed from an early land bridge between the Pacific Ocean and the South China Sea into a beautiful chain that we now call the Philippines.

This archipelago was inhabited by people known linguistically and racially as Filipinos, who were primarily of Malayo-Polynesian descent. Speaking eighty-seven dialects sprinkled with Chinese, Arabic, and Spanish, the Filipinos have been bound together by a common religion; over 88 percent of them are Catholic. They enjoy a casual lifestyle common to those who live in a year-round climate of warm days and balmy evenings, enjoying a healthful diet of fresh fish and fruit—mangoes, guavas, pineapples, bananas, coconuts.

In 1935, the Filipinos began to move toward independence from the United States, which had seized the islands from a collapsing Spanish empire. Though the terms of independence had been established and the date for its formal effect agreed upon by both parties, U.S. military bases remained in the country. The first president of the Philippine Commonwealth, Manuel L. Quezon, invited an American, General Douglas MacArthur, to help with the building of a Filipino army.

MacArthur was certainly qualified for the job. He understood the value of having a home guard, he knew combat tactics as well as Filipino culture and history. He had hereditary claims (his father, General Arthur MacArthur, had been the Commonwealth's first military governor), and his own ties went back to 1904, when he was stationed there soon after graduating from West Point. His second tour of duty in the Philippines came in the 1920s. A bold and brilliant tactician with dramatic leadership abilities, Douglas MacArthur was a wise choice. Still, with obsolete weaponry and little money, his assignment was not easy.

He began his ten-year program by building a defense force modeled on the Swiss citizen-soldier concept. But as an aggressive and powerful Japan escalated its war with China and Manchuria, it quickly became apparent that he did not have the luxury of ten years.

The "Field Marshal," as the Philippine government referred to him, began demanding heavy support from Washington. By 1938, as his demands continued to be ignored, he resigned his American Army commission. Independently, with only a small contingent of U.S. troops, MacArthur continued to train the Filipinos.

Off-duty, he and his men enjoyed the dark-sand beaches, explored extinct volcanoes and cloud-topped mountains cut by clear streams and crashing waterfalls. They marveled at rice terraces carved from hillsides 3,000 years before, becoming enchanted by the bright hibiscus and bougainvillea, the tree-sized poinsettias and exotic wild orchids, and of course the beautiful women with sparkling dark eyes.

Who would want to destroy such a paradise? Unfortunately for the Filipinos, their strategic location, coupled with the presence of American military bases, would spell their doom.

By February 1941, Japan's aggressive moves began to worry the United States government. General George Marshall ordered an army formed from Filipino reservists, with Douglas MacArthur as its commander, placing the headstrong general back on active duty. The Philippine Army was inducted into the United States

Army, and the combined American-Filipino unit became known as the United States Army Forces in the Far East (USAFFE).

Demands from MacArthur for more troops and equipment rained upon Washington. Startled U.S. citizens, most unaware of the danger from Japan, questioned why National Guard units were leaving for islands over 10,000 miles away . . . islands whose history and importance they knew little about. By September 1941, MacArthur had about 108 light tanks, over 13,000 U.S. servicemen, 20,000 Filipino regulars, and 100,000 raw Filipino reservists. But housing, equipment, vehicles, and roads were poor. Added to the deplorable situation was the fact that none of the units had ever trained together and those eighty-seven dialects produced a tangled mess of misunderstandings.

The Field Marshal complained that his Far Eastern Air Force (FEAF), consisting of thirty-five B-17 Flying Fortresses and seventy-two fighters (mostly Curtiss P40 "Kittyhawks" and a variety of obsolete fighters, including World War I biwinged planes), represented only a third of what he needed to repel a Japanese invasion.

USAFFE also had to abide by Washington's various defense plans for the Philippines. First was "War Plan Orange III," to be superseded by "Rainbow V" in October 1941. Both plans called for the abandonment of Manila and a strategic withdrawal into the Bataan Peninsula and the little island of Corregidor off the tip of Bataan. Thus, access to the valuable Manila Bay could be denied an enemy until the Pacific Fleet at Pearl Harbor, 5,000 miles away, arrived to relieve the "defenders." Rainbow V covered a situation wherein America might be engaged with both Germany and Japan. Germany would be considered the main enemy.

Meanwhile, the Japanese military had agreed on a plan of action—a sudden coordinated attack on Pearl Harbor, the Philippines, and Malaya followed by assaults on Burma and the Dutch East Indies. A bold chain reaction a quarter of the way around the world would be unleashed in a matter of hours on both sides of the International Date Line, December 7–December 8, depending if one was at Pearl Harbor or Manila.

It was 0300 (3:30 A.M.), December 8, in the Philippines when the official War Department message notified units of USAFFE:

"Hostilities have commenced by an air attack on Pearl Harbor and a state of war exists between the United States of America and the Japanese Empire." For those who believed in "War Plan Orange III" or Rainbow V, it was now obvious that no help would be coming from the U.S. Pacific Fleet.

At dawn on Formosa, Japanese pilots waited for a fog to lift before they could launch a massive air attack on the Philippines. Most of their 751 bombers and fighters were to attack American air and naval bases on Luzon, the main target being Clark Field.

Fate or luck more than any other single factor no doubt governed the events, which occurred between dawn and 1:00 P.M. on December 8, 1941 (December 7 in Hawaii). The Japanese, delayed by fog, knew they had lost the element of surprise. The commander of the Far Eastern Air Force, Major General Lewis H. Brereton, requested permission to attack Formosa. He had no desire for his planes to be destroyed on the ground as had occurred in Hawaii a few hours earlier. MacArthur denied permission for the attack, fearing his FEAF lacked adequate photographic data of Japanese airfields on Formosa to assure definite targets. Instead, all of the American planes were ordered into the air to conduct "reconnaissance."

On Formosa the fog began to lift and the Japanese planes took off, heading out over the China Sea toward Luzon. At 11:20 A.M. American planes were ordered back to their bases for refueling. As strange as the circumstances may be, by 11:30 practically the entire Far Eastern Air Force was on the ground while pilots rested.

Anxiety filled the Japanese pilots as they cruised in perfect V formation at 22,000 feet (safely out of U.S. obsolete gun range) a few miles from Clark Field. It was noon and they had not been challenged by a single U.S. fighter. At 12:15 they were over Clark Field and could not believe what sat below them. By the end of the day two-thirds of America's Far East Air Force was completely destroyed. On December 10, the Japanese under the command of General Masaharu Homma began their land invasion of Luzon. By Christmas Day, with USAFFE down to only four P40 fighter aircraft, Manila had been declared an "open city" for the Imperial Army, and General MacArthur's troops were withdrawing to Bataan and Corregidor. On Corregidor, or "the Rock" as it was called, USAFFE had stored a six-month food supply—enough to feed 10,000 men until help arrived. Bataan, a peninsula ideally suited for a long holding action, is scarcely twenty-five miles long and twenty miles wide. Through its center, two mountain ranges were covered with thick forest and jungle. Rugged peaks rise over 4,700 feet only to slope sharply to narrow coastal plains on the China Sea and Manila Bay side.

USAFFE had lines of defense on Bataan, dug in and prepared to delay the Japanese. Yet as well stocked with supplies as Bataan seemed to be, many important items did not exist. There were practically no mosquito nets and very little quinine. Malaria quickly spread as exhausted men easily fell victim to disease. Besides almost 90,000 soldiers on Bataan, USAFFE had some 26,000 civilians to feed. There was only enough food for 100,000 people for thirty days. MacArthur placed everyone on half rations. This allowance was soon to be cut in half again—then again and again until it all was gone. But if Bataan fell, the tadpole-shaped island of Corregidor could still hold for another month until help arrived from America. The American-Filipino forces of USAFFE were confident. America had never deserted her men before in any war.

The main Japanese assault began on Bataan on January 9, 1942, resulting in a staggering defeat for the Imperial Army. And the United States radioed that help was on the way. But by the end of January, USAFFE was forced to withdraw to the southern half of the peninsula. During mid-February a stalemate in the fighting developed, with neither side making substantial progress. Now the USAFFE troops, weakened by hunger and disease, were running dangerously low on ammunition.

General MacArthur, following direct orders from President Roosevelt, evacuated Corregidor with his family and President Quezon and arrived safely in Australia on March 17. There he faced a press conference and announced to the world: "The president of the United States ordered me to break through the Japanese lines and proceed from Corregidor to Australia for the purpose, as I understand it, of organizing the American offensive against Japan, a primary objective of which is the relief of the Philippines. I came through and *I shall return!*"

MacArthur left Lieutenant General Jonathan M. Wainwright on

Corregidor as commander of USAFFE. The army on Bataan was given to Brigadier General Edward P. King, Jr. Answering to King were Major General Albert M. Jones, I Corps commander (Western Front), and Brigadier General George M. Parker, II Corps commander (Eastern Front). But Washington had written off USAFFE as expendable. The remaining 90,000 American and Filipino soldiers on Bataan and Corregidor were doomed.

BATAAN, THE PHILIPPINES
(April 1942)

A realistic, courteous man from Atlanta, General Edward King reminded his troops more of a college professor than a hardened field commander. The tall, mustached officer had never faced combat before the Japanese invasion but was an expert in the use of artillery. Unfortunately, the rag-tag army he commanded in Bataan possessed few artillery pieces. Without this important war equipment, King appeared convinced that his men could not hold even a single major thrust by the enemy.

And while USAFFE waited, the Japanese planned their last major assault around a special date. The birthday of their first emperor, Jimmu, would fall on April 3. This attack must begin then, and all the Americans must surrender by April 29 to honor Emperor Hirohito's birthday. Homma was now months behind schedule. His honor was at stake and the American surrender would make a grand birthday present for their god emperor.

At 0900 (9:00 A.M.) on Good Friday, April 3, 1942, 156 Japanese artillery pieces began the heaviest bombardment of the war on Bataan. Over 100 planes of the Imperial Air Force, now completely unopposed in the sky, dove upon the U.S. trench positions while Japanese tanks clanked down the highway in the II Corps area firing cannon and machine guns at every suspected American position.

On the morning of the fifth, as Easter services were conducted under fire, two Japanese columns ran into the U.S. 21st Division, which put up stubborn resistance. However, by noon the 800 men left in the 21st, finding themselves outflanked, finally broke and retreated in disorder. At 12:15, the 21st Division ceased to exist as a unit.

Up until this time, activity on Jones's I Corps front in the western area had been light. With the first hint of Japanese movement, Jones's infantry counterattacked with orders to charge all the way to Olongapo. They were stopped after proceeding only 500 yards. The U.S. left flank began to disintegrate as starving, sick men collapsed on the field while attempting to charge enemy positions.

Throughout Easter Sunday, bloody hand-to-hand battles developed all along the combat line, which ran north by a few hundred yards. USAFFE counterattacks were using up the last of the ammunition as the Japanese continued to push ahead.

By the close of April 5, the worst blow came: The Japanese finally took Mount Samat, though at a tremendous cost to their infantry. Still, the enemy was now in a position to charge down both sides of the mountain and attack the flanks of the defenders.

Complete catastrophe overtook the Americans by the morning of April 6. The Japanese, using Banzai suicide charges, rushed at U.S. positions occupied by the engineers. These men fought back with pistols, bolos, and entrenching tools until they, too, ceased to exist as a unit.

Colonel Whitford P. Johnson, a slim man in his mid-thirties from Chicago, was in command of one of the Filipino units during the last desperate days of fighting on Bataan.

Johnson surveyed his troops before issuing his command. They were mostly boys in their teens, peering anxiously over the edge of foxholes, dust-caked faces streaked with perspiration.

"Fix bayonets," he shouted.

Before them, stretching for 500 yards, was a smoldering no-man's-land separating the two warring armies. Once a thick, green jungle filled with the heavy scent of flowers, it had become a desertlike place with smoldering tree trunks serving as markers for the hundreds of Japanese, American, and Filipino soldiers whose corpses, twisted into grotesque rigor mortis, lay rotting in the tropical sun. In the distance, Johnson and his troops could hear the faint chattering of machine gun fire and the occasional sharp cracks of rifles.

One of the boys under Johnson's command, seventeen-year-old Private Adriano Olivar, Jr., reached nervously for his long blade, fastening it to the end of his ancient (1903) Springfield rifle.

"Prepare . . . to charge!" Johnson yelled.

The young Filipinos behind him licked cracked, sunburned lips, praying that their American colonel would be nearby as they rushed the enemy. They trusted Pete Johnson implicitly; he was a man to truly admire. He never complained about being hungry, eating his meager portion of rice along with his men when all other food was gone. He never said a word when that small ration was cut in half, to less than a handful a day. He had promised them that other Americans, thousands of them, would be coming soon from the United States to throw the hated enemy into the sea.

"Charge!" Johnson yelled again.

Private Adriano Olivar and twenty of his comrades leaped to their feet and, with rifles held straight out, began to run into the field toward the Japanese positions. Their cries of "Mabuhay!" sounded strong from those eager, parched young throats.

Johnson was maybe twenty yards ahead, waving his .45 automatic pistol. "Come on, men! Come on, let's get 'em!" he exhorted.

But scarcely had the words left him when a tremendous explosion caught up dirt and smoke on his right flank. Japanese artillery was back in action. Explosion after explosion erupted in front of the small band.

Private Olivar began to run faster, trying to ignore his aching muscles and rasping breath. The quick, whirring sound of shells hitting all around Olivar and his fellow soldiers was deafening, raining chunks of earth on the racing young men.

A particularly violent blast near Olivar caused him to twist sideways and stumble. He saw Colonel Johnson crumble to the ground without a sound. Olivar ran past the dead American, leaping over a fallen tree, continuing his charge scarcely aware of his actions.

Then he heard the roar of another shell. He felt his body being lifted, tossed into the air like a bag of rice. He crashed to the ground in an unconscious heap.

When he came to a few moments later, he could see that the shell had torn away one leg at the knee, leaving nothing but crimson shreds of clothing matted with bits of flesh and muscle. Using his bayonet, he managed to slice some material from the uniform on his good leg. He was just beginning to tie a tourniquet when a combat medic materialized next to him.

Hours later, as he was being carried into a battlefield operating room, the half-conscious young Filipino heard an American voice say: "Olivar, Adriano, casualty number 2,017. . . ."

At dusk on April 7, the Japanese had driven the II Corps to a line running from Limay across Bataan, leaving only nine miles of land held by USAFFE.

Around 3:00 P.M. on the eighth, Japanese tanks penetrated the center of the American defense line, cutting through 1,360 men of the II Corps in combat positions. All the rest of the Luzon force were in full retreat down several trails heading for Mariveles.

The two field hospitals on the south slope of Mariveles Mountain received General King's orders late in the day on the eighth. All medical officers and female nurses were to evacuate to Corregidor at once. The medical officers, weak from lack of sleep, some wounded by fragments from Japanese bomb attacks, elected to stay with their patients, who included a number of captured Japanese wounded. The nurses, after bidding tearful goodbyes to their teams, left for Corregidor by small boats at nightfall.

The order for the destruction of coast artillery and all remaining antiaircraft equipment was given at 9:30 P.M. Their crews became foot soldiers moving inland with an assortment of other military personnel: aircraft mechanics, clerks, cooks, men who picked up any weapon they could find en route to fight one last battle against the enemy. The Americans now held only seven miles of land.

On the Rock, Wainwright told General Beebe to try to reach King's headquarters. Wainwright wanted to make certain King followed orders. Under no conditions was he to surrender. But explosions had disrupted the communications lines and Beebe was unable to reach King.

King's headquarters did manage to call Wainwright at 0600 (6:00 A.M.), to advise the commander of USAFFE that General King, feeling he "had no further means of organized resistance," had sent a flag of truce to the Japanese.

General King, dressed in his last clean uniform, surrendered his troops unconditionally at 12:30 P.M. on April 9, 1942.

Second Lieutenant Robert Lapham, along with thirty-seven other men, had volunteered to join their commander, Colonel Thorp, for a daring commando mission. They were going to raid Clark Field and destroy as many of the Imperial Air Force planes as they could before being captured or killed.

With luck and careful deception, the group managed to slip between Japanese positions to begin the attack on April 9. The surrender of Bataan rendered the plan useless. Colonel Thorp left the decision to his commandos. The mission had always been unorthodox, his unit on Bataan no longer existed, and he knew that once they were discovered, the Japanese would show no mercy.

"Well," he began, "which will it be? Do you want to surrender or would you rather disband and take your chances alone?"

The decision was unanimous. They would split up and journey north in the hope of joining up with Filipinos who had reportedly already begun guerrilla action against the enemy.

Captain R. W. Volckman, the 11th Division's intelligence officer, sat in his office on the southwestern side of Bataan and waited for the Japanese to accept his unit's surrender. Several hours earlier, white flags had been strung around the camp's perimeter, as ordered by headquarters. There was nothing left to do but wait and think about the plan he had discussed with his signal officer, Captain Donald D. Blackburn.

Being in the intelligence section, Volckmann had the advantage of information not available to everyone. He knew that guerrillas were already fighting the Japanese in northern Luzon. He had requested permission from his commander to attempt escaping from Bataan to join them.

Soon Japanese infantry approached the camp, pausing momentarily to study the white flags. Then the troops came rushing in, charging wildly. Volckmann and Blackburn took advantage of the chaos to roll into a creek bed where they were hidden from the enemy by trees and vines tangled in heavy brush.

While the Japanese continued their assault, the two officers crawled slowly for a few yards along the creek bank before beginning their dangerous journey through the jungle.

A similar scene was being repeated in the southern part of Bataan as Air Corps First Lieutenant Bernard Anderson made good his escape, beginning an extraordinary odyssey north.

In all, about a hundred Americans would succeed in eluding capture. More than half of these would die by 1945.

Sometimes I think we all died on the march . . .

—Sidney Stewart, *Give Us This Day*

At 10:00 A.M. April 9, 1942, while General King began his negotiations with the Japanese near Cabcaben, Bataan, small skirmishes continued throughout the lower peninsula. But except for occasional cracking rifle shots, the quietness of the morning bore mute testimony to the stories spread by the "bamboo telegraph" among the 26,000 civilians as they began to assemble in family groups along the east road—the same road that had been cluttered with the retreating Luzon force the previous afternoon. The Americans had surrendered.

Six miles north of where General King listened to the unconditional surrender terms of the Japanese, Colonel Imai requested that the radio message he had just received be repeated and stood impatiently next to the operator as the words came clearly again over the field phone. "Kill all prisoners!"

Colonel Imai frowned with bewilderment. He was very familiar with the plans for prisoners under formal surrender.

Major General Yoshikata Kawane, General Homma's transportation staff officer, assigned the personal responsibility for prisoners of war, had informed all key officers of his detailed plans days before and insisted they be strictly adhered to. According to this plan, POWs were to be moved on foot, carrying their own food rations, to the border of Bataan and Pampanga. There, some 200 trucks would transport them to San Fernando where they would board the train to Capas in Tarlac province. Then it was only a seven- to eight-mile march to Camp O'Donnell where they were to be interned.

Imai knew there was to be a field hospital at Balanga, the capital of Bataan, only twenty-eight road miles from Mariveles. There was even to be another field hospital erected at San Fernando and medical aid stations set up every few miles along the entire route. With such elaborate plans for prisoner movement, the "kill" order was not logical.

Colonel Imai turned to his radioman. "Tell them I will not obey the order unless it is in writing from General Homma himself!"

Colonel Imai was correct with his doubts. Homma had not issued the order. A few days before, visiting officers from Tokyo succeeded in convincing several junior staff officers that their war with the Americans was a racial one. The only solution, they proposed, was the extermination of the enemy. As their ideas flashed across the battlefront in Bataan it apparently became the personal decision of each field commander whether the decree had, in fact, originated from General Homma's offices.

Most Japanese officers considered the order a misunderstanding. They began to make their own plans that essentially followed the master plan from Major General Kawane. At least his orders had been approved by Homma in writing.

Soon after this, Imperial Army officers across the peninsula began to receive another piece of disquieting news. Rather than the 20,000 to 25,000 prisoners they had expected, they now learned that the total number might run to more than 70,000 men. Handling that many prisoners could present enormous problems, requiring extraordinary measures they had never anticipated.

Within an hour after the American surrender, the first Japanese troops approached USAFFE Luzon Field Hospital Number 2. The facility sat half a mile from Hospital Number 1 and one mile up the road on the southern slope of Mariveles Mountain. It was located right by the road where thousands of men were beginning their death march.

Private First Class Eugene Evers, a medical corpsman, watched as several army tanks lined up in front of the primitive hospital buildings. The tanks came to a noisy halt, their turrets turning so that each small cannon pointed toward the medical headquarters. But Evers, like the rest of the hospital staff, had little time to worry about what might happen next. Every day, he and his colleagues were watching men die, on the wards as well as on the operating table. If this was the end, he could only pray that it would come quickly for himself and his 4,000 patients.

But the cannons did not fire. To Evers's surprise, a high-ranking Japanese officer climbed out of a tank and, surrounded by several soldiers, approached the American hospital commander. The six-foot-tall frame of Colonel James Duckworth filled the doorway of the small headquarters shack.

The two officers saluted each other.

"I understand that you have Japanese wounded in this hospital, Colonel," the tank commander barked in perfect English.

Colonel Duckworth frowned, and his piercing eyes froze on those of the enemy officer.

"This is correct. We have forty-two Japanese soldiers receiving treatment for wounds here." Duckworth's massive square jaw jutted outward. "You would have received forty-three, but your own bombers killed one only two days ago. They also killed 101 other patients as well!"

"That was a mistake. We announced our apologies by radio for the bombing of Hospital Number 1," the Japanese snapped back.

"And I suppose it was a mistake when your planes bombed our hospital on April 5?"

"Yes . . . a bad mistake."

"And," Colonel Duckworth's attack continued, "I suppose you are also sorry about the bombings of noncombatants here on March 27!"

"Colonel, we are so sorry for all the unfortunate bombings of your hospitals. Now, where are the Japanese soldiers? I wish to see them immediately!"

Colonel Duckworth pointed to a large nipa building surrounded by a high fence some twenty-five yards away where the enemy soldiers were receiving treatment from two American corpsmen. The fence had been erected more to keep vengeful Filipinos out than to contain the enemy.

The Japanese casualties were brought to the USAFFE hospital over a period of weeks, all with massive wounds and too weak to resist the surgeon's attempt to clean the dirt and maggots from damaged flesh. As they began their recovery the soldiers revealed they had been told by superiors that Americans tortured and killed all POWs. They were deeply impressed with their treatment.

After an hour of inspection and interviewing, the Japanese tank commander entered Colonel Duckworth's office and advised, "Your Japanese patients report to me that they were treated well. I have decided to make my camp here to insure that no harm comes to you and your men. Your command will be transported by vehicle to a prisoner of war camp just as soon as practical."

The stub of the amputated leg of Private Adriano Olivar had healed satisfactorily under the care of the American doctors. He sat on the edge of his bed and watched as seven Japanese soldiers walked through his ward at Hospital Number 1 searching for weapons. The enemy soldiers apparently had some sympathy for the fourteen amputees in Olivar's ward, for the Filipinos were not mistreated in any way.

After a few minutes of casual searching, one Japanese noncommissioned officer informed them in Tagalog, "You may stay here if you wish . . . or you may go and join your friends who will march like soldiers to the concentration camp. I understand that some Filipinos have made good their escape along the route by mingling with civilians. Perhaps you can also be lucky."

Olivar stroked his crutch as the Japanese squad left the ward and he began to wonder how far he could walk on one leg. At seventeen, he knew he was perhaps the strongest of all his fellow amputees but that story about mingling with the civilians sounded like a trick to him. Amputees would easily stand out in a crowd of civilians. He tried to explain his concern to his comrades, but to no avail. They were all still soldiers and if the other USAFFE Filipinos were forced to march somewhere, then they too must march with them.

The amputees began to file out the door. As Olivar hobbled down the steps he found himself confronting a Japanese soldier sitting on a large crate, his face wearing a grin, a samurai's sword across his lap. At his feet lay the decapitated body of a Filipino medical corpsman.

Private Olivar moved around the body and continued down the trail to join the other thirteen one-legged men.

By the third day of the march, April 12, the first column of Luzon prisoners entered Pilar after traveling twenty-six miles from Mariveles.

Surely the brutality and callousness displayed by the Japanese troops on Bataan defies comprehension by Western minds. In 1942 Japan was a self-critical country and indifference to sufferings had been deeply entrenched in custom for hundreds of years. In their crowded land, human life was cheap. The millions of uneducated peasants, farmers, laborers, and small businessmen had been thoroughly indoctrinated by a small group of leaders into believing that they were great and all other Orientals should be their slaves. Americans, they believed, were "soft degenerated animals" who deserved nothing but hatred and death before they polluted the entire world with silly democratic ideas.

The Japanese had been forced into the twentieth century with a feeling of inferiority, vanity, and frustration. Naturally, they became obsessed with the idea of eliminating the white man who had interfered with all their plans for so many years. Japanese society thrived on discipline and quick, unquestioning obedience to superiors. The harsh treatment of their own simple people was necessary to control a swelling population faced with many shortages—of raw materials, food, and space. The tough training of the multitudes, beginning at infancy, had always produced individuals who would blindly follow the orders of those few leaders.

For the Japanese soldier, this unquestioning obedience had reached a zenith in the 1930s and 1940s. In the early days of military recruit training, many subordinates were accustomed to being beaten for minor infractions of regulations. If they were lucky, they would be struck only with the hand, bayonet case, or stick.

There was no tradition of mercy or compassion in their medieval "Code of Bushido" (the way of the warrior), only loyalty and self-sacrifice. Revenge was honorable under the code. Thus, the Japanese soldier's process of thinking and action was not the end product of their war with China or the campaign in the Philippines. The ability of the U.S. Luzon force to hold out, delay, and inflict heavy casualties upon the Imperial Army only antagonized the Japanese.

Perhaps the individual Japanese soldier desired to live as much as any human being, but he was trained to believe that if he permitted himself to become captured he would suffer the worst insult possible and disgrace his emperor, country, army, and family. Surrender was a criminal act. If his enemy did not execute or torture him to death, as fully expected, then he might be executed by his own army if recaptured, or even worse, he might be permitted to live in disgrace.

It became, therefore, impossible for the average Japanese soldier to understand the complete surrender of the Americans. In his medieval mind he had the right to reduce the prisoners to any degree he desired.

For the more educated officers (and a small percentage of NCOs), especially those acquainted with Western society and history, frustration set in. Some actually issued orders forbidding cruel treatment of prisoners and were prepared to face ridicule for this compassion. Strangely, there was no general pattern of behavior toward prisoners in Bataan. While some guards clubbed, bayoneted and hacked the prisoners, a few POWs found themselves picked up by military or civilian vehicles and given rides all the way to San Fernando.

The majority of gaunt, red-eyed moving skeletons in the death march approached Balanga with practically all hope for survival gone.

The stench of unburied dead in the fields along with the dust choked and ate away at raw, parched throats. Open wounds, caked with dust, throbbed as gangrene spread rapidly and numb, bleeding feet moved without calculated motivation. Only the strong and determined had made the twenty-eight miles from Mariveles to this capital of Bataan.

Balanga, according to Major General Kawane's plan for the handling of POWs, was to be the first major phase for organization, but the plan was a terrible failure. The Japanese had expected the first column of POWs to arrive in Balanga in one day. After all, twenty-eight road miles was not considered a long march for the average Japanese infantryman.

It normally would not have been a great distance for the average American or Filipino, but these men, wrecked with disease and malnutrition, exhausted and wounded, could not be considered average. What was to have taken one day had taken three.

There was to have been a field hospital at Balanga, and there was none. There were to have been vehicles, two hundred of them, to transport the POWs to San Fernando, yet few could be spared.

Again, an effort was made to separate the Filipinos from the Americans, and the Japanese partially succeeded in this endeavor.

At Balanga, each prisoner was to have been given another ball of rice, salt, and water, but, again, there was not enough rice for all the POWs.

In the morning the march continued north toward Orani, and the road dissolved into a sandy, yellow-white dust. Between the small wood and bamboo homes, whose structure began at the very edge of the trail, Filipinos lined up as before, cheering and shouting, "Victory, Joe!" expecting, perhaps, this zombie army might rise, phoenixlike, and save them.

A few hours before dawn on the sixth day after the surrender, dark figures moved quickly, silently between towering acacia trees, whose drooping branches sheltered the road in Hermosa. As one figure placed an object along the road and disappeared in the darkness, another came forward and did the same—then another and another.

As the first rays of sunlight cut through the old trees, all was still except for the rustle of massive banana leaves caught in the morning breeze. The muffled sounds of hundreds of footsteps in the dust broke the silence as men marched down the road near the city.

When the column of POWs entered Hermosa they were greeted by a strange assortment of containers side by side on the edge of the road—bottles of every shape and variety, rusty tin cans, coconut halves, and dented canteens filled with water.

The first prisoners grabbed for the containers, but were shoved back into formation by guards who kicked the precious rations aside.

The POWs had now walked a total of forty-three miles.

From there the column moved on to Dinalupihan and then crossed the provincial border into Pampanga, where the road narrowed and began to wind toward Lubao and Guagua.

After Guagua, it was Bacolor, and finally the tall smokestacks of the San Fernando sugar mills could be seen in the distance. On the ninth day of the march, what was left of the first column, having traveled eighty-five road miles, came to a halt in the San Fernando railway station. Here, in this industrial town, the Japanese again issued balls of rice, salt, and water while thousands of cheering Filipinos lined the streets chanting their "Victory, Joe!"

After a two-hour wait, the POWs were counted into groups of 100 and crammed into small boxcars for a forty-mile ride to Capas. They were forced to stand rigid because of lack of room in the boxcars, and screams of panic drowned the whimpering cries of others as everyone gasped for air in the darkness and sweltering heat.

When the first trainload of prisoners arrived at Capas, the doors were opened and those who had not suffocated tumbled out. They were hastily reformed for the eight-mile march to their next destination.

Along this last road they discovered the Filipinos had again left cans of water and food, spread neatly on glistening green banana leaves. Here, some of the Japanese guards were more compassionate, allowing the prisoners to pick up what food they could before entering their next area of punishment—Camp O'Donnell.

Private Forrest Dreger, of Milwaukee, walked ahead of Corporal Albert Charmelo in the last group of prisoners to cross the Bataan-Pampanga border and glanced over his shoulder occasionally to be sure his Chicago friend was still in the march. Charmelo had fallen out several times during the last two days but somehow had always mustered enough strength just in time to escape death and continue.

He blinked his dry eyes and tried to carefully rub the dirt from his lids. Not far from the road sat a dusty, dented Red Cross ambulance and next to it, leaning over an American soldier, he thought he saw a young Filipino girl in a nurse uniform. It must be an apparition, something only his partly conscious mind could create, and then his eyes returned to the road.

Third Lieutenant Josefa Hilado had finally caught up with the death march and sadly realized there was little she could do with her small supply of medicines and bandages. A bright, attractive girl of twenty-one, Nurse Hilado had been reassigned from an aid station in Cavite Province to Bataan. The soldier at her feet was dead of heat exhaustion, and she wondered if the same fate or worse had befallen her brother, who was with the Luzon force in Bataan.

Miss Hilado brushed her thick black hair from her face with a fast motion of her right hand and began to walk toward the staggering prisoners.

Another American soldier lay beside the road. She started to kneel next to him, reaching for an arm to check the pulse. She looked up for some unexplained reason just in time to see a guard swing at her with his rifle. She leaped backward. His bayonet ripped the sleeve, narrowly missing her breast.

She stood there, staring coldly into the eyes of the Japanese guard, who shouted at her, then made a short lunge with his bayonet. Again, she leaped backward and the blade missed by inches.

The guard lost his patience and drew his rifle to the rear, preparing to make a long thrust. Suddenly, he was pushed aside by a Japanese NCO, who barked an order at the man and pointed up the road.

Miss Hilado's bravery had obviously impressed the NCO, who now motioned for her to come forward. He knelt and picked up the feet of the unconscious American and nodded to her with a smile. She reacted by slipping her hands under the armpits of the prisoner, and they carried him to the ambulance. Then the NCO bowed sharply from the waist and joined the march, shouting orders, accented by violent arm movement.

Lieutenant Hilado realized at that moment that if she was to be of further help to her country, she must learn to speak the strange language of the enemy. From then on, every spare minute would be devoted to the task of becoming proficient in Japanese. She already spoke several Filipino dialects fluently. It should not be difficult to learn Japanese.

For the next three days, Miss Hilado's ambulance followed the march while she and two other Red Cross workers risked death, giving out food and treating what few wounded they could. And all the time she repeated every Japanese word she heard over and over to herself.

When the last of the POWs reached San Fernando, Miss Hilado received her next orders from the Red Cross. She was to proceed at once to Capas and assist in establishing a Red Cross center there.

Little Adriano Olivar paused for a moment only 300 feet from the main gate of Camp O'Donnell. He dared not place much weight on his crutch for he had bound its cracks several times with fine strips of cloth from his uniform during the last few days. The crutch was now seven inches shorter than its original length when he left the field hospital twelve days ago, and he feared it would not hold together much longer. At first he felt like crying, but then his youthful round face broke with a slight smile of pride.

So it had taken him three or four days longer than the other POWs to reach O'Donnell. He had proven to himself that a one-legged man could be a soldier too. He had survived that eighty-five mile hike from Mariveles to San Fernando, survived the suffocating forty-mile train ride to Capas, survived those last miles to these gates.

Of the fourteen amputees from his ward who had left the hospital on crutches, he was one of six who did survive. The others, with broken crutches, lay dead somewhere along that road in Bataan.

Now he knew he could survive most anything and perhaps

someday would live to study and become a doctor like the American surgeons who had saved his life. It was not an impossible dream for a seventeen-year-old who had already experienced so much.

Olivar clutched at the bulge in his ragged shirt where he had hidden a brown bottle of pills found in the road dust during his journey. He planned to keep the bottle until someone could unlock the mystery of its contents.

But now the gates of the next level of hell stood open for Private Adriano Olivar.

Of the over 72,000 Filipinos and Americans who began the march of death in Bataan, only 52,000 arrived at Camp O'Donnell: 9,200 Americans and about 42,800 Filipinos. Within a few days approximately another 9,000 Filipinos suspected by the Japanese of being members of USAFFE were rounded up in Luzon and forced into the concentration camp.

The exact number will never be known, for during those few hours before the surrender most American records were lost, destroyed, or sent to Corregidor. Records in the Filipino units simply disappeared during the retreat.

The Imperial Army, shocked by the unexpectedly large number of POWs, apparently did not take time to keep records regarding those who began or completed the march. After all, a few thousand dead more or less could make little difference to the race who planned to write all future history books in Asia.

Further complicating the issue was the fact that large numbers of Filipinos were successful in disappearing into the jungle during the surrender or escaped the march with the help of civilians.

Just how many of those 9,000 Filipinos later imprisoned at O'Donnell were actually military is also unknown.

In spite of the lack of Japanese records, the best data available indicate that between 9,000 and 14,000 Filipinos and 2,275 Americans died during those horrible days of the infamous Bataan Death March.

The Filipino never really had a country. All he had was his family and his town mates, whom he treated like relatives, because most usually were distant kin. MacArthur knew the Filipinos would fight ferociously to protect family and barrio. For the Filipinos, there was no longer any question concerning their future course of action. Mere affection for the Americans was not the deciding factor. Nor was freedom, as guaranteed by the Americans and now promised by the Japanese, the driving force.

The vicious and inhuman Japanese treatment of the gentle Filipinos had sparked a flame that in a short time developed into the most violent, organized system of guerrilla warfare ever experienced by any nation in recorded history.

NUEVA ECIJA, THE PHILIPPINES
(April 1942)

Lieutenant Juan Pajota, a twenty-four-year-old member of the Filipino 91st Infantry, had been trained by the 45th Division, Philippine Scouts, in communications and basic infantry tactics. When the Japanese invasion began he and his unit were ordered out of the Cabanatuan Training Camp next to the little Barrio Pangatian, in Nueva Ecija province, to line defenses in western Luzon.

En route, his column was attacked by Japanese dive bombers and several Filipino soldiers were killed. Pajota received a wound in his left leg, yet was able to lead his unit in several skirmishes with the enemy as the Filipinos withdrew toward Bataan.

Pajota's band of seventy-five men arrived at the Bataan border on January 2, only to find that the Japanese had completely sealed the entrance to the peninsula. Most of his men were unarmed, having discarded their malfunctioning rifles during the withdrawal. The lieutenant had only his .45 automatic pistol and a few rounds of ammunition.

Pajota had heard rumors of guerrilla warfare developing in the central and northern parts of Luzon and decided to divide his unit into groups of five and return to the vicinity they knew best—their old training camp at Barrio Pangatian near Cabanatuan City.

The Filipinos successfully completed the zig-zag 125-mile hike across open country and arrived in the Pangatian area on February 5. As Pajota suspected, Camp Cabanatuan was now occupied by a small unit of Japanese soldiers who were busy installing rows of barbed-wire fencing around the compound.

Lieutenant Pajota gathered his small group and began to seriously discuss plans for an organized resistance movement. But Japanese patrols were everywhere throughout Nueva Ecija province. Pajota's newly formed guerrilla force was forced to stay on the move—from barrio to barrio—until a network of communication could be effected.

By April 1, guerrilla recruitment was well under way.

3

Before the thundering altar, god of war
Forlorn, afraid and lost, I kneel to pray.
From such a god as thee, I beg not life.
My life is forfeited, the hour is late.
Thou need not swerve the bullet, dull the knife,
I ask but strength to ride thy wave of fate.
And one thing more, to validate this strife,
And my own sacrifice—teach me to hate!

—Lieutenant Henry Lee, POW Camp O'Donnell, 1942

CAPAS, THE PHILIPPINES
(April 1942)

Captain Tsuneyoshi completed a long drag from his cigarette, which he held tightly between his thumb and index finger in a perfect perpendicular to the highly polished narra wood floor. His hand moved slowly several inches from his large round face, then dropped in a quick jerking chop to the front as if he were attempting to jam the thing into his bulging abdomen.

The smoke was held deep in his lungs, while perspiration rolled from his long sloping forehead. It flooded his bushy eyebrows and flowed in little streams to the corner creases of narrow slit eyes. Those eyes seemed to be fixed on something far out in the dry treeless plains beyond the high barbed-wire fence that separated them from the rest of Tarlac province.

The commander of the Imperial Japanese Army Prisoner of War Camp O'Donnell repeated his exaggerated smoking exercise until a burning sensation at the fingertips warned that the time had come to flip another butt out the screenless window of his headquarters building.

He had been standing and staring into that desolate plains area for over an hour attempting to compose a proper speech in a mind saturated with humiliation and worry. Indeed, it was demeaning for the aging captain to have the assignment of commanding a prisoner of war camp. General Homma's staff told him the job was a great honor, but the staff also said he could expect only 25,000 prisoners. Now, his aides advised that they had lost count of the total. Was it actually possible that his compound held over 62,000 POWs?

While Captain Tsuneyoshi meditated, his short bowlegged frame blocking the afternoon breeze, the staff sat patiently upon small wooden stools placed strategically according to rank in a wide semicircle about the room. His four junior officers, backs rigid, feet wide apart and flat on the floor, studied their commander and wondered what he intended to say to the thousands of Filipino-American prisoners whom the guards had assembled in the boiling sun some two hours before.

Captain Tsuneyoshi finally turned, nodded sharply at his men, pulled his wide brown leather belt up another inch over his belly, and started for the open door. Out into the bright sun and through a row of saluting guards the staff followed. They tried not to notice the thin trail their captain's long samurai sword cut in the dust as his short legs carried him in peculiar style to the crest of a small mound of earth from which he intended to address the prisoners.

Before him, row upon row of USAFFE men, their bony frames scarcely protected from the sun by perspiration-soaked, tattered uniforms, waited for the weird little figure to speak. Throughout the ranks, bodies of those who had collapsed and died from heatstroke and exhaustion lay unattended, their comrades forbidden to move until the camp commandant delivered his speech.

Suddenly, Captain Tsuneyoshi began to scream orders in Japanese, and the interpreter, who stood statuelike by his side, told everyone to salute.

The captain then started to swing his arms in short, choppy motions as if he were directing some invisible orchestra. His entire body jerked while a flood of Japanese sentences broke from frozen lips.

"You are enemies of Japan! You are not honorable prisoners of war! You are captives and you shall be treated as captives. . . ."

The interpreter struggled to keep up with the raving commandant.

"There is no escape from this place! Anyone who tries to escape will be shot. Your country has forgotten your names. . . . Your loved ones no longer weep for their loss. . . . You will soon be joined by others. . . . Those who survive the Imperial Army's invasion of Corregidor. . . ."

On and on for twenty minutes the lecture continued. Finally, Captain Tsuneyoshi spun around and waddled toward the shade of his headquarters, the long sword still dragging the ground behind him.

The condition of the unfinished barracks of Camp O'Donnell was, at first, of little concern to the POWs. Roofs certainly would need repair before the late May rains arrived, but for now, at least the crude grass and bamboo structures offered welcome shelter from the scorching sun.

During those first few days the POWs, weakened by sickness, starvation, and the March of Death, could do nothing but rest and attempt to regain some element of strength. But, strength did not come to the majority.

Some managed to crawl or stagger out across the dusty yards to water faucets that dotted the camp area—there were three such faucets for every 8,000 men. The others had to rely on the unpredictable charity of their comrades.

There were no toilets and no tools to dig latrines or graves—and no one had the strength to dig anyway. Pleas to the guards for medicine went unanswered, but requests for food, by the third day, resulted in the distribution of quantities of worm-infested rice. Those who refused to eat died in less than a week, and the death rate continued to climb as malaria and dysentery took their toll. A few were able to carry the dead outside where corpses were first laid side by side and then stacked upon one another to rot in the sun. By the end of the first week the deaths were averaging fifteen a day.

Millions of the black files swarmed into O'Donnell, spreading more disease. Soon the hot April breezes carried only the sickening, horrible smell of rotting flesh.

Slowly, a small percentage began to gain some strength by choking down their measly portions of rice. The strong of heart and mind would survive, but in less than three weeks, 23,000 Filipino and American prisoners would be dead.

CORREGIDOR, THE PHILIPPINES
(May 1942)

The three-and-one-half- by one-and-one-half-mile island of Corregidor, pounded into a barren wasteland of smoldering tree stumps, buildings reduced to rubble, its big guns silenced by bombs, stood like a wounded gladiator, waiting in Manila Bay for the final death blow.

But deep within Malinta Tunnel on "the Rock" and crouched in trenches and foxholes along her shell-pocked beaches nearly 15,000 men, half-starved, numb from the five months of day and night bombardment, sat by their remaining assortment of weapons to prove to the world that they could take some of the enemy with them when that blow fell.

On May 1, waves of Japanese bombers continued the attack while 240-mm cannon, accompanied by smaller artillery, began a two-day barrage. On May 2, some of the 3,600 artillery rounds fired at the Rock that day finally smashed through concrete and steel ammunition dumps, detonating such violent explosions that the entire little island appeared to observers on the mainland to have erupted in flame.

At 9:30 P.M. on the fifth, the first Japanese assault boats approached Corregidor, heading for the central area where they knew the USAFFE main headquarters was located. But a current swept them in the direction of the eastern tip, and there, illuminated by bright moonlight, they came into the weapon sights of the beach defenders, a strange army composed of U.S. Marines, sailors, Filipino Scouts, and civilians who proceeded to easily annihilate the enemy in the water.

Before midnight, while the eastern battle continued, about 1,000 Japanese did manage to land undetected near the center of Corregidor and began to work their way inland. Before dawn they succeeded in bringing in three tanks and a few artillery pieces. With all of their communication gone the American defending forces did not realize, at first, that they had been cut in half.

Although the exhausted men of USAFFE attempted attacks on the Japanese wedge, they stood no chance against the murderous fire from the imperial artillery and advancing tanks. Near dawn, May 6, 1942, General Wainwright knew he must take the only step left to avoid the massacre of some 5,000 American wounded and female nurses in the caverns of Malinta. He surrendered the Corregidor garrison and all of the USAFFE in the Philippines.

Within a few days the surviving 14,000 defenders of the Rock found themselves en route to prisons in Manila and to Camp O'Donnell.

CAPAS, THE PHILIPPINES
(May 1942)

When Colonel Duckworth, his hospital staff, and patients arrived at O'Donnell in captured American trucks they found some semblance of a hospital already set up and staffed with other medical personnel. They were doing their best without the benefit of medicines or surgical equipment. The fourteen-by-fourteen-foot hospital wards each housed at least ten patients, all near death.

Even though Colonel Duckworth had been allowed to transport the entire stock of his Bataan hospital supplies to O'Donnell, he discovered with frustrating disbelief that Captain Tsuneyoshi's staff had confiscated the complete lot.

Now, with no medicine to control the amoebic and bacillary dysentery, no fly screens for windows, and inadequate cooking facilities, the daily death rate increased, fed by the new arrivals from the Bataan hospital and Corregidor. Hearts of men, weakened by prolonged starvation, dilated and ceased beating. The lack of protein prompted more cases of beriberi, and lungs, flooded with fluid, permitted pneumonia to easily conquer the weak.

But the human spirit for survival still flowed in a surprisingly large number, and these men began to organize the camp with basic plans for existence. They established small work details, counting on only an hour's work per man per day. Large stoves of clay were constructed. They were primitive but adequate to cook rice and boil contaminated water. And, from parts of wrecked automobiles inside the camp, they fashioned crude shovels and waited for permission to bury their dead.

Finally, in late May the rain came, flooded the camp, and carried with its waters the bloated corpses so near the Japanese guard quarters that Captain Tsuneyoshi was compelled to issue permission for burial details to begin. Lines of men able to walk or dig began the sickening task of carrying the dead out from O'Donnell to a spot designated as the camp cemetery.

Pleas to the Japanese to furnish some meat were eventually answered. Every four weeks, slaughtered carabao meat was distributed—one-fourth of a carcass for 500 men. It was enough to make a meat broth to saturate rice. For some it was just enough nutrition to sustain life.

Yet on the Filipino side of the camp the death rate began to reach 550 men a day.

Private Adriano Olivar, from his bed in one of the hospital wards, volunteered for the burial detail, insisting that he was in better physical condition than the rest of the 4,650 patients in his area. He was fully convinced that his one leg was strong enough for him to hop with the assistance of the crutch. He tried to explain his calculations to the doctors. The long bamboo pole, from which hung the dead in canvas sacks, could be braced upon the shoulder above his one leg.

But the doctors found another assignment for the young private. In desperation for medicine, it occurred to the medics that some of the patients from the Bataan hospital or Corregidor might have brought with them their personal drugs.

As word spread through the wards, Private Olivar gladly turned over his large brown bottle of pills, still unaware of the treasure he possessed. The doctors informed him that the bottle contained sulfa pills, the drug they most needed for treating pneumonia and intestinal infections.

Since the bottle rightfully belonged to Olivar, he would be given the required dosage for his own survival and could help control the distribution of the quantity remaining.

NUEVA ECIJA, THE PHILIPPINES
(May 1942)

During April and May, about forty miles northeast of O'Donnell, Lieutenant Juan Pajota continued his vigorous recruitment campaign of a guerrilla army in Nueva Ecija province.

On May 7, Lieutenant Pajota was in the little barrio of Macatbong only two miles due east of his old camp Pangatian-Cabanatuan when a runner brought the news from the bamboo telegraph—Wainwright had surrendered Corregidor.

There was only one conclusion for Pajota. He must fight the enemy regardless of what the Americans might do. He confronted his small army, which was waiting patiently in the cool shade of a nipa hut.

"We must," he began with little expression to his face, "continue our recruitment for the resistance movement. Everything will move exactly on my orders and precisely at the time I designate."

Pajota pointed to the dial of his Lord Elgin wristwatch. "From this day, when I say nine o'clock, I mean, on the dot!"

"What on the dot?" one of his men interrupted.

Pajota's stern eyes changed quickly and the high cheeks moved upward, causing his eyes to narrow with a mild, friendly grin. He was concerned with his men's ability to comprehend the importance of punctuality, for time, to most Filipinos, was very uninteresting. If someone said "nine o'clock" about the only thing necessary to know was whether the appointment was for morning or evening. Once this was determined, the general custom of "Philippine time" applied—it was acceptable to report after nine, at the convenience of the one reporting. In the tropics, no one really cared to frustrate life with promptness.

Pajota's eyes changed to the stare of a cat. "'On the dot' is an American expression," he replied. "It means that you must be where you are told to be, exactly at the time you are told to be there! If your superiors say 'nine o'clock,' they mean nine o'clock—not nine-thirty or ten!"

Through the first two weeks of May, Pajota and his men moved from barrio to barrio generating support for his plans while runners kept him advised of enemy activity at nearby Cabanatuan City.

But the most important news received from the bamboo telegraph was that a few American soldiers were making their way north to link up with guerrilla units such as his own. Pajota sent runners to all surrounding villages. He must make contact with those Americans as soon as possible.

By May 14, Pajota's army had grown to a strength of twenty, and they stopped that day on the edge of the small barrio of San Juan near Laur to celebrate the lieutenant's birthday. War or no war, a birthday is an important event to Filipinos and a good excuse for a happy gathering. As customary, the villagers went all out in the preparation of a feast for their guests and there was ample "lambanog," a potent distillation of "tuba" (coconut wine), for everyone.

The following morning the little army proceeded toward Bacao, but his men were suffering from the exhaustive recruitment campaign (as well as a few hangovers), and Pajota declared the fifteenth a day of rest. In the early afternoon a runner caught up with the guerrillas and informed Pajota that five Japanese soldiers, led by two pro-Japanese Filipinos, were already at Bacao on their way to the Bato Ferry. The lieutenant instructed the runner to return to Bacao and be sure that the enemy take a short cut, using a special trail he suggested.

The timing and location for a first guerrilla encounter with the Japanese in Nueva Ecija were perfect. There were two basic things Pajota's men needed—weapons and combat experience for the new recruits.

He assembled his men that afternoon and presented a simple plan for an ambush. "That trail the Japs will take is narrow. They will be moving in single file, so it is important to position ourselves in order that we not be hit by our own fire. I will show you these positions when we reach our ambush point."

Pajota squatted on his haunches in typical Oriental fashion, feet flat upon the earth, buttocks near the ground, body leaning slightly forward, and he began to scratch his plan in the soft dirt as his men joined him in a tight circle.

"You must learn this now," he continued. "The Japs have a will to fight unlike anyone else because they do not wish to surrender. Even if they are wounded, if they can crawl, they will hit back. They may pretend like they are dead and strike when you come close. For this reason at least two of you will aim at each single enemy. We have little ammunition, so aim carefully!"

"What about the two Ganaps?" one of the guerrillas asked.

Pajota stared at the ground a moment, sickened by the thought that some of his countrymen had sided with the Japanese. He glanced up at the young men across from him. "They are traitors. They will die also!" His eyes moved from face to face, testing the reaction to his order. None of them liked the idea of killing fellow Filipinos, but the collaborators must be eliminated.

"Now," Lieutenant Pajota broke the brief silence, "the Ganaps will, no doubt, be leading the patrol. The Japs are clever. They have an alert sense for danger and will force the Ganaps to walk ahead. Sergeant Sicadsicad will be next to me and we will allow them all to pass until the last Jap is directly across from us. When you hear my shot at that last Jap you must shoot quickly!"

The guerrillas soon split into pairs, casually proceeded in the direction of Bato Ferry, and then materialized out of the brush near the trail approximately three-fourths of a mile from Bacao. There they took the assigned positions and waited calmly for the enemy.

Within a few hours the Japanese approached the site, the two Filipinos leading by some twenty paces, exactly as Pajota had predicted. When the last soldier crossed the sights of Pajota's .45 automatic, he slowly squeezed the trigger. As the Japanese soldier sprang into the air from the impact of the first bullet, a barrage of fire followed so rapidly that it was impossible to distinguish individual shots. The seven-man enemy patrol crumpled to the ground, all killed instantly.

Now, the guerrillas had five additional rifles. While they divided up the ammunition, Pajota sent one man to evacuate the barrio of Bacao with instructions for the citizens to mingle with those of the next village, Sagana. If the Japanese intended any reprisals upon Bacao they would find nothing but an empty town to burn.

After Pajota had complimented his men for following orders perfectly, they divided into small groups, dissolving again into the brush, and moved on to Kukong Kabayo to continue recruitment. The entire ambush, search, and dispersal had required less than two minutes.

CAPAS, THE PHILIPPINES
(1942)

In the center of Capas the Japanese guards from Camp O'Donnell established a headquarters in one large school building directly across the street from a wood frame two-story home.

Doctor Romeao Atienza and his wife, along with Josefa F. Hilado, began their Red Cross functions in that home the same week the last of the Death March survivors staggered into the prisoner of war camp, seven miles away.

From the beginning, the three Red Cross workers begged the guards to speak in their behalf to Commandant Tsuneyoshi. In the name of humanity, the Red Cross must be allowed to perform the harmless administration of medical help to the dying POWs.

Doctor Atienza even journeyed in their ambulance to O'Donnell for a face-to-face confrontation with the camp commander, but Captain Tsuneyoshi's mind was made up. No civilians would be permitted to enter the compound except those who came to the front gate to sell food. The Japanese desired to buy fresh vegetables and fruit.

In the meantime, Josefa Hilado agreed to treat minor wounds and ailments of the Japanese guards and even convinced them that she was half Japanese. Her mother, a pure Japanese, had died long ago in Manila, she lied, before any of the children had the opportunity to learn the Japanese language fluently. And all the time she continued to memorize new Japanese expressions, becoming so proficient that she could comfortably carry a simple conversation.

She learned that most of the guards were about her age, and some were even younger. And she discovered that they were plagued with the same worries that have concerned all soldiers since the beginning of recorded history. The majority were homesick youngsters, pressed into service for their emperor, and detested their assignment of guarding prisoners. Each possessed dreadful fear of their superiors but, most of all, they worried about contracting diseases, which were killing so many in the camp.

Using any excuse from their details they could get away with, the guards would climb the wooden steps leading up into the Red Cross building and come to their new friend, Miss Hilado, exercising polite manners, requesting medicine for anything from upset stomachs to scratches and blisters. She would always greet them in their language and make a small attempt to help before sending them on their way.

For a while, isolated in the Red Cross house, it was almost difficult to believe that these soldiers were of the same army that had conducted the March of Death, starved her countrymen at Camp O'Donnell, and were committing atrocities throughout the country.

The bamboo telegraph was hot with stories. It told of the slaughter of entire villages in northern Luzon by the Japanese and of a recent atrocity in a barrio near Capas where a man and his wife, suspected of communicating with guerrillas, were brought to the center of town. There the wife was repeatedly raped by a platoon of Japanese infantry while her husband and villagers were forced to stand helplessly and watch.

But Miss Hilado put aside her bitterness and concluded that if the telegraph related such things, it could provide a far more useful service. It could carry out, through its tangled network, important information needed by the guerrillas. She also had a personal concern. Somewhere among those dying men at O'Donnell, her brother, Carlos, might be still alive. She finally asked the guards if they would locate her brother and deliver a message. They agreed, happy to return help for her kindness.

The guards spent three weeks searching for Carlos Hilado and eventually reported one day to the Red Cross building saying that they had "very bad news." Private Carlos Hilado had died around the first of May of exhaustion from the march out of Bataan to O'Donnell.

Sympathizing with her loss, they inquired if they could do anything to ease the sorrow. She glanced at the stack of thousands of telegrams and letters from concerned loved ones and nodded, yes. Would they try to locate a few more Filipinos in the camp or at least confirm their deaths?

They agreed and she typed a short list on a piece of brown paper. It was the first of hundreds of notes to follow.

In a few days, the note was returned with an "X" placed in front of three names. Apparently, the other two should be considered dead. Miss Hilado handed the guards several more lists, thus beginning a strange relationship.

Late June brought a major change to Camp O'Donnell. A new Japanese commandant was assigned, with definite orders to begin a phase of pacification with Filipinos but no particular orders on the disposition of Americans.

Colonel Ito, a tall, slim officer of fifty-five, spoke broken English in short staccato sentences. His first order presented a slight ray of hope for those who were still alive within the barbed-wire enclosure. All medicine and medical equipment previously held by the commandant would be released at once for use by the prison hospital. Next, food ration quantities were to be increased.

Colonel Ito came to visit the Red Cross station in Capas, thanked them for their kind treatment of Japanese guards, and surprised everyone with the announcement that the Red Cross would now be allowed to go into the camp with a special pass. There were, of course, certain conditions. The Filipinos must not deliver or carry out messages (written or verbal), nor were they to take in weapons, food, medicine, or supplies. Their job was simply to aid the sick POWs, using the medicines existing in the camp. "Any infringement" of the regulations would "result in death to the offender"!

In addition to Ito's proposal, Doctor Atienza was told that Japanese guards would continue to visit the Red Cross Capas headquarters and bring with them a few American prisoners. These POWs might perform various cleaning duties after they completed a similar task at the Japanese guard headquarters across the street. Should an American escape, the *entire* Red Cross staff would be held responsible.

As Colonel Ito finished his announcement to the Red Cross unit, Miss Hilado thanked him in Japanese. The startled colonel removed his eyeglasses and stared at the young nurse for a moment. "Ah, so!" he exclaimed. "You speak Japanese *and* English. Good! I will return and you will teach me more English—agreed?!"

Miss Hilado nodded, content with the thought that another link was about to form in the telegraph's communication system.

For the next six weeks, Doctor Atienza, his wife, and Nurse Hilado, along with several other nurses, traveled into the hell of Camp O'Donnell, extending their humanitarian efforts to the POWs. And, each time, hidden in their old ambulance they smuggled precious supplies of medicines—quinine for malaria, sulfa, money, and guava leaves for raw wounds and dysentery. With the money, the POWs could buy additional food from the hundreds of civilians who were now allowed to gather every day just inside the gate. The food price to the POWs was only a token, but the Japanese always received the maximum retail price plus whatever percent the individual figured he could bargain for.

But not all the civilians were there to sell food. Their disguise as vendors allowed them to slip fresh clothing to many Filipino POWs, who then mingled with the crowd and casually departed when the civilians were ordered out. The names of the escapees were simply added to the death list, substituted for those who had died earlier.

Seven days a week, in the blazing sun and the breath-snatching heat inside the medical wards of the camp, gentle, small hands of the Red Cross assisted the American medics, treating the sick and comforting the dying.

Time and again, Miss Hilado stuffed notes and letters into her underclothes and, upon her return to the Capas headquarters, turned the small scraps of paper over to runners who began the distribution of long-awaited news to grieving relatives. And, in the process, she passed on verbal information about the number of Japanese at the camp and the number and conditions of American and Filipino POWs.

Untiring, these young "Little Brown Angels of Mercy," as the American POWs called them, continued their gallant task until one morning two of Miss Hilado's close Red Cross friends failed to report for duty. It was not until her return to Capas late in the day that she learned of their fate. Her friends had been arrested, accused by the Japanese command in Capas of smuggling medical supplies into O'Donnell, and were taken to Fort Santiago in Manila—a place where the Japanese took special prisoners and a place from which no one ever returned. After five long days the Capas Red Cross unit received the news. Mr. and Mrs. Antonio L. Escoda had been beheaded.

That night, the remaining Red Cross staff, now sure they too were under suspicion of the same crime, held a meeting. The Red Cross unit's decision was unanimous. Regardless of the danger, they must continue the smuggling. The lives of many depended on their sacrifice.

For the next few months, while some of the Japanese guards pretended to search her ambulance, Josefa Hilado's work went on. The guards were unpredictable. They always searched the vehicle thoroughly when she left the camp. It was then that she sweated with fear the most. If they forced her to disrobe, as some nurses were made to do at other stations in Luzon, then they might discover those notes, and even the friendly guards would be in no position to help.

Each afternoon, upon returning to Capas, she treated the ailments (many of which were imaginary) of the Japanese soldiers or entertained Colonel Ito, who paid an occasional visit. The commandant always brought a gift for his English tutor, and if the gift had some value to the POWs, it ended up the next day in the camp.

There was one guard who even developed a crush on Miss Hilado and came to court her one rainy evening in early August.

She and the would-be suitor engaged in a polite conversation in Japanese. The soldier spoke of his family in Japan and gave her some exciting news. The Filipino prisoners, he said, might soon be released. Before the guard departed he handed her a photo of himself taken at a studio in Capas. It was indeed a compliment, for he had just mailed an identical one to his mother.

She thanked him as he stood to go and told him she would treasure it always. The soldier blushed, bowed stiffly, hurried out the door, and crossed the street to his quarters.

A few days later Miss Hilado was confronted by several grinning guards on the Red Cross center's front porch. They explained that they, too, had photographs for her. She knew they had each helped in the past by ignoring the smuggling and now they beamed with excitement as they handed her the pictures. Actually, the visit was serving as a "goodbye," for these guards had received orders transferring them to a new post.

At Camp O'Donnell, rumors spread among the remaining 6,500 American prisoners—rumors that they were to be sent to a new death camp, a place where they must work and die in secret, hidden from the eyes of the rest of the world, a place the Filipinos called *Cabanatuan*.

4

⭐

There can be no greater, more heinous or dangerous crime than the mass destruction under guise of military authority or military necessity, of helpless men incapable of further contribution to war effort.

—From General Douglas MacArthur's "review" of
General Masaharu Homma's case, War Trials, 1946

NUEVA ECIJA, THE PHILIPPINES
(Summer 1942)

Since his first encounter with the Japanese, Lieutenant Juan Pajota had been anything but idle in Nueva Ecija province.

Shortly after midnight on August 1, Pajota was awakened by one of his men who related exciting news from the bamboo telegraph: Two American officers were traveling cross-country in the night, heading in the direction of his temporary headquarters.

At 0300 (3:00 A.M.), United States Army Captain Harry M. McKenzie and his companion arrived with their guide at Pajota's camp to find the guerrillas all wide awake and waiting for them with food, fresh water, and a meeting place prepared.

A conference began in the early morning hours that was to tie Pajota and his men into the growing web of organized guerrilla resistance. The Americans explained that they had escaped

Bataan and since January, with the help of civilians, were moving north to link up with another American officer, Robert Lapham.

Until after daybreak, the men discussed plans and reviewed in every detail the results of Pajota's campaign. McKenzie was impressed with the accomplishments of the Filipino commander and promoted him to the rank of captain. It was a field commission, for which official orders were later drafted.

Pajota was instructed to continue his recruitment and break his command into small units. At all times he was to emphasize the importance of supporting only the Americans and avenge Japanese atrocities.

On August 5, after the Americans moved on to meet with Lapham, Captain Pajota began to commission a few of his most able men as first lieutenants and placed them in command of subdivided units. Pajota had an unending attention to detail. He remembered that most of the 91st Filipino Infantry documents and records had been captured by the Japanese. Since his men were primarily former members of the 91st, it was imperative to deceive the enemy no matter how trivial each method might seem. He elected to use the designation "squadron" for his newly formed units rather than more common infantry identification. Each squadron had a three-digit number based on a system. With such designation true strength and type of weapons would be difficult for the enemy to determine.

To further intentionally complicate the system, he selected a letter suffix for each squadron number. Squadrons 201 and 201A, therefore, became two separate units with different commanders. Each squadron, armed with bolos, captured Japanese rifles, and old American (USAFFE) Springfields, had responsibility for a particular area, but they remained basically mobile.

Captain Pajota would maintain overall command of his squadrons and answer to the American officer, Robert Lapham. Pajota's area consisted of almost thirty square miles, which varied in terrain from flat open fields (mostly cultivated with rice), to dense forest over rolling country, to the high rough country of the Sierra Madre mountains on the east. All the area must be traveled on foot or horseback.

Pajota's command was just one of the guerrilla units that prepared to rain destruction and frustration upon the Japanese. Other guerrilla units, whose commanders were mostly former USAFFE Filipino officers, began activity throughout Luzon and other islands, some before Bataan fell.

On Luzon a major link in the chain of command and communication began as Robert Lapham established mobile headquarters in the northern section of Nueva Ecija province. This six-foot, twenty-four-year-old blonde soldier had successfully avoided capture since the aborted raid on Clark Field. Once situated with a band of followers, he promoted himself from lieutenant to major and assigned Captain Harry McKenzie (a former American civilian) as his executive officer.

To the west, Bernard Anderson, an Air Force lieutenant, promoted himself to the rank of colonel and began activities against the enemy.

Far to the north, Captain R. W. Volckmann completed his odyssey to the Mountain province, organized his followers, and promoted himself to the rank of colonel. Donald D. Blackburn, who escaped Bataan with Volckmann, succeeded in reaching northern Luzon and established a guerrilla army.

There was a certain charisma about these men that attracted the Filipinos in magnetic fashion. Definitely, their original status as American officers in the USAFFE played a big part. They possessed all the natural traits of a good leader in the eyes of the Filipinos. They were handsome, brave, brilliant in their planning, imaginative, and determined to fight the Japanese. The Filipinos were impressed with an open, honest face but for them to follow such men into combat would require something more than all of this.

The Americans must first prove themselves to be not only worthy of trust but sincere in the desire to continue fighting the Japanese. The stand at Bataan was almost proof enough, but when the Americans exhibited their determination to fight and die for freedom as guerrillas then all suspicion disappeared.

The American guerrilla officers coordinated attacks on the enemy even as they maintained separate commands and generally operated independently of each other. When MacArthur finally learned of their actions, he officially recognized the ranks these men had awarded themselves.

For those Americans still suffering from disease and battle wounds, the adjustment to the rugged guerrilla life was no simple matter. Despite the devoted help of the Filipinos, many died of their wounds or from beriberi, malaria, and dysentery. Still others were eventually captured by the Japanese.

But all who could, without any prior training in guerrilla warfare, set about using the bamboo telegraph, establishing field units, maintaining records, and building the nucleus of a fighting force that gained them a well-deserved place in the history of unconventional warfare.

The guerrillas soon found that they had the support of the majority of Filipinos. Of course, as one would expect among any people, there were those who did side with the Japanese. Some of those were forced into supporting the enemy by torture. And some did elect to die rather than betray the Philippines. Others, called Makapili, were bought with money or promises of prominence in the new government Japan was to establish.

The guerrillas feared these traitorous Filipinos the most, even more than the Imperial Army troops. Their mere existence in any locale threatened not merely the safety of the guerrillas but also their supporters and families.

The American-led guerrilla forces were not the only problem the enemy faced on Filipino soil. The Huks were another troublesome Filipino group for the Japanese.

As early as the 1930s, a man named Luis Taruc and several other socialists broke away from the American ideal of government and began to recruit farmers and small-town businessmen to join their movement. Luis Taruc wanted to establish his own political party by the time Philippine independence was granted by the United States.

He assumed that America, a capitalist country, would hand over all power to the oligarchy that had controlled the Philippines for centuries. Therefore, he wanted the socialists to have a strong voice in the nation's future to insure a better life for the common people.

But Taruc's vision of socialism differed from that of others in the rest of the world. He injected strong Christian religious views into his movement. He, himself, was a deeply religious man. And he knew the rest of his countrymen felt the same.

In 1938, facing the very real possibility of Japanese aggression against the Philippines, Taruc formed an alliance with the communists. It was never a happy union; their widely divergent views on their mutual goals led to bitter disagreements.

Luis Taruc was a man of considerable intelligence, warm and sensitive toward his followers' needs. He was also a spellbinding orator. Peasants flocked to him, believing his strongly articulated ideas of a Christian-style socialism. He clearly understood the needs of the poverty-stricken masses.

The communists were quite different, perhaps more pragmatic but also considerably more cold-blooded and cruel. They had their own followers, enough in number to impress the socialists. But their godless attitude, the lack of any religious beliefs, was extremely difficult for the deeply devout Taruc to tolerate. Nevertheless, after the Japanese invasion, the alliance held for a while.

At the age of twenty-eight, Luis Taruc was appointed commander of the combined socialist-communist force. He formed well-disciplined squads of fighters from his peasant volunteers. He called the army Hukbo Ng Boyan Labon Sa Hapon (the People's Army to fight the Japanese). Eventually, the organization became known as Hukbalahap, with the name finally shortened to the more manageable Huks.

Like Pajota, Commander Taruc also divided his army into squadrons. Each squadron consisted of 100 men and was subdivided into platoons and squads. A battalion of Huks was composed of two squadrons.

At least in the beginning, the Huks and the USAFFE guerrillas had one interest in common—the disposal of their mutual enemy, the Japanese.

CABANATUAN, NUEVA ECIJA, THE PHILIPPINES
(September 1942)

Light, steady breezes always drift across the central plains of Luzon, appreciated especially by youngsters who fly small kites made from scraps of paper and thin strips of bamboo. The Nueva Ecija children spend hours assembling these kites, often no larger than a book cover, and launch them from string of grass, cotton, or bits of cloth, all twisted carefully by hand into varying lengths.

The breeze that morning in late September 1942 was perfect for kite flying. The fields along the highway connecting Cabanatuan City to Cabanatuan-Pangatian were speckled with scores of boys and girls who clapped and giggled in excitement while their simple toys tugged in the wind.

The children's attention was distracted by the sound of hundreds of people marching. They pulled their kites down to watch the procession moving along the gravel highway.

The main group of the surviving 6,500 American prisoners of war had arrived in Cabanatuan City by rail cattle car from Capas and now were in their final march to Camp Pangatian three miles down the road.

These POWs were the first Americans most of the children had ever seen. The sickly, gaunt figures stumbling before them bore little resemblance to the powerful white men they had heard so much about.

Originally, there were three work camps prepared for the Americans in the Cabanatuan area: the large camp, Pangatian (the former base of Juan Pajota and part of the 91st Infantry), and two other smaller camps hastily organized from warehouses. From all three, the Japanese planned to send POWs for various construction projects.

But the angel of death spread his wings of welcome mostly over Cabanatuan-Pangatian. Here, the bulk of POWs arrived and discovered that over 1,000 Americans had already been deposited by truck some weeks earlier. All of these were hospital cases, unable to work.

Corporal Eugene Evers reported with about 200 other medics to the rear of Camp Cabanatuan, which had been designated as the "hospital" area.

The wards of this hospital were nothing more than sixty-foot-long buildings constructed of woven bamboo on bamboo frames with nipa grass roofs. Like the wards at O'Donnell, these too had no screens over the windows—only large thatched shutters that could swing down from a hinged top. These shutters, Corporal Evers learned, were suitable for blocking out the hot afternoon sun and heavy rains but could not hold back the blue-black flies. The insects swarmed by the millions into the wards and crawled upon the faces and lifeless forms of the hospital's 2,500 patients.

At the front of Cabanatuan the rest of the 4,000-odd American POWs were assigned to their sixty-foot-long nipa barracks, 100 men to a unit.

Sergeant Abie Abraham climbed the three wooden steps that led into his barracks staggering from his own weakness and the weight of another POW he had half-carried the final mile to the camp.

Once inside he noticed that a narrow aisle ran the complete length separating two decks of bamboo racks on each side. The floor was constructed of bamboo strips nailed on a base frame a fraction of an inch apart. Since all of the units were elevated two to three feet from the ground, these cracks permitted some circulation of air.

Abraham gently laid his companion upon the first vacant space he found on a lower-level rack, climbed to the upper level, and collapsed into a deep sleep.

The stockade, which now had become known as Cabanatuan POW Camp Number 1, sat on flat land on the south side of the highway approximately four and three-fourths miles east of downtown Cabanatuan City. Along that same highway, a few hundred yards away, was the little barrio of Pangatian, and another mile east was the barrio of Cabu. The larger town of Bongagon was nine additional miles east.

The Japanese had made only a few changes at the camp in preparation for the POWs. First, they enclosed a 600-by-800-yard section with three rows of barbed-wire fence eight feet tall. The fence rows were four feet apart. Inside, they divided sections by single rows of barbed-wire fence, six feet tall and erected to contain the POWs in the northeast section.

Over 6,000 POWs were thus crammed into an area approximately 180 yards by 380 yards. Their north boundary was the rows of fence along the highway, and their east boundary the three rows lining the eastern perimeter. One row of fence separated them from the Japanese troop quarters at the south, and one row of fence along the central, north-south road that divided the camp.

At the front gate, the only entrance from the highway, the Japanese constructed a twelve-foot-high guard tower, and they built a second tower at the northeast corner of the camp. These two towers were each originally manned by four sentries with rifles and machine guns. They commanded an excellent field of vision over the POW section, the highway, the main gate, and a good distance across the open fields that stretched north two miles to the Pampanga River.

About halfway down the POW section's perimeter on the east was a large open pillbox, slightly elevated above ground level and surrounded with sandbags. From here, four sentries with rifles and a machine gun had perfect vision of the southern half of the POW area (which contained mostly the hospital dispensary, operating hut, and wards) and the eastward terrain, which also was flat country.

It was this east area, beyond the perimeter, that most concerned the camp commandant. Less than fifty yards outside the fence rows a small creek cut through a gully running practically parallel to the east fence from south to north. Its bed varied in depth from about two feet deep at the south end of the camp to nearly six feet near the front where it passed under the highway and continued to the Pampanga River.

Fearing that Filipino guerrillas might attempt to approach the camp from the east (using the creek bed for concealment), the Japanese made sure that the cogon grass was always cut close to the ground. Several sentries were assigned to patrol this area on foot, night and day.

At the far southeast corner of the camp, they erected another twelve-foot tower whose guards could keep a watchful eye on the few buildings to the south, just beyond the fence where the livestock (mostly carabao) was kept. An elevated pillbox was also constructed at the rear gate.

There was yet another purpose for the rear guard tower and pillbox. In the flat area outside the southeast section the Japanese planned to allow the Americans to bury their dead. The burial details would need tools and even the most primitive tools might suddenly become weapons in the hands of desperate men. The machine gunner in the southeast tower was instructed to watch those burial details carefully.

The remainder of the camp belonged to the Japanese. They quartered enlisted men and guards in the southeast section. In the southwest section they erected their communication center and turned the barracks there over to transient troops. The motor pool was located in the west central area. The northwest section was saved for the officers quarters, headquarters, and a few barracks for the front gate guards.

By the middle of September, the seasonal rains that had pounded Luzon almost every day since the end of May ceased.

Cabanatuan lay shrouded in ghostly silence that morning as Sergeant Abie Abraham scanned the sheets of paper on which he had recorded so many names of dead American soldiers. Now, he must add more numbers—those figures given to him by the earlier arrivals at the camp.

By the time that the last of the American POWs arrived from O'Donnell in September, Abraham had recorded the names of over 1,000 dead comrades. They had all been carried out to the muddy field at the end of the camp and buried in a common grave, dug by the POWs, first with bare hands, later with shovels made from wood and scraps of metal.

On September 20, Sergeant Abraham buried his notes in their secret hiding place beneath his barracks. He stepped out into the hot morning sun, which already had begun to boil moisture from the rain-soaked buildings and saturated earth.

He turned east to face the long Sierra Madre mountain range and thought for a moment how beautiful, how tranquil they appeared. Quickly he glanced in the opposite direction toward Mount Arayat as if to assure himself that nothing had changed— that he had not dreamed into a peaceful death.

Motivated by his deep religious beliefs, the sergeant made the sign of the cross, then walked slowly to the fence that separated his area from the center road and the Japanese camp headquarters.

"It's 0900," he heard someone say, and he wondered how any POW had managed to have a watch after so many searches by the Japanese since Bataan's surrender six months before.

He joined the crowd of hundreds who had been gathering along that fence since daybreak, keeping a vigil for three officers who had been caught while trying to escape under the wire fences.

The day of their capture they were dragged from the headquarters building, bleeding and unconscious, and tied to posts in full view of their comrades across the road. For three days they had been hanging there, feet several inches from the ground. But everyone knew they were not dead because occasionally a guard would pass and jab with his rifle to be sure they were still breathing.

Abraham had considered staying in his barracks that morning in order not to view more torture and death. It was not morbid curiosity that brought him to the fence. It was a determination to etch forever in his mind the details of Japanese brutality. He could never be sure that his notes would survive the months to come. Sergeant Abraham prayed that *he* be spared only long enough to testify against the enemy someday.

Several guards, led by an NCO, came out from the headquarters building and cut the ropes that held the American officers. They crumpled to the ground. As they tried to get to their feet the guards were upon them, tying their arms behind their backs.

Then the long walk began toward the rear gate. Abraham moved slowly with the multitudes along the wire, following the procession.

The guards and their three prisoners approached the cemetery and the Americans were lined up, side by side, their backs to a shallow trench.

"God, give them strength!" Abraham heard the man next to him whisper.

"Our Father, who art in heaven . . ." Abraham began the prayer, which was picked up by a few around him.

Most simply stood with blank expressions, their shriveled hands clutching the barbed wire.

At the graveyard the Japanese NCO held out a pack of cigarettes, offering to place one between each prisoner's lips. Two POWs stared ahead, their eyes apparently not seeing the final gesture. The third looked up slowly, then managed to spit at the feet of the NCO with a jerk of his head. The NCO performed a neat turn, walked a few paces to the side, and barked three orders.

The sound of eight rifle shots cut the quiet morning and rolled with a haunting echo through the valley.

Life at Cabanatuan, for those who were not admitted to the hospital, consisted of five to seven days' labor, depending on the mood of the Japanese. Constantly, work details were marched or trucked throughout Nueva Ecija province to cut firewood, clear bamboo thickets, build airstrips, and reconstruct buildings damaged or destroyed during the invasion.

By the last of September 1942, the Japanese officially changed the classification of the Americans from "captives" to prisoners of war and began to issue pay in Japanese occupation peso currency. A PFC received fifteen centavos a day, NCOs twenty-five centavos, and officers sometimes as much as ten pesos a day.

With these funds the POWs were free to buy food, fruit, and tobacco from the Filipinos who were occasionally allowed to gather along the highway fence or at the main gate. As usual, the Filipinos had two prices—one for the Americans and a highly inflated one for the Japanese. Bananas and other fruit, which the Filipinos had in abundance, were usually given to the POWs only to be confiscated by greedy guards.

Some semblance of a POW command organization began, hampered by the continual shifting of details to and from the other POW camps in the area and the relocation of numerous groups to Manila or major construction projects throughout Luzon.

The work details suffered such severe beatings that the balance between those in the hospital and those available for work swung back and forth. Actually, none of the POWs were in condition to perform hard labor, and when American officers protested the assignment of sick men to details, they were beaten and placed on even tougher labor assignments.

By October, when Lieutenant Colonel Mori took command of Cabanatuan, the POWs had a farm of over 300 acres under cultivation. They worked the fields using sticks and hoes made from scraps of metal for seven to ten hours each day. Since there was no irrigation, the entire farm had to be watered by hand. And when the first small harvest came, the Japanese guards took most of the vegetables. Discovering this injustice, the Filipinos in the area began to leave food at the worksites at night to be smuggled by the POWs back into the camp.

Through it all, however, many of the Americans managed to maintain some sense of humor and even nicknamed their most hated guards by appearance or mannerism—"Half pint, Donald Duck, Big Speedo, Little Speedo. . . ." Jokes about these guards produced a few smiles and an occasional laugh for the POWs.

In the camp, efforts to organize and improve morale, spearheaded by the clergymen, medics, and a few enthusiastic POWs, were successful. First, the clergy finally convinced Lieutenant Colonel Mori that the men should be allowed to worship their God, and regular church services were held.

Stoves of clay and metal were built, replacing open-fire cooking, and the bakers and cooks learned new methods, using the small rations issued by the Japanese.

Meat was mostly the heads and intestines of carabao—350 pounds per week per 2,000 men. Sometimes only fish powder was issued instead of meat, and often weeks went by without even fish powder. The POWs devised ingenious traps for rats, lizards, and an occasional dog or cat that wandered through the wire fences. The grand total of meat usually averaged out to five ounces per man every three days.

From the farm the Japanese eventually allowed the Americans to keep the camotes and casaua. The POWs stole whatever they could of the okra, peppers, cucumbers, eggplant, onions, and radishes. This was a dangerous game, for to be caught stealing usually resulted in a fatal beating.

Starting in October, the Japanese made periodic issues of eggs and canned milk, but as the starvation diet continued some turned on their own. A few accepted special favors from the enemy—food for information. Some stole from their buddies and traded for food and tobacco or those hard-earned centavos so they could buy necessities from the guards. When caught, these POWs were warned that they might stand trial by court-martial. Cases were even prepared and hidden for future reference.

In December 1942, competition games of golf, baseball, and volleyball began and tournaments of chess, Monopoly, checkers, and poker were under way with handmade equipment. Prizes were usually one precious egg or hand-rolled cigarettes.

But the POWs grew tired of the activities, and when they did, classes in astronomy, radio repair, music, horse raising, and cattle breeding caught on. The U.S. Navy POWs who had arrived late at O'Donnell from Corregidor had been allowed to keep most of their musical instruments, which they carried on to Cabanatuan. A camp band was established.

These Corregidor POWs managed to smuggle in something far more valuable to morale. Hidden under their clothes and in some of those musical instruments they had placed parts of radio equipment. While others attended classes on how to make dog tags from leather, combs from carabao horn, or razors from GI mess kit knives, a special team of technicians began to slowly assemble a radio receiver.

The possession of a radio or even knowledge of the location of a radio would mean instant death. But these technicians ignored the threat and worked through the nights on their electrical contraption. Unfortunately, they did not have all the necessary parts, especially tubes or wires for a decent antenna. A brilliant plan was devised. They instructed the workers in the small power station on how to overload the camp electrical circuits and soon every personal radio owned by the Japanese began to blow tubes.

The guards were then advised that there were a few among the POWs who knew how to repair radios. A steady stream of radios needing repair began to flow to these POWs, who reported the name and type of tubes or parts needing replacement. Of course, there was nothing wrong with some of the parts, and as the replacements arrived from nearby Cabanatuan City or Manila, the POWs retained what they needed.

During this time, small bits of copper wire were stolen and woven into an antenna that was hidden within a long, heavy rope.

One guard inquired about the purpose of the coil of rope. He was informed that some of the POWs had requested permission to commit suicide by hanging. Little by little the radio was assembled into a very compact unit and concealed inside three canteens that had been cut in half. They were hidden in separate areas, to be connected at some future date. But since so many POWs were transferred in and out of Cabanatuan, it would be almost a year before the engineering marvel would receive its first broadcast.

At Cabanatuan City the Bureau of Constabulary was reorganized by the Japanese to augment the Imperial Army and reestablish a law enforcement group, led by Filipinos. They placed as provincial commander former USAFFE major Godofredo G. Monsod, who, being very pro-American, quickly formed his staff with other USAFFE officers.

A tough former member of the 88th Field Artillery, Philippine Scouts, Third Lieutenant Mario S. Garcia, had survived the Death March and incarceration at O'Donnell and remained a backer of the guerrilla movement for almost a year. In 1943 the Japanese became suspicious of Garcia's activities and again imprisoned him for a month in his hometown of Cabanatuan City where guards tried beatings, starvation, and torture in an effort to learn of the young officer's true allegiance.

Finally convinced that he had no guerrilla affiliation, the Japanese set Mario Garcia free and allowed him to join the Philippine Constabulary along with Monsod. It would be another year before the Japanese learned they had made a big mistake.

Pajota's direct information concerning Japanese activities around Cabanatuan City dated back to September 1942, when Juanito Quitives joined the constabulary. With brave men like Monsod and Garcia in the intelligence network, Quitives stood an even better chance of relaying important data to the guerrillas. For, unknown to the Japanese, First Lieutenant Juanito Quitives also commanded Pajota's Squadron 200.

Lieutenant Merle Musselman arrived at Cabanatuan in June 1943 and immediately went to work with the other doctors at the camp hospital. The smaller Camp Number 3 where Musselman had been assigned for a year was about to be closed.

Doctor Musselman had heard of the deplorable hospital conditions at Cabanatuan through various members of work details who had been transferred back and forth between the two camps. But seeing thousands of bed patients dying slow deaths from lack of medicines and guard brutality shocked the young officer. Visions of those early days at O'Donnell flashed through his mind.

At least at Cabanatuan there were some medicines (though never enough), and the hospital staff was well organized.

But the black flies, lice, bedbugs, and mosquitoes continually spread disease. Handicapped by meager laboratory facilities and lack of cooperation of Japanese officers, the camp doctors and medics worked in twenty-four-hour shifts. Soon, deaths resulted among their own staff.

The worst slow killer was beriberi. It was probably the most dangerous vitamin deficiency disease encountered at Cabanatuan and was directly responsible for more deaths than any other illness. It was chronic in nature, and the POWs who suffered from it and did not die were either incapacitated for months or permanently disabled.

Generally speaking, the POWs' diet was deficient in all vitamins as a result of their lack of meat and vegetables. The rice issued by the Japanese was of medium mill, most of the Vitamin-B-containing pericarp removed.

A few days after his arrival, Doctor Musselman was advised that the last of the precious vitamins and medicines received in Red Cross 1942 Christmas packages were gone, and everyone began to pray that the Japanese would allow 1943 packages to be distributed.

Depressed with the news that the staff was once again out of supplies, Doctor Musselman returned to the laboratory, where he found three men busy manufacturing strange-looking tablets from handmade molds. The pills were "sulfa tablets," he was informed.

The Japanese guards were constantly trying to buy medical items from the lab, for they also had shortages. As frightened as the guards were of the hospital area, they did often venture into the lab and had been paying handsome prices for the "sulfa." With the money from the sale of the pills, cigarettes were purchased at the camp commissary—cigarettes the Japanese had stolen from Red Cross packages.

The Japanese never discovered that those sulfa pills they lined up to buy from the POWs were actually counterfeited from nothing but starch.

December arrived with its usual pleasant, balmy weather in 1943. Two thousand six hundred and fifty-six Americans lay buried in the POW Camp Cabanatuan cemetery.

Only 3,844 remained alive.

5

I wouldn't take the whole damn Jap Army for one Alamo Scout!

—General Walter Krueger, spring 1944

NEW GUINEA
(1943)

James Canfield Fisher's concern for humanity and a gifted mind guided him successfully through Harvard Medical School. After his internship, Boston City Hospital assigned Dr. Fisher to its surgical staff, where he served for two and a half years until World War II interrupted a promising career.

The only son of novelist Dorothy Canfield Fisher spent his early years in France, where his father served for three years as an ambulance driver with the French Army during World War I. After that, James traveled Europe extensively with his parents. In fact, his early schooling was in Europe, and when the Fishers finally returned to their native Vermont, young James's friends had a little trouble understanding his heavy French accent.

James was an amiable and curious fellow, full of desire to continue his untiring search for knowledge, doing his part for mankind in the process. He considered World War II only a temporary interruption in life. He never seemed to waste a minute, possessing a marvelous ability to turn every new encounter into something of lasting value. And, armed with an infectious grin, he managed to make every person he met feel that he was the most important individual on earth.

Like many intelligent men preoccupied with deep thought, Dr. Fisher was terribly absentminded. He had been that way since early childhood, often to the amusement of both teachers and friends. It was not that forgivable fault that produced his overseas assignment during the war. It was the irony of events and that mysterious system of selection executed by some unknown individual in the high command of the U.S. military.

By all logical thinking, James Fisher should have been assigned to a medical unit in Europe where his proficiency in languages would have been most beneficial. At least he should have been assigned to a major medical staff somewhere, so his surgical skills could be put to good use. Instead, he ended up in New Guinea as commanding officer, Medical Detachment, 98th Field Artillery Battalion, Pack. Captain Fisher did not complain. He shrugged off the peculiarity of the assignment with the thought that he must be needed in an artillery battalion. Why else would fate send him there?

The 98th Field Artillery Battalion, Pack, left Camp Carson in December 1942, arriving with their 1,000 mules and mountain guns at Brisbon in January 1943.

Sixth Army commander General Walter Krueger had planned to use the 98th in the Salamaua campaign but by February, when the battalion arrived in New Guinea, the Salamaua battles were practically over. Having already crossed the mountains, Allied troops were dealing the Imperial Army a major land defeat. For the time being, the 98th and their equipment were useless in New Guinea.

But Frank Dow Merrill was busy training a regimental-size group of American volunteers in the rough mountainous Burmese jungle and desperately needed the 98th's special equipment to fight the Japanese there. The 98th's mules were quickly reassigned to "Merrill's Marauders." This action left Sixth Army at a complete loss for what to do with the troops of the 98th.

A short, husky Captain Fisher went about his duties dwarfed by the former muleskinners in his battalion. With the exception of most of the officers and a handful of men everyone in the 98th was at least six feet tall. Considering the laborious tasks usually confronting a pack artillery outfit, the Army had established a minimum height requirement of five feet, ten inches and drafted these tough, healthy individuals from the rural farms or mountainous areas of America.

It would not be easy for men accustomed to a life of hard work to lie around and wait for the Army's new plans. Soon, morale began to slip, and Dr. Fisher found his duties far more complex than expected. In the field, personal health is so entwined with spiritual health that the medical officer often supersedes the chaplain. The simple fact is that men sometimes find it easier to talk with one who is more acquainted with the realities of war and life and . . . waiting.

The low morale situation brought the big men of the 98th to Dr. Fisher, and everyone soon developed deep admiration for their medical officer. Yet, when they called him "Captain Fisher," he politely suggested a different title. "Just call me Jimmy," he would say. Not all the men could allow their military or common courtesy to slip that far. So Captain James Canfield Fisher became more popularly known as "Captain Jim" or, of course, simply "Doc."

NUEVA ECIJA, THE PHILIPPINES
(1943)

In Nueva Ecija Province on Luzon, eighteen-year-old Jesus Bondoc did not have a rifle, but he was, nonetheless, a guerrilla in Major Robert Lapham's army.

A squadron commander had sent Bondoc to the city of Guimba to procure some quinine for the ailing American and when the young guerrilla returned he found the camp in a flurry of excitement. While he was gone some of his countrymen had turned over to Lapham a damaged radio transmitter unit. Not only did the major manage to repair the equipment, he had even succeeded in establishing contact with MacArthur's headquarters in Australia.

By late August 1943, Colonel Anderson and Colonel Volckmann, still operating in separate areas of Luzon, had likewise made contact with Allied headquarters using primitive, practically homemade radio units.

At first, Allied headquarters refused to believe the American guerrillas' communication, fearing that it was a Japanese trick. The reluctant headquarters demanded names of the Americans' girlfriends and schoolteachers, and a variety of information to be verified. Often answering in a barrage of typical American profanity (motivated by both frustration and an effort to be believed), the guerrillas finally convinced MacArthur's staff.

Contact was now established (and maintained) with an army MacArthur had previously hoped, but could not be sure, existed. It represented the first confirmation that an active, vigorous guerrilla campaign was in full swing on Luzon.

Overshadowing the first communication of important data was the heartbreaking news of the Bataan Death March, the death camps, and the atrocities committed by the Japanese on civilians in reprisal for guerrilla activities. Because of those brutal retaliations, MacArthur was compelled to issue what became known as the "lay low order."

In essence, the guerrillas were instructed to cease their direct attacks on the enemy until arms and munitions could be supplied from Australia. In the meantime, the guerrillas were to increase the sophistication of their units, intensify surveillance, and send as much information on the Japanese as possible.

Two basic factors forced MacArthur to radio the "lay low order." First, the guerrillas, with all their small victories considered, might quickly become extinct without adequate weapons. The Allies desperately needed detailed information concerning enemy troop concentrations, troop movements, beach defenses, and air base locations before the liberation could be undertaken. Thus, survival of a well-organized resistance movement was paramount for intelligence purposes.

Second, MacArthur would need the support of the entire population of the Philippines when the time for invasion arrived. He had had that support once and was convinced that it could be maintained with the majority of Filipinos. But those reprisals for guerrilla activity upon thousands of civilians might jeopardize the feeling of allegiance to the United States. MacArthur assured the guerrillas, however, that they would be unleashed on the enemy again . . . when the time was ripe.

Captain Juan Pajota received his orders from Major Lapham. Until otherwise instructed, Pajota and his men were to avoid contact with the Japanese, engaging instead in intensified intelligence gathering.

Using an obsolete map of the province of Nueva Ecija, Pajota began to make his own "operations map" to cover each square mile of his area of responsibility. Without the aid of a compass he and several teams recorded every road, trail, river, stream, and town on the new map, traveling some twenty square miles on foot to do so.

The guerrilla command posts and special landmarks were all listed, and enemy positions marked on thin paper overlays. Pajota's operations map would take almost a year to complete, but the end result was surprisingly accurate.

A mile north of POW Camp Cabanatuan, the Imperial Army engineers stayed busy through the rainy season of 1943 reconstructing the bridge over Cabu River, at the same site where Filipino USAFFE engineers had destroyed the old bridge during the retreat in 1941.

Since the reconstruction required much more time than originally anticipated, the Japanese decided to erect a temporary bridge to handle the flow of traffic between Cabanatuan City and Bongabon.

The engineers selected a spot for this wooden bridge some 300 yards northwest of the highway and detoured vehicles along a dirt track from Barrio Cabu to the river. Once across the river, traffic proceeded on another dirt road at an angle to where it connected, once again, with the highway.

NEW GUINEA
(October 1943)

To many in the military it seemed as if Lieutenant General Walter Krueger was born in the United States Army. Emigrating to the United States from West Prussia, Walter Krueger volunteered as an enlisted man in 1898 during the Spanish-American War. While serving in Luzon in 1901 at the peak of the Philippine Insurrection, Krueger was commissioned a second lieutenant. Later, he was appointed chief of the newly formed "Tank Corps" in World War I.

Known both for his skill as a tactician and as an excellent trainer of troops, the sixty-two-year-old Krueger was appointed as commander of the U.S. Sixth Army early in 1943. By October of that year, his well-organized army had moved to New Guinea and, winning one battle after another, gradually forced the Japanese into overland retreat.

General Krueger's concern and love for his enlisted men was a well-known fact. Having come up through the ranks, unlike most generals in the Pacific, he could appreciate the hardships the soldiers endured both in training and in combat. He looked forward to future invasions, but the loss of a single man weighed heavily on him at all times.

Early in October 1943, Lieutenant General Krueger studied a special problem confronting his headquarters. True, his campaign was progressing well. Salamaua and Lae had fallen, but the rest of New Guinea was loaded with Japanese. Sixth Army knew where they were, but exactly how many, their activities, physical condition, and morale were not known.

Information was flooding his headquarters in the form of captured documents, prisoner of war interrogation reports, and air reconnaissance. It was all general information—not specific enough to satisfy Krueger. Air observations were fine, but much could not be seen from the air. Documents and reports from prisoners or natives were stimulating, but reliability was questionable. To gamble even so much as a company of men on that kind of data did not sit easy with General Krueger.

He had also studied the results of a secret experimental group formed by the Navy and decided to discuss the information with his staff.

The "Amphibious Scouts," as the Navy called their team, was formed by Commander William Coultas and had begun operations in July. The concept was basically simple, but the missions were some of the most dangerous of the war. A small group of men, all volunteers with special training, would land by night in enemy territory, reconnoiter for several days—weeks if necessary—and bring out firsthand information. This temporary unit was composed of men from both the U.S. Army and the Australian Army as well as several Navy adventurers. After considering the success of those early missions by the Amphibious Scouts, General Krueger concluded that the Army needed such an organization on a permanent basis.

To find the right men and keep the program secret at the same time would be quite an undertaking. Commanders must sift carefully through their troops in the Southwest Pacific to find men most suited and, of course, those men must be willing to volunteer. Krueger outlined the basic requirements for the type of men he wanted—courageous, but not foolhardy, rugged, healthy, good swimmers, intelligent, and expert marksmen.

When asked what he proposed to call this new unit, he replied, "They'll be called the Alamo Scouts. I've always been inspired with the story of the Alamo and those brave men who died there. Our Alamo Scouts must have the courage and qualifications of Crockett, Bowie, and Travis!"

By December 3, construction of the training site was well under way near a small native village on Kalo Kalo off the east coast of Fergusson Island. Here, isolated but within a half-hour boat ride from Sixth Army headquarters, the Alamo Scouts began their training in secrecy and without interruption. The six-week course started with an intensive physical conditioning program, especially strenuous in the sapping heat of the tropics.

Then there were swimming tests, rubber boating, marksmanship—emphasizing quick firing from the hip as well as conventional methods—and familiarizing the men with every small weapon in the U.S. and Japanese arsenals. Exercising razor-sharp teamwork, the men learned to move like ghosts in the jungle.

Long marches, accuracy drills in grenade tossing, hand-to-hand combat, and courses in blinker signaling, field radio operation and repair, message-writing methods (using a variety of codes), and map-compass reading sometimes lasted for a full twenty-four-hour period. As a small reward, the Scout trainees were seldom required to stand formal formations and there was rarely a prescribed uniform. Pay was the same as for any foot soldier in the Pacific.

Simulated missions with PT boats dropping them off on deserted islands were repeated over and over, always with enthusiastic support from the Navy. Conditioning under fire was the final phase. To add realism to the training, live ammunition and full-charge explosives were used. The swimming test, for example, included a course requiring a team to swim out in the surf underwater for fifty yards, then come up together. Upon a signal the men surface dived while sprays of lead from several Tommy guns whined into the water where they had submerged.

All the trainees who finished the six weeks were good, but some way had to be devised to select the best of the good. The democratic process solved this selection dilemma. Each enlisted man candidate was asked to name, by secret ballot, three officers, in order of his personal preference, he would be most willing to follow on a mission. He was also asked to name five other men into whose hands he would entrust his life if he worked with them as a team member. Student officers, in turn, were asked which men they would wish to have with them on a mission. To this was added the staff officers' recommendations, and the total votes were counted. The result was a Scout team consisting of one officer and six men.

For the next several months, with the help of the daredevil PT boat crews, the Alamo Scouts investigated enemy positions under the very nose of the Japanese. Dropped off with their rubber rafts at night from the PT boats, Scout teams would paddle through often violent surf, hide the rafts, carry out their mission, and then return to the beach at the appointed hour trusting the Navy would always be there to pluck them from the danger of eventual detection.

Knowledge gained on hundreds of enemy positions by the daring Scouts was of tremendous value in the planning of many invasions. Within nine months various Scouts had earned a total of nineteen Silver Stars, eighteen Bronze Stars, and four Soldiers' Medals without losing a single man.

Scout Headquarters once reported to General Krueger that they knew where they could kidnap a high-ranking Japanese officer. All plans for a raid on the enemy camp had been carefully drawn and two Scout teams were standing by, dressed in special camouflage jungle suits.

Krueger studied the report and request with great interest. The capture of the particular enemy officer would have excellent propaganda value but little tactical value. Weighing the odds, he decided the mission was too risky and informed the disappointed Scouts that he could not authorize the raid. When a staff officer pointed out the possible success of the mission might cost only a few men, General Krueger snapped, "I wouldn't take the whole damn Jap Army for one Alamo Scout!"

CABANATUAN, NUEVA ECIJA, THE PHILIPPINES
(January 1944)

By late January 1944, the Americans in POW Camp Cabanatuan on Luzon had given up hope for 1943 Red Cross Christmas packages. Word circulated that both mail and those cherished packages had arrived, but for unexplained reasons, the Japanese commandant elected not to release them.

After continual pleading by camp medical officers, the commandant did finally agree to distribute small supplies of medicine. However, the remainder of valuable goods—vitamins, shoes, blankets, toilet articles, and cigarettes—would be held for some future date.

But the Filipinos from Pangatian and her nearby barrios did their best to pass on small Christmas gifts to the POWs with permission from the commandant. Medical Corpsman Eugene Evers received a broken phonograph complete with hand crank and records. He and his buddies managed to repair the old machine and even made workable needles from bits of wire. The records were cracked but the music was to bring many hours of enjoyment.

The secret radio in the camp, at long last, was in working order. The static-filled news broadcast from Australia informed the POWs of MacArthur's campaign progress and news of the war's progress in Europe.

But the majority of prisoners in Cabanatuan were still unaware of the radio's existence. When news of Allied victories was passed from man to man, many were skeptical of the truth.

Most of the prisoners had now been confined for over nineteen months. Although the death rate was no longer spiraling, conditions in the camp had not improved.

Food—that is, food without meat—was still rationed and medicines remained in short supply or completely nonexistent.

6

I'm going to turn you men into Rangers!

—Lieutenant Colonel Henry Andrew Mucci, April 1944

NEW GUINEA
(April 1944)

A year had gone by since Captain James Fisher and the 98th Field Artillery Battalion arrived in New Guinea and the Army had still failed to find some practical use for them. Bored, and with morale dangerously low, the husky fellows occupied their time by making the most of any project, regardless of how trivial.

Dr. Fisher had a passion for carpentry. Among the tall pines in the Red Mountains near his home in Arlington, Vermont, were numerous small cabins he had built as a youngster. His skill with a hammer and saw stayed with him, as did that passion for constructing things. So it was only natural for him to find a spot and erect a "clinic" during those months of waiting.

The site was a small hill on the bank of a fast-flowing, shallow stream directly across from the battalion headquarters. In this little shelter, Fisher planned not only to treat the minor ailments and injuries of the 98th, but to expand to accommodate the needs of local natives.

Members of his medical detachment and many others offered to help with the clinic's construction, but Captain Fisher really preferred to do the work himself.

Several times a day "Captain Jim" would wade into the clear, cold waters and splash back and forth from headquarters or the supply area to his little hospital, usually forgetting an item each trip. The men, unable to do much with the construction of the clinic, decided to build a small bridge. At least they could contribute something for their doctor's efforts.

A day after the completion of the bridge, several men on a detail near the headquarters watched with amusement as Captain Fisher emerged from his clinic, strolled to the stream, and began to wade across. As he reached the opposite bank, he was confronted by the detail. They knew he was absentminded, but this was too much.

"Why didn't you use the bridge?" one soldier asked.

Captain Fisher scratched at his close-chopped black hair and grinned. "Oh! The bridge . . . I forget about the bridge!"

The men of the 98th Field Artillery had wasted away fourteen months mostly at Port Moresby, through no fault of their own. Without real purpose for existence, only the strong moral fiber of the men and officers held the unit from becoming a battalion of troublemakers.

Morale is a command responsibility, and it was not one to be shed or ignored by General Walter Krueger. In fact, Krueger had a plan for the men of the 98th and was only waiting for a few more details to develop before placing his ideas into action.

The success of the elite Alamo Scouts pleased Krueger. The small-team surveillance of the enemy had yielded magnificent results in those early months of 1944. Now, to complete his well-organized Sixth Army, General Krueger needed something else. The plan for the invasion of the Philippines would necessitate the training of another elite unit—a highly trained combat unit for assignments too large for the Scouts to handle. After all, the concept and purpose of the Scouts centered on reconnaissance and surveillance, not major assault missions.

General Krueger's colleagues in England planning the invasion of Europe already had such battalion-size units undergoing special training. They called the units Army Rangers.

For some months, Krueger worked on a plan to establish his own Sixth Army Ranger battalion. The most logical group from which to form the nucleus of a Ranger unit was, of course, the idle 98th Field Artillery's battalion of husky giants.

But an army does not convert a bunch of big men into Rangers without considerable effort. The key would lie with intensive training by an excellent cadre and a commander with unusual qualities.

For the 98th, a leader must be chosen who could churn the men into an effective fighting force—a leader of special caliber and personality who would gain respect, maybe even admiration, through personal participation. Krueger knew he needed a man with dramatic leadership abilities but insisted that the battalion commander also possess genuine interest and concern for the men. Few of the officers in the 98th were infantry trained. Most, naturally, had been schooled in artillery. Krueger concluded it would be better to find someone from outside the Sixth Army command staff, a stranger who had no obligations or allegiance to other officers. The man finally selected was West Point graduate Lieutenant Colonel Henry Andrew Mucci.

When Lieutenant Colonel Mucci arrived at Port Moresby to take command of the 98th in April 1944, he had just turned thirty-three years of age. With a high, receding hairline, though, he appeared much older.

Since his graduation in 1932, Mucci had held a number of less glamorous and certainly less demanding positions. He had been a company commander at Fort Warren, Wyoming, and later went to Fort Benning, Georgia, for additional infantry training. The final assignment before New Guinea was Hawaii, where he received concentrated schooling in jungle warfare and Ranger-type tactics while serving with the military police staff.

The first day of the new command Lieutenant Colonel Mucci stood off on the sidelines calmly puffing on a pipe. His dark piercing eyes, accented by heavy brows, studied the men as they formed directly in front of an eight-by-eight-foot platform that stood some four feet high. When the battalion was called to attention, Colonel Mucci tapped the ashes from the silver-rimmed pipe on his heel and crammed it, stem first, into his shirt pocket. With a swaggered gait he strutted toward the front of the assembly and in one quick leap, aided by placing his hand on the deck, was standing on the platform.

Now, the 98th had a clear view of their new commander. It was a sight most of the men had never seen, but one they would never forget. There Mucci stood, a trim, small man with fists clenched and placed on his hips, causing his elbows to jut outward, clearly revealing a .45 automatic hung low in its leather shoulder holster under one armpit. Mucci raised a hand and scratched at his dark mustache, then returned the hand to his hip.

The small figure on the platform shouted, "AT . . . EASE!"

There was a moment while the men relaxed their position and waited for what they expected to be a few uninteresting announcements.

"I am Lieutenant Colonel Mucci . . . your new commanding officer. I'm going to turn you men into *Rangers!* From now on, the 98th will be known as the Sixth United States Army Ranger Battalion. For the next few months we will be going through some of the toughest training you can possibly imagine. We're going through it together! You men are big and healthy . . . you can take it. And when we're through you'll be the roughest bunch of soldiers in the Sixth Army.

"I'm not saying this is going to be any picnic. But you are going to learn things that no other soldier knows how to do. You are going to see action and plenty of it.

"You're going to learn about new weapons," Mucci continued, "new ways to kill Japs . . . and how to stay alive in the process." Colonel Mucci paused and glanced down at one of his staff NCOs standing beside the platform. "Toss me your knife, Sergeant!"

The Sergeant swung a large trench knife he was holding up to his commander.

Mucci pulled the double-edged blade from its sheath. "You have heard that the Japs are good with bayonets and knives. Well, you're going to be better. You're going to learn to kill so fast with this knife that the Nip won't have time to yell. . . ."

Chuckles erupted from a few NCOs in the first line.

Colonel Mucci looked at Staff Sergeant Mike Koren. "Come on up here, Sergeant. I want you to try and get me with this knife!"

"Go up and get him," Staff Sergeant W. R. Butler teased.

"*You* go get him, Butler!" Koren replied. Sergeant Butler climbed onto the platform and stood before Mucci.

Colonel Mucci's dark eyes squinted as he looked up into the face of the six-foot-four-inch soldier. "What's your name, trooper?"

"Butler, sir! Staff Sergeant Butler."

"Okay, Sergeant Butler," Mucci said as he handed him the knife, "try and cut me!"

"Are you sure, sir?"

"Cut me, dammit!" Mucci shouted.

Sergeant Butler lunged forward, aiming the blade at the commander's arm.

Mucci moved with lightning speed. Before anyone could determine what happened, Butler was flipped, landing on the ground in front of the platform.

A roar of laughter was silenced by Mucci, who raised both hands and yelled, "At ease! At ease!"

Sergeant Butler dusted himself off and stepped back into the formation.

"Now," Mucci went on, "the reason I could do that to Sergeant Butler was because I was trained how to do it. I guarantee you that in a few weeks you'll be able to make the enemy eat his own knife. But there are a few other things to learn first. I may be Colonel Mucci, but don't dare call me that in the field. The first one who calls me 'colonel,' I'll call him *general,* and we'll see who the Japs shoot first!

"Soon . . . you'll wear no insignia . . . no rank at all on your combat uniforms. You'll call each other by nicknames, rather than rank. That means you really get to know one another and learn to work together as a team. You don't need to worry about your identity. Everyone in the Pacific will know who you are because you'll be the most dangerous men they ever met. To get you accustomed to some of these changes, we're not going to be tough on military courtesy. I don't want some fool saluting me in the field . . . the Japs may see you do it.

"I'll see to it that you get a good ration of beer from now on. If you are man enough to fight, you are man enough to drink. But . . . you had better be standing tall the next morning or . . . no more beer! I have two little whistles, which make a lot of noise. If I blow this black one, it means, hurry up! If I blow this brass one, it means you had really better hurry up! And . . . one thing more. If you want to talk to me about something, just come up and knock at my tent. I'm always interested in what you have on your mind!"

By the end of the first week a few men in the new Ranger battalion requested transfer to other units. A few others were transferred out by Colonel Mucci for various reasons, which he held as a secret between them.

Though it was not a requirement of the Army or Mucci, married men were encouraged to give their situation serious thought before they elected to stay in the unit. By the end of the month, though, everyone who remained was a volunteer.

The final Ranger battalion was to consist of approximately 600 men. Each of the former artillery "batteries" became a company containing sixty-three to sixty-five men. A Ranger company consisted of a company headquarters with one officer and three men, two platoons with one officer and thirty-one men each. Each platoon was divided into a headquarters, a special "weapons" section of six men, and two "assault" sections of eleven men each.

The assault section had a headquarters of one man, an assault squad of five men and a light machine gun squad of five men. Machine guns, however, were soon replaced with the easier-to-manage Browning Automatic Rifle (BAR). The firepower of a Ranger company, with their mixture of thirty two M1 semiautomatic rifles, BARs, M1 carbines, and Thompson submachine guns (Tommy guns), equaled that of a 180-man regular infantry company.

For support, the 6th Rangers had their own medical detachment under Captain Fisher, a communications section, a headquarters unit, and a motor pool.

First Lieutenant Robert W. Prince was a likable young officer. The men of his "C" Company considered Prince a strict disciplinarian, but fair in his decisions and concern for their welfare. The other officers knew Robert Prince as a quiet, serious man possessing the rare quality of a calm, natural leader.

Prince never wasted time with dramatics or exaggeration. Perhaps this serious attitude left him vulnerable to Colonel Mucci's magic personality. For Bob Prince, at age twenty-three, was also very impressionable.

No doubt the Army could have used Lieutenant Prince during

that year the 98th sat around with nothing to do. Prince had received an ROTC commission after graduating from Stanford University and then intensive artillery training at Fort Sill. He was a bright artillery officer, ideally suited for combat. But fate had held him with the 98th and now fate was about to tie him with the most unusual and exciting officer he had ever met.

Colonel Henry Mucci possessed a natural ability to motivate people. He was a born politician who knew what to say, and when and how to say it. He knew the art of leadership and when to turn charming, rather than dictatorial, if the occasion called for such personal tactics. To get morale on the upswing while turning the 98th into Rangers would require a good cadre. No one appreciated this fact more than Mucci.

Colonel Mucci looked down his Roman nose at Lieutenant Prince and then broke into a large grin as he began their first interview.

Since Bob Prince was married, Mucci explained the option to transfer to a different unit, but quickly added, "I need good men like you, Lieutenant. You stay with the Rangers and I promise you'll be two grades higher in rank by the time we are through liberating the Philippines!"

Mucci, as usual, was convincing, and Bob Prince decided to stay. Not because of the promise of promotions—even Mucci knew it was not the key—but because the challenge seemed interesting. And Prince had become attached to his men of C Company. He would like to see them through the war.

Everyone was to learn that Colonel Mucci was full of wild claims, yet each claim had an element of truth so heavy that it was often difficult to separate fact from fiction. He was equally full of promises—promises he always had a way of fulfilling.

When the Ranger training began with the grueling hours of calisthenics, Mucci was there, going through the exercises in the hot sun with the men. Often, he would even be on the platform leading PT. When one man yelled, "Dish it out, you son of a bitch! We can take it!" Mucci increased the "pushups" from 100 to 150, keeping pace with the strongest.

Whatever Mucci told the men to do, he also did. He seemed to be everywhere—on each twenty-mile hike, in the middle of bay-

onet training, jogging along on the five-mile runs before break-
fast, crawling through the mud to participate in attacks on simulated Japanese pillboxes, firing a variety of weapons and scoring
some of the highest grades.

Some men, of course, originally resented their battalion
commander's Napoleonic personality. They called him "little
MacArthur." Yet one fact was obvious. Unlike generals, Mucci
was there to be seen.

Often quick-tempered and emotional, Mucci had learned
somehow to control the faults. And those who were critical discovered that behind the colonel's flamboyant front was an individual who was honest and kind to the lowest-ranking soldier.

So the big men of the 6th Rangers, happy to find a place in the
war at last, followed their commander—and learned fast.

Twenty-six-year-old Staff Sergeant Norton Most rubbed his
blond crew cut hair as he studied the technical manuals that
came with the 6th Rangers' new radio equipment. After weeks of
training with the old SCR 284 radios, Sergeant Most and the other
members of the communication section now must learn the pec-
ularities of the SCR 694.

Basically the two radios functioned the same, but the three
new sets had a much longer range for both voice and key transmission. Ideal for the Rangers, the SCR 694 unit was equipped
with pack boards (canvas stretched on a light frame) for comfortable portage in the field.

Three men would be required to carry all the equipment for
one SCR 694 unit, and each must understand its operation and
maintenance completely as a safety measure should the other two
men be killed in combat.

Sergeant Most was an inquisitive and intelligent man, always
working on some mathematical problem with a slide rule. Headquarters was delighted when they learned that the sergeant had
not only mastered the use of the SCR 694, but increased its normal transmission range from twenty miles to twenty-five miles
through slight modification.

Sixth Rangers F Company had their own priest. Well, though
his buddies called him "Father Schilli," Tech 5 Sergeant Francis
Schilli was not a real priest. Raised a strong Catholic on a Missouri

farm, T/5 Schilli had memorized practically every sacrament and ritual of the church.

During those long, boring days before the 98th became the 6th Rangers, he was often called upon to quote a special passage, amazing Protestants and Catholics alike. But the men always remarked that he should have brought his violin to New Guinea rather than sending it home when they left the States. The powerful hands of the big country boy could make that violin answer his every demand with tunes like "Wabash Cannonball" and "Red River Valley." He played it as a fiddle and to the other muleskinners, Schilli's music was the best they had ever heard.

Those same fingers that guided a violin bow, repaired delicate wood cases, and rehaired bows could also repair heavy farm equipment with equal skill. It was no wonder, therefore, that he could take apart and reassemble an M1 rifle blindfolded faster than most men in F Company.

T/5 Schilli gladly demonstrated his art to his best friend, Corporal Roy W. Sweezy, and soon Sweezy was just as proficient with the weapon drill.

Both men were quiet and serious. They were the kind of soldiers everyone liked because they cooperated and did not bother anyone; the type of men one often meets in the military, yet learns very little about.

If Schilli was quiet, Sweezy was even more of an introvert.

Corporal Sweezy was also raised on a farm, but in the far north country of Michigan. Except for what he confided in his friend, Roy Sweezy's thoughts were mostly his own. He stayed to himself, even blushed when someone told a dirty joke, but was learning to be a good Ranger.

No one ever teased the big easygoing farm boys much. No one was that crazy, for they were powerful enough to break a man's back, though it's not likely that the thought ever crossed their minds.

Lieutenant Colonel Mucci called Charles H. Bosard "the kid," but not because of his age. At twenty-six, Bosard was, in fact, a few years older than most of the others. The affectionate nickname Mucci bestowed on the first sergeant of F Company was in reference to Bosard's size. Yet the wiry five-foot-six-inch Bosard could move about with tremendous speed as he maintained relentless pressure on his men in the field.

Typical of so many tough first sergeants, Bosard's size had nothing to do with his ability to train and lead. Mucci knew the value of a good noncommissioned officer and, to him, Bosard was worth every bit of his 140 pounds in gold.

Somehow, at the end of practically every training day, Sergeant Bosard managed to find a few quiet moments in his tent and maintained a field diary.

"*May 8, 1944*—Having a big general inspection today—Have been firing all our weapons, going over Misery Hill, through Torture Flats, landing nets, obstacle course—ran about ten miles. We are all darn good swimmers now—250 yards with a 50-pound pack. *June 4*—Working very hard—going through grenade course and bayonet course. Getting ready for amphibious training. *June 19*—Getting ready to go out on a night problem . . . night patrol, perimeter defense, etc. We are all *Rangers* now!"

Staff Sergeant August T. Stern and the men of C Company's weapon section finished their familiarization with flame throwers, machine guns, and both .90- and .60-mm mortars by the last week of July 1944.

Each Ranger, before completing his training, would fire every weapon. For this reason, Sergeant Stern's group and the other weapon sections must not only be proficient in the operation of the weapons, they must be able to instruct their buddies as well.

Of all the new weapons developed for the U.S. foot soldier, one of the most interesting was the one they nicknamed the "stove pipe." It had no impressive technical nomenclature, unless it was "Rocket Launcher, Shoulder Type," but few ever called it that.

More popularly known as the "bazooka," the 2.36-inch rocket launcher was simply a smoothbore steel tube about five feet long, open at both ends, and equipped with handgrips, shoulder rest, trigger mechanism, and simple sights. The bazooka gained its name from its resemblance to the crude musical horn of the same name used by a radio comedian of the day, Bob Burns.

The military bazooka was developed chiefly for attacking tanks or fortified positions at short range. Weighing a little over fourteen pounds, the launcher could be disassembled and carried in two sections. The nineteen-inch-long rocket it fired weighed about three and one half pounds and carried eight ounces of a powerful explosive known as pentolite. Traveling at 300 feet per second, it was capable of penetrating five inches of armor plate at 300 yards.

About the only disadvantage of the bazooka was the "back blast," a burst of flame out the rear of the weapon as the rocket ignited and sped toward the target. A bazooka team was usually composed of two men, one man to carry and fire the weapon and one to carry and load the rockets.

Japanese tanks had operated successfully in the Far East largely because they had little opposition until the Americans arrived. Against American tanks the Japanese armor was no match due to their thin steel skin and lack of speed and power. But the American foot soldier could not always rely on his tanks to be present in the jungle to back him up. The bazooka, therefore, became the Japanese tankers' worst enemy.

NUEVA ECIJA, THE PHILIPPINES
(August 1944)

During mid-August 1944, Luzon guerrilla Major Robert Lapham received confirmation on his primitive radio that MacArthur and the U.S. Navy were ready to supply the guerrillas in the Philippines with the promised weapons and munitions. The only possible way this could be accomplished was by submarine.

Major Lapham requested Captain Pajota to select a suitable site for the rendezvous, and plans were made to pick up the important deliveries. Although the dropoff point was definite, the Navy could not guarantee the exact time. Too much depended on weather and Japanese air or naval activity around Luzon.

Colonel Bernard Anderson also was promised delivery of supplies and selected the mouth of the Masanga River on the east coast of Luzon. To reach this scheduled point, Colonel Anderson and his men successfully avoided Japanese patrols and bands of

Huk guerrillas as they crossed over fifty miles of open country on foot. Once in the safety of the eastern mountain range, they were able to move down to the coast, make contact with the U.S.S. *Nautilus,* and return with the valuable equipment without incident.

For Major Lapham's contact, Pajota suggested a cove known as Debut Bay near the town of Baler about midway along the east coast of Luzon. Debut Bay is a narrow cove with waters deep enough to easily accommodate the *Nautilus.* Surrounding the cove, heavy forest providing excellent concealment stretched up into the high Sierra Madre Mountains.

Major Lapham and Captain McKenzie arrived at Debut Bay and, along with Pajota, established a temporary headquarters . . . and waited. When the *Nautilus* arrived, she was able to maneuver to within twenty-five yards of shore and docked at a primitive raft Pajota's men had constructed of bamboo.

The joy of the two Americans at meeting countrymen for the first time in almost two and a half years was, understandably, overwhelming. The excitement continued as the Filipinos began to unload a fantastic assortment of weapons and supplies.

There were Thompson submachine guns, .45-caliber "grease guns," M1 carbines, and Browning Automatic Rifles (BARs), plus what seemed to be an unending quantity of ammunition. The small, lightweight carbines with their fifteen- and thirty-round magazines were perfectly suited for guerrilla warfare and the little Filipinos. And there were even supplies that answered to personal requests—American-made leather shoes for the sandaled or barefoot Filipinos and a new pair of binoculars for Pajota.

Many cartons of a very special item were unloaded—American cigarettes. The U.S. psychological warfare teams had not missed a trick. On each pack of cigarettes was the picture of General Douglas MacArthur, and clearly printed beneath his profile were his words, *"I SHALL RETURN!"* In a matter of days the cigarettes would be handed out one at a time all over Nueva Ecija. Each happy recipient was shown the pack with the promised pledge reconfirmed.

Major Lapham, Colonel Anderson, and some of the other American guerrillas could have evacuated the Philippines on the *Nautilus* and left the fighting to the Filipinos. No one would have condemned them. Each American was plagued with at least one tropical illness. That was enough reason to leave. Each had been in the combat zone since December 1941—almost three years—under the most trying and unusual conditions. That was surely reason enough to leave.

Of course, MacArthur's headquarters had already commended them highly for their outstanding sacrifices. The ranks they bestowed upon themselves, qualified by their duty and performance, had been recognized by the U.S. Army. It was a small reward, but they asked for no more—only the privilege to continue to serve their country. Whatever motivated these men of unusual caliber, their decision to stay and fight rather than evacuate certainly impressed the Filipinos.

But now that the Filipino guerrillas knew American subs could deliver supplies, they were puzzled by an interesting question. If the United States could get the *Nautilus* in and out of Debut Bay, and the American guerrilla commanders would not leave, then why must the sub return empty? Why could it not evacuate the American POWs at Cabanatuan?

The idea was not completely new. Colonel Anderson had drawn attack maps and all the plans for a raid on the POW camp to free those poor individuals who were still half alive. Major Lapham, whose command area actually included the POW camp, likewise had maps and plans. He and Captain Pajota discussed the idea many times during August and September 1944. If the attack on POW Camp Cabanatuan was executed at once, over 3,000 Americans could be set free.

Pajota's squadrons and Lapham's other units in the Guimba area of Nueva Ecija could easily overpower the Japanese garrison at the POW camp. The evacuation of 3,000 sick men across the mountains to the sea while under pursuit by the Japanese, of course, presented the greatest worry. Most of the POWs were not capable of walking that distance. They would have to be carried.

In the Guimba area, Major Lapham had another brilliant guerrilla captain, Eduardo Joson. An average-size Filipino with a pleasant personality, Joson was an excellent organizer and a fearless leader. With the help of Joson and Pajota, Major Lapham knew enough civilians could be mustered to carry the POWs. Assuming the guerrillas could, in fact, deliver all the 3,000 POWs to the sea, another major problem would face the Navy.

It would be impossible to risk the twenty or thirty subs required to evacuate all the men at once. Never could enough seaplanes be expected to land and take off in enemy waters without detection. However, it was believed that one or two subs might be able to shuttle the POWs far out to sea to a waiting transport ship.

The American guerrillas knew the time for an Allied invasion of the Philippines must be close at hand. Would the Japanese execute the prisoners at Cabanatuan? Based on past performance of the Imperial Army in Bataan and O'Donnell, there was good reason to study the future of the Cabanatuan inmates with great concern.

Colonel Anderson pleaded by radio with MacArthur's headquarters. In order to save the POWs, a raid must be carried out immediately. Anderson was ordered to "hold off." Major Lapham also presented his plan by radio, and he too was instructed to "hold off."

The risk, in the eyes of headquarters, was too great. No one doubted the guerrillas' ability to overpower the Japanese garrison at the POW camp. Nor did headquarters feel that Anderson or Lapham would be unsuccessful in delivering at least a large percentage of the POWs to the ocean. But the U.S. Navy could not yet guarantee a successful evacuation by sea.

At POW Camp Cabanatuan, cigarettes were still at a premium. The Japanese, in a generous mood, turned over to the prisoners shredded leaves of tobacco, which had been processed by the Imperial Army while manufacturing insect repellent. From this, the Americans rolled an ample supply of cigarettes using scraps of paper. The end product in no way resembled American cigarettes, but, for those who had never been able to rid themselves of the smoking habit during twenty-eight months of confinement, the garbage was better than nothing.

The death toll leveled. Now, only a few a month withered into death from beriberi, malnutrition, dysentery, and malaria. The numbers of these dead and dying had to be added to those who were failing fast from the beatings. Maintaining the list was still complicated by the continual rotation of men for work details. Some names were simply missing from rosters of returning work groups. It was difficult to ascertain if these men were dead or had been sent to other details elsewhere in the islands.

By September 1944, POW Camp Cabanatuan had become a mixing bowl of Allied prisoners. Many American civilians who were interned in other prisons in Manila suddenly found themselves in the Cabanatuan hellhole. And there were even a few British, Norwegians, and Dutch, most of whom had been plucked from the sea by victorious Japanese naval vessels.

Uneasy without some remembrance of their ships, several Navy POWs constructed a large gong bent into the shape of a triangle from scrap iron. Taking turns at standing "watch" over the prison yard, they struck out the time of day on their gong. The resulting sound had a strange similarity to navy "bells."

By the first of September 1944, the fourteen-month-old "lay low" order imposed on the guerrillas in the Philippines was lifted.

The new instructions received by radio came as welcome news to the men who were forced to play hide and seek with the Imperial Army for so long: "Destroy all enemy lines of communication, harass, delay, and destroy enemy troops and supply movements." Now, the guerrillas were on the offensive again.

There was good reason for the major change in American strategy. Since late in July, President Roosevelt had held a plan of MacArthur's under deep consideration while the U.S. Joint Chiefs of Staff debated the idea. MacArthur, in the spring of 1944, had been given the approval to bypass many Japanese-held islands in the Pacific that were no longer considered important to the overall objective—the invasion of Japan. A target date for the invasion of Mindanao in the southern Philippines was set for November 15, 1944.

But as MacArthur proceeded with his plans for the invasion, a new theory was advanced by Washington. Admiral Ernest J. King, chief of staff of the U.S. Navy, suggested that the Philippines should be bypassed altogether and Formosa be considered as the next target. If MacArthur would not agree to this, then Admiral King recommended that at least Luzon should be forgotten for the time being.

The Filipino guerrillas, regardless of the cost in lives, must keep the Japanese busy in Luzon until the end of the war. Formosa, according to Admiral King, would allow a faster end to the war due to its strategic position within easy air range of both Japan and China.

Naturally, MacArthur was furious with the King plan, arguing that the only logical procedure was to capture all the Philippines with his own plan. Japan could also be struck by air from Luzon as well as Formosa, he pointed out. And, MacArthur reminded, the United States had a "moral" obligation to liberate the Philippines.

The arguments continued from spring through early summer while the future of an American possession depended on MacArthur's ability to convince Washington. Everything came to a head by the end of July as President Roosevelt met with MacArthur and Admiral Chester W. Nimitz, commander of the Pacific Ocean Area, at Pearl Harbor. MacArthur, with his usual dramatic flair, presented his plan—Mindanao, then Leyte, then Luzon.

As a compromise, Nimitz suggested his plan—Mindanao, Leyte, bypass Luzon, and hit Formosa. Roosevelt declined to announce a decision at that meeting.

For the next two months, Third Fleet Commander William F. Halsey's carrier task force (under Nimitz's command) began launching their planes to strike at the central and southern Philippines. So successful were Halsey's planes in destroying both Japanese air bases and aircraft that he suggested a new plan—bypass Mindanao and invade Leyte in the central Philippines, thus cutting Japanese communications and lines of supply in half.

The invasion of a major Japanese-held island, right in the middle of the Philippines, without the support of land-based planes was a bold idea, indeed. Finally convinced, Washington advised MacArthur: The Allied invasion of Leyte was to begin October 20, 1944. A decision on Luzon would come later.

NUEVA ECIJA, THE PHILIPPINES
(September 1944)

Second Lieutenant San Pedro, of guerrilla Squadron 201A, supervised as his men enthusiastically carried out the orders of Captain Juan Pajota. The temporary wooden bridge spanning the Cabu River, about a mile from POW Camp Cabanatuan, was no longer in use now that the Japanese had reopened the main bridge.

For practice the guerrillas proceeded to destroy the temporary bridge anyway. All the planks were quickly ripped from the structure, while a few men chopped away at the girders with their bolos. When they had completed their task they moved to their next objective—the main bridge.

The Imperial Army was proud of the new Cabu Bridge, which stretched some eighty feet across the river at the main highway. They had devoted almost two years to the leisurely work on its reconstruction.

Like large brown termites, the Filipinos chopped into the wooden girders until they had cut a little more than halfway through each beam. Then they withdrew into the brush. It was lunchtime and their task was complete. It would be up to the Japanese to finish the destruction.

Around 1:00 P.M., an Imperial Army truck loaded with supplies left Cabanatuan City headed for Bongabon. By 1:15, the truck passed the POW camp and continued north, passing onto the Cabu Bridge. As the guerrillas expected, the weight of the truck was sufficient. The bridge, with the vehicle, crashed into the river.

By midmorning of the next day, the Japanese engineers were once again at the river, removing the damage and hauling fresh lumber for their second reconstruction of Cabu Bridge.

The parade ground, looking much like a football field from the air, was located on the far west side of POW Camp Cabanatuan. Very few American prisoners ever saw the parade ground or, for that matter, any of the enemy facilities west of the road that split the camp in half. If they did, it was only because they were there on a work detail, digging zig-zag trenches for the Japanese near the rear of the camp or performing some maintenance duties. The Japanese troops stationed at the POW garrison through September 1944 did not hold parades on that level stretch of earth within the barbed-wire fences. But they did make good use of it.

The parade field was ideal for what the Imperial Army called "Dog Day" training—hours of strenuous exercise for the troops during the hottest time of the day.

Spartan in their concept of physical fitness, Japanese soldiers would form at the parade field and begin the exercise with an hour's calisthenics. Then they continued with thirty minutes of jujitsu, followed by an hour of bayonet drill.

The Japanese bolt-action rifle, though smaller in caliber than the American semiautomatic M1, weighed almost ten pounds. Considering the average size of the Japanese infantryman to be about five feet, four inches tall, the rifle was, indeed, a heavy weapon for him to lug about. And the rifle was only balanced when affixed with its long bayonet (which brought the total weapon weight to over ten pounds).

Trained to believe that the bayonet was his most valuable and effective weapon, the Japanese soldier went through his hour's exercise each day with a tremendous amount of enthusiasm. While the bayonet was the individual soldier's most valuable weapon, the soldier, himself, was the most valuable, yet expendable, weapon to the Imperial Army.

If the Americans planned to invade the Philippines, every soldier in the Imperial Fourteenth Area Army would be physically and mentally fit to meet the challenge. Each man was fully prepared to fight to his last breath. There was to be no unit or individual surrender in the Philippines.

7

People of the Philippines . . . I have returned!

—General Douglas MacArthur, October 20, 1944

NEW GUINEA
(September 1944)

First Sergeant Charles Bosard of the 6th Rangers F Company opened his diary and glanced over the brief remarks he had entered during the last few days:

"Sept. 24—Will go somewhere in two weeks. Everybody excited. Fired mortars today. Sept. 27—Today we had bayonet drill again—assault tactics—plenty rough. Oct. 7—Photographed by Associated Press as being the 'biggest and roughest men in the Army.' We leave tomorrow for the Philippines! We'll be the only men there for 3 days . . . been working hard to get this outfit ready for combat."

On October 3, Lieutenant Colonel Henry Mucci had called his officers into the "war room" for a briefing. The Rangers were finally going into action.

A successful invasion of Leyte, Mucci informed his staff, depended on the Rangers' ability to take two small Japanese-held islands, Dinagat and Homonhon, and hold them until relieved by other Sixth Army troops. These target islands actually guarded the entrance to Leyte Gulf, affording key radio and navigation positions for the enemy. The Rangers were scheduled to attack on October 17—three days before the major Leyte invasion.

By October 7, all the Ranger equipment was loaded aboard assigned ships and at 0800, October 9, the battalion formed for the last time in front of their headquarters to stand retreat before moving to their point of embarkation. At 5:00 P.M., their convoy pulled out for sea and proceeded for Hollandia. That night General Krueger surprised Colonel Mucci with a change in strategy. There was to be a third island for the Rangers to take. Accordingly, Mucci drew the necessary plans for one company to land on Guiuan, twelve miles north of Homonhon.

A few days out to sea, Captain Bob Prince (Mucci had kept his promotion promise so far) and the other company commanders reluctantly invited Colonel Mucci into their quarters for a game of bridge. They all knew their battalion commander was uneasy with the thought of dividing his troops for an attack on three islands simultaneously, and the rough seas the convoy encountered on the twelfth had not helped his disposition at all.

The officers considered Colonel Mucci a lousy bridge player. They even maintained a record of his losses, which irritated the colonel no end. But they thought a card game might be just the thing to divert his troubled mind.

"Why don't we play hearts?" Mucci asked as he sat down in the empty chair waiting for him.

Prince shuffled the cards and no one answered.

"I'm tired of bridge," Mucci persisted. "Let's play hearts!"

"This will give you a chance to cut what you owe." Prince smiled as he spoke and began to deal. "Besides, your game of hearts is nothing to brag about anyway."

Colonel Mucci, obviously disgusted with the game selection, sat through one poor hand after another. Finally, after two hours of losing, he stood and tossed his cards on the table. "To hell with bridge! I'm not going to play with you guys anymore!"

The infuriated colonel stormed from the room and as the steel door slammed behind him, uncontrollable laughter broke out among the staff.

On October 15, the winds, reaching gale proportions, lashed

at the Allied convoy, but by 0800, on the seventeenth, as naval guns hammered away at the three small islands selected for the Rangers, the sea suddenly became calm.

Under a heavy overcast sky the first assault waves of Rangers approached what appeared to be perfect beaches. A hundred yards offshore their landing craft grounded on coral reefs, forcing the men to wade the rest of the way. By noon, all of C Company were on Dinagat and had established their battalion command post, thus far completely unopposed. Three companies then moved out to find the Japanese and gain control of the upper end of the island.

Company D landed on Guiuan and Company B, reinforced with a platoon composed of men from the motor pool, landed on Homonhon, also unopposed. Within an hour they were combing the jungle for the enemy.

During the next three days, the 6th Rangers hunted down and killed over 700 Imperial Army soldiers, destroyed several radio installations, and set up valuable navigation lights to guide the arriving invasion convoy heading for Leyte.

Early on the morning of the eighteenth, two days before the major Leyte invasion, Lieutenant Joseph Therrien checked over an assortment of articles left by the fleeing Japanese. In an officer's trunk he found an American flag, neatly folded according to prescribed American Army regulations. At 0855 a small group of 6th Rangers assembled around a hastily constructed flagpole and saluted while Sergeant Francis Anderson raised the flag.

Officially, the Americans had returned to the Philippines.

Leyte, a narrow island some 115 miles long, is located almost in the center of the Philippines.

To take this strip of land and its valuable airfields General MacArthur planned to commit 200,000 men of General Walter Krueger's Sixth Army along with 2,500 combat aircraft from the Far East Air Force and 1,500 aircraft from the Seventh and Third fleets.

General Tomoyuki Yamashita arrived at his new headquarters in Manila in early October to assume command of the Imperial Army's Fourteenth Area operations. By October 20, the Japanese had fewer than 150 conventional combat planes throughout the Philippines and only about 300 planes on Formosa for backup protection. The Americans were now clearly the masters of the Pacific sky.

Of Yamashita's 500,000-man army, about 200,000 were scattered in the southern Philippines. Only 20,000 were on Leyte on October 20 to greet the giant Allied Army invasion force.

By midafternoon of the twentieth, the Allies had established a large beachhead on Leyte's eastern shore. Just before 2:00 P.M., staff officers, newspapermen, and the president of the Philippines, Sergio Osmena, joined General MacArthur in a landing barge. (Sergio Osmena became president of the Commonwealth of the Philippines in 1945. Their first president, Manuel Quezon, who escaped Bataan with MacArthur in 1941, died of TB in 1944 scarcely three months short of seeing the Americans return to the islands.)

Touching sand some fifty yards offshore, the barge's steel door splashed down and the party, led by MacArthur, waded ashore. After wandering about for a few minutes, the Field Marshal stepped before the microphone of a portable radio. His rough voice cracking with emotion, he began his speech: "This is the Voice of Freedom, General MacArthur speaking. People of the Philippines; I have returned! By the grace of the Almighty God, our forces stand again on Philippine soil . . . soil consecrated in the blood of our two peoples. We have come, dedicated and committed to the task of destroying every vestige of enemy control over your daily lives, and of restoring upon a foundation of indestructible strength, the liberties of your people. . . . The hour of your redemption is here!"

By the end of October, the Allies had completely secured the Leyte valley. By December 10, the Japanese had lost 50,000 men, including reinforcements Yamashita reluctantly committed. The remaining 15,000 Japanese were sick, short of food and ammunition, and no longer functioned as organized units. Yet for the next twenty days they would hold out until finally hunted down by Filipino guerrillas or American patrols. Almost none survived. Now MacArthur had Washington's approval—Luzon could be liberated.

NUEVA ECIJA, THE PHILIPPINES
(October 1944)

At POW Camp Cabanatuan, the canteens containing the home-made secret radio were carefully placed together and the long rope with its antenna was connected. The few POWs who kept the secret of the radio could not, at first, believe their ears as the rebroadcast of MacArthur's speech from Leyte's beach came through.

It was much too dangerous to keep the radio going for any length of time so the operators worked in shifts. Each shift transported the radio to a new location and strained to pick up every word of the exciting news on the Voice of Freedom. Still, most POWs did not know of the radio's existence. Others, fearing punishment, chose to believe it did not exist.

But American planes had been spotted flying over at high altitudes and all the prisoners began to hold to the hope that liberation was truly close at hand.

Sergeant Abie Abraham stood at the open window of his hospital ward and watched as the long line of 1,500 POWs formed along the road inside the camp. The tough little boxer had finally fallen seriously ill from combined complications of asthma, beriberi, and malnutrition. Running a high fever, he was confined to the camp hospital, removed temporarily from any work detail rosters. Thus his name also was deleted from a new list the Japanese were hurriedly compiling.

"Where in hell are the Japs taking all those guys?" Sergeant Abraham turned to ask the ward medic, PFC Eugene Evers. "That's too many for any work detail."

Evers joined the sergeant at the window. "I heard Dr. Musselman and Dr. Weinstein talking this morning. Apparently, they are shipping all of us to Japan or Manchuria little by little. Only the fellows who are too sick to travel will remain here."

"What about you medics?"

"I guess some will go and some will stay. Weinstein is going, but Lieutenant Musselman and several others will stay for a while."

Sergeant Abraham had mixed emotions. His family was still either hiding in Manila or in prison somewhere in Luzon. "I'm not sure if those boys are lucky or not," he said.

"Wherever they are going . . . it couldn't be any worse than this place."

During the last week of October 1944, over 1,800 American prisoners of war, mostly from Camp Cabanatuan, were packed like fish into the lower level of a 5,000-ton freighter in Manila Harbor. A few hours out into the China Sea, the vessel was spotted by a lone U.S. submarine, which had no way of knowing of the freighter's human cargo. Direct hits were scored by two torpedoes and within minutes, the ship—and its prisoners—disappeared beneath the waters. Five American POWs survived and were picked up by Chinese fishermen.

Meanwhile, the Japanese imperial headquarters ordered the evacuation of all Allied POWs in the Philippines to continue as fast as practical.

Captain Pajota's men reported the departure of that first group of American POWs from Cabanatuan to Major Lapham. Once again, Pajota and Lapham reviewed their plans for a raid on the POW camp. They were certain that if they could attack now, while the Japanese attention was on Leyte and the defense of Luzon, it was still possible to rescue the 2,000 POWs remaining. A number of radio messages shot back and forth between Major Lapham and Colonel Anderson. They agreed. An attack on the camp must come now.

Another radio plea for permission to carry out the attack went to MacArthur. Again, Allied headquarters radioed the guerrillas to "hold off."

Apparently, headquarters still felt that it was impossible to guarantee the necessary naval support for a successful evacuation of the prisoners. The invasion of Luzon was now only two months away. The guerrillas were assured that the rescue of all Allied POWs would receive top priority once that invasion began.

Tremendous pressure was upon the imperial Japanese engineers at Cabanatuan City to finish repairs on the bridge over the Cabu

River. Their Manila headquarters insisted that the highway from Cabanatuan to Bongabon be open for heavy military traffic before the end of November.

By November 15, the engineers proudly tested their new bridge by permitting two tanks to follow one another across its wooden structure. Everyone was satisfied that all specifications had been met. The bridge could support their armor and the road to Bongabon was once again open.

The new Cabu bridge, constructed mostly of heavy timber, was approximately seventy-five feet long and twenty-one feet wide, spanning the muddy river about ten feet above the water. The engineers had even included a chest-high wooden handrail along both sides. Now, the Japanese hoped that the bridge would not fall victim to those troublesome Filipinos again or be destroyed by American planes.

On the morning of December 15, the Americans landed on Mindoro. Now, everything was ready. The invasion of Luzon could begin on the new target date—January 9, 1945. The Japanese no longer possessed an effective air force or navy in the Philippines area to stop the Americans.

8

Any nationalist who makes an ally of the Communist is going for a ride on a tiger!

—Huk commander Luis Taruc: *He Who Rides the Tiger*

In Manila, on December 12, 1944, a group of more than 1,600 American POWs were loaded into a converted prewar 15,000-ton ocean liner for evacuation to Japan. Again, many of the prisoners were from Camp Cabanatuan. Before the vessel could pull into the bay, it was sighted by U.S. warplanes returning from a mission. The fighters broke from formation and dove in for the attack.

With the noise of the battle erupting above and exploding bombs in the bay around them, panic spread throughout the liner. For many who had survived the Death March and the concentration camps, this new hell was too much.

Low on fuel and ammunition, the U.S. planes were forced to call off the assault, but before they did, more than 100 of their countrymen suffocated or were trampled to death as men tumbled and scrambled over one another in a hopeless effort to claw through the ship's steel walls with bare hands.

During the night the liner safely maneuvered through Manila Bay and out into the China Sea. By dawn, she was far up along the west coast of the Bataan Peninsula, scarcely more than a mile from Subic Bay. But, with the dawn, the U.S. planes returned, now determined to finish the enemy ship.

Trapped in the dark holds, where the temperature was over 100 degrees Fahrenheit, the POWs climbed upon one another to reach the upper deck. In order to drive them back, Japanese guards opened the hatches and began to fire rifles and pistols wildly into the screaming crowd. Suddenly the ship ran aground in the sand less than a quarter mile offshore. The Japanese then decided to allow the POWs to climb out, twenty-five at a time. In the sky, horrified U.S. pilots finally recognized their mistake and called off the attack.

The 1,300 surviving American prisoners who swam or waded ashore were quickly rounded up and held in various areas around the ruins of Subic Naval Yards until a new plan for evacuation could be instituted.

By the end of 1944, only a little over 500 Allied POWs were left at Camp Cabanatuan. The majority of these were much too sick to send anywhere (not that those evacuated were in much better physical condition), and their life expectancy was, indeed, short.

Now, a gradual change developed in the behavior of the guards at Cabanatuan. Their arrogant and belligerent attitude toward the POWs was not replaced with kindness. But the prisoners detected nervousness and worry in their faces. The activity of the sentries became spasmodic, almost haphazard.

Work details and beatings, for the most part, ceased. Red Cross Christmas packages marked "1943" were even distributed to some of the men as the first POWs departed in late 1944. A few of those 500 who remained in the camp found themselves in possession of American-made shoes from those packages. The majority stored the shoes carefully for some future use, electing to move about the camp barefooted or with handmade sandals as they had done for so long a time.

LUZON, THE PHILIPPINES
(January 1945)

It was almost January 1 before the Japanese could spare the time or ships to evacuate the 1,300 American POWs who survived the December 12 U.S. aircraft attack on the prison ship at Subic Bay. These POWs, along with a few hundred taken from various work details about Luzon, were divided into two groups. Slightly over 1,000 were packed in the hold of a large freighter, and the balance were crammed into smaller ships. The 500-odd Allied prisoners remaining at Cabanatuan were, with few exceptions, former military personnel.

In Manila the Japanese held over 3,500 Allied civilians at Santo Tomas University and approximately 1,300 civilians at the old Bilibid Prison. Another 2,200 civilians were interned at Los Banos Prison on the south shore of Laguna de Bay about forty miles from Manila. Most of these civilians were Americans—men, women, and children who were trapped in the Philippines during the Japanese invasion in December 1941. They were a mixture of businessmen, educators, engineers, journalists, and dependents of the original USAFFE force.

With the exception of Camp Cabanatuan, therefore, there were only a handful of American military POWs still scattered about Luzon.

All of the civilian prisoners were, by comparison to the Cabanatuan POWs, in reasonably good physical condition though a majority suffered from malnutrition and lack of adequate medical attention. The Japanese calculated that these civilian prisoners would present no real embarrassment for either the Imperial Army or Tokyo should Luzon fall to the American forces. Japan had every right to hold civilian prisoners. After all, American-born Japanese were still being held in "detention camps" in the United States.

So the last load of American prisoners leaving by ship virtually eliminated the remaining military personnel, except for those at

Cabanatuan who were not expected to live much longer anyway. As before, little preparation had been given to the care of the POWs crammed inside the ships. As a result, over ten a day would die from lack of water during the trip to Japan.

Most of Imperial Fourteenth Area Army commander Tomoyuki Yamashita's sixty years had been devoted to military service for his emperor, and a great number of those years had dragged by with the sounds of battle thundering in his ears. The world once called Yamashita the "Tiger of Malaya" after his brilliant but brutal victories in that jungled part of Asia. His troops had smashed Singapore, dealing the British one of their worst defeats in history.

Yamashita understood Western mentality and the strategy of those hated white men. He knew the secrets of breaking American and British fighting spirit by permitting his army to commit atrocities. His army thrived on winning—on the offensive—and each warrior deserved to draw blood in any way he desired.

When Field Marshal Count Terauchi departed for Saigon to control the Southeast Asian war in late November 1944, he left orders for Yamashita to continue to fight on Leyte. General Yamashita argued against the plan, insisting that Luzon should be the great battlefield. It was not until December 21 that imperial general headquarters finally gave in and granted full control of the Philippines defense to Yamashita, turning over to him what was left of the Fourth Air Army. By then, it was too late for the Japanese in the Philippines.

Although Yamashita had over 250,000 soldiers under his command on Luzon, imperial headquarters had not given him control of the large group of naval troops stationed in and around Manila. Nor did Yamashita have the superior army he once commanded on the mainland of Asia. More than half his Luzon force was poorly led and all units were short of supplies and munitions as a result of Field Marshal Terauchi's orders for the suicidal stand at Leyte. Most of Yamashita's three months in his new command had been devoted to satisfying Terauchi's demands, leaving little time for organizing an effective defense of Luzon.

With the fall of Leyte, the Japanese were left in a stalemated position. To meet MacArthur's massive army and devastating fire-power on the beaches of Luzon no longer seemed practical to Yamashita. A great effort at the beaches would cost far too much in equipment and men.

Japan had been unable to succeed in its lightning war of conquest in Asia. MacArthur's early offensive from Australia and many U.S. naval victories saw to that. Without the necessary raw materials for a continual campaign, forced to the defensive, and lacking sufficient industrialization to match the Americans, the Imperial Army was essentially doomed to eventual destruction. The awesome capacity of American industry, as some Japanese leaders feared, would cost them the war. The Japanese had also grossly underestimated the Americans' will to fight for islands or peoples so far from their main continent.

The Imperial Army's equipment on Luzon was basically the same they had used during their invasion three years before. True, tanks and planes had been modified and updated. A better rifle and a new, small, deadly mortar had been introduced. But this was nothing compared to what American industry had produced for MacArthur.

Yamashita calculated correctly that MacArthur would attack at Lingayen Gulf, where General Homma's invading armies had landed three years earlier. Other than a small delaying force, Yamashita did not plan to meet the Allies at Lingayen.

The best he could do, he figured, was to delay the Americans' conquest of Luzon, inflict as many casualties as possible, and tie down as many American units as he could. Thus, mainland Japan would have more time to prepare for an inevitable invasion.

Unlike MacArthur in 1942, General Yamashita did not intend to retreat into Bataan. The situation was different in 1942, for then even the Japanese lacked sufficient air power and mechanized equipment to deal with the Americans quickly. His forces could be easily annihilated in Bataan by the superior American military. Yet the Fourteenth Area Army commander appreciated the fact that Manila Bay and her harbors could be denied the Americans with some harassment.

For the defense of Manila, Yamashita knew he could rely on the 17,000 naval troops under the fanatical Rear Admiral Sanji

Iwabuchi. Yamashita stationed 6,000 soldiers on the island of Corregidor and assigned only 1,000 to Bataan. These should be sufficient to delay the Allied foot soldiers and the U.S. Navy as well.

Yamashita also planned to leave the central plains area defended by only small delaying forces while the bulk of his quarter million men moved to three mountain strongholds. The majority of these men began a withdrawal from previously assigned positions to the rugged wilderness of northern Luzon, including the valuable and fertile Cagayan Valley, from which they hoped to draw food during their long stand. To defend the hilly area east of Manila, the second-largest force prepared fortifications in cliffs, caves, and tunnels. The mountainous terrain just west of the central plains that overlooked Clark Field was where the third, smallest force withdrew. If the Americans moved down the central plains for Manila, as Yamashita expected, their right flank could easily be threatened.

As for the Allied strategy, to attack Luzon, Vice-Admiral Thomas Kinkaid's Seventh Fleet, consisting of more than 850 vessels, was in charge of providing protection and delivering General Krueger's 200,000-man Sixth Army. While this major assault was under way, Admiral Halsey's Third Fleet carriers would launch their aircraft to strike at Formosa and northern Luzon.

General George Kenney's Far East Air Force would bomb and strafe Luzon from its new bases on Mindoro and Leyte. Kenney was to move his airplanes up to Luzon as soon as engineers completed construction of bases.

The battle for Luzon was to become the largest of them all in the Pacific as troops locked in combat numbered more than six times those engaged in 1942. On Luzon, for the first time in the Pacific, the employment of corps, divisions, and regiments would more closely resemble that under way in the European theater. And, against the largest Japanese force ever assembled on one island, more American fighting men were to be committed than in North Africa or Italy.

On January 4, four large landing craft (LCIs) containing the 6th Ranger Battalion hauled anchor and joined the forty-mile-long convoy heading for Luzon.

At 0700, January 9, 1945, the Allied forces entered the calm waters of Lingayen Bay and the Navy began their barrage of the beaches while aircraft pounded suspected positions farther inland.

At 0900 the first assault craft moved toward the shore. At 0930, the first wave of American liberating forces hit the Lingayen beaches almost completely unopposed. By nightfall over 68,000 soldiers, including MacArthur, were on Luzon.

The 6th Rangers were deeply disappointed when they learned that they must wait until January 10 before going ashore. At noon that day, the first landing craft carrying A Company beached in surf that had churned up ten-foot waves overnight.

DWAKS (amphibious tanks) were called in to deliver the Rangers and by 1600 (4:00 P.M.) all companies were ashore. The battalion moved 1,000 yards inland and found Colonel Mucci with the advance quartering party standing in an area he had selected for a bivouac site.

Everyone was ordered to dig in and get some rest. The orders came not a moment too soon, for at 2200 (10:00 P.M.) a Japanese plane strafed their area and dropped one bomb, which, luckily, landed in an isolated area and did no damage. But there was little sleep that night for the Rangers. The next morning the battalion moved farther inland, establishing a new perimeter near the town of Dagupan.

By the thirteenth, their equipment had arrived, and the Rangers were advised that they were to serve as the main guard for General Krueger and the Sixth Army headquarters. Now, the Rangers moved two miles south of Dagupan to the vicinity of Calasio and began to erect a "semipermanent" camp. It would be three more days before the battalion received their first combat mission.

No sooner had General Walter Krueger settled in his new headquarters than he found himself in the presence of some very distinguished guests.

First, guerrilla leader Colonel R. W. Volckmann came to visit and wanted to know why the Navy had bothered to use such a massive bombardment preceding the Lingayen landing. Only a few weeks before, Volckmann and his men had recovered documents from a downed Japanese plane. The papers turned out to be a full report of General Yamashita's defense plans for Luzon, which were en route to Tokyo when the plane crashed. Colonel Volckmann had radioed MacArthur's headquarters advising that there was no organized resistance planned for the Allies at Lingayen.

Also on hand to welcome the Sixth Army commanding general was guerrilla leader Colonel Bernard Anderson, still wearing his 1941 Air Force cap, and Major Robert Lapham, wearing his old campaign hat. New orders were issued for the guerrillas. "Effective at once you and all elements of your organization are placed under command of the commanding general, Sixth United States Army."

The war was not yet over for the Americans who had survived the hardships of a thirty-one-month guerrilla campaign against the Japanese.

By January 10, the slow and careful advance of the American forces into Luzon was making good progress against light enemy resistance.

On the right (southern) flank, moving toward Tarlac, Clark Field, and San Fernando was Major General Oscar W. Griswold's XIV Corps, which included the 37th and 40th infantry divisions.

Major General Innis P. Swift's I Corps, including the 6th and 43rd infantry divisions, began to push north into the mountains toward Baguio and east through the Cabaruan Hills toward San Jose. It was in these mountains that the Americans would run head-on into the largest concentration of more than 158,000 Japanese soldiers.

As I Corps entered the Cabaruan Hills, the Japanese opened up with a heavy bombardment from a series of caves, pillboxes, and tanks. Short of fuel, the Japanese had buried their armor on the mountainsides leaving only their turrets exposed. The I Corps advance slowed and MacArthur became impatient.

General Krueger explained to the Field Marshal that he was worried mostly about his flanks, fearing that a fast drive for Manila might leave his lines of supply and communication vulnerable.

"Go to Manila," MacArthur ordered. "Go around the Nips, bounce off the Nips, but go to Manila!"

General Swift's I Corps was then reinforced with the 25th Division, and he immediately launched all three divisions at the Japanese fortifications in the Cabaruan Hills.

Griswold's XIV Corps, meanwhile, continued south for thirty miles losing only a little over twenty-five men in the advance. His troops rolled through Tarlac, hardly noticing the abandoned camp known as O'Donnell. But on January 23, XIV Corps encountered heavy opposition near the town of Bamban. They had finally contacted the 30,000-man force General Yamashita had left in the mountains to guard Clark Field.

Of all the Allied troops fighting their way inland from Lingayen Gulf, none had a greater variety of combat experience than the men of the Signal Corps Photographic Service.

Since Australia, these daring photographers had been in the midst of practically every battle. They had flown over the battles in planes, jumped into it with the paratroopers, landed on the bloody beaches with the liberating armies, and were on hand to record most of the major naval engagements.

To accomplish the mission assigned the Signal Corps of producing a photographic record of the war on Luzon, a total of fourteen combat units, two newsreel units, two mobile labs, and one photographic repair section landed with the first invading wave. Two additional units were assigned aboard ships of the U.S. Navy. The men of the 832nd Signal Service Battalion had traveled great distances with their equipment to keep up with General MacArthur's leapfrogging campaign.

The average strength of a combat photography unit was one officer and five enlisted men. The enlisted ranks were composed of two still and two motion picture photographers, plus a utility man. Each unit was self-sustaining, packing thirty days of field rations, plus their cameras and film. For protection, each man carried a .45-caliber automatic pistol and, under certain conditions, was issued a carbine or M1 rifle. But their cameras were their most prized possession, seeming often more valuable than life itself.

The delicate equipment had to be protected from salt water, concussion, and fungus, which of course was no easy matter during battle in the Pacific.

Having shared the grim life with the fighting men of the Sixth Army, the men of the 832nd were proud of their accomplishments. And by the time they staggered from the weight of their equipment through the waves at Lingayen, they were equally thankful that, to this point, the battalion had not lost a single man.

Now separate photo units began to push along with the Army,

employing their special technique of becoming almost part of the countryside to obtain accurate, candid photos. It became the responsibility of "Unit F" of the 832nd Signal Service Battalion to go with the 6th Rangers and record every action on film, no matter how dangerous the mission.

A few miles into Pangasinan province from Lingayen Gulf, Filipino villagers had practically recovered from the excitement of the Allied invasion. The rapid advancing American front-line troops had passed through several days before. Waving and shouting "victory" to the steady stream of military support traffic moving into the central plains had become routine.

Each day, the Ilocanos in Pangasinan believed that they had seen every piece of American equipment. But the next day brought some new, strange instrument of war and the excitement began again. As the sun sank low over the waves of the South China Sea beyond the Zambales Mountains, beyond Bataan province and Corregidor, slowly their entire world seemed to be flooded with saffron glory. It was dusk, January 15, and the Ilocanos' conversation in one village in Pangasinan shifted to a discussion of one of those new American war machines. It was time for the "Nangisit Law wa–law wa" to appear as she had each evening for the last three days.

The machine was a dreadful-looking thing that thundered into the evening sky to kill the Japanese. The natives knew she did not return until almost dawn. Surely it would come again this night.

None of the Filipinos had ever seen such weird-looking airplanes before. It even became a game to stand outside the huts and count them as they flew overhead, and some of the children tried to stay awake until the killers returned. But it was impossible to count them once the darkness gained control of the land. Then the killers could not be seen—only heard. The Filipinos named the airplane as it appeared to them, "Nangisit law wa–law wa": "black spider." The Americans called her the "Black Widow."

The "Dark Lady," the "South Pacific Sandman," the "Black Widow," whatever they called her, the P61 Night Interceptor Pursuit Airplane had proven to be one of the most valuable aircraft in the Pacific war. In late 1940, the brilliant engineers at Northrop

Aircraft began their project to give the U.S. Air Corps a very special night fighter. It was not until October 1943 that the first P61s were delivered to the military. They were, indeed, no ordinary aircraft.

Painted glossy black, the P61's twin 2,000-horsepower Pratt and Whitney radial engines were mounted in the wing in low-slung nacelles that tapered back into twin tail booms. A long, pod-shaped fuselage projected front and back of its inner wing sections and was accented by a long, blunt nose and a greenhouse-type, two-level canopy. Though capable of reaching speeds of 375 miles per hour, she could circle at extremely slow speeds without a stall. Altitude ranges were just as impressive. She was comfortable at 30,000 feet or at tree-scraping 100-foot levels.

The final design was a ship with a length of nearly fifty feet (extremely long by comparison to the famous thirty-seven-foot P51), a wing span of sixty-six feet, and a height of fifteen feet. But this 30,000-pound craft held many "secrets."

One of the secrets was a new "spoiler"-type aileron made from perforated magnesium and located on the rear third of the wing. The spoiler permitted her to function at very low speeds (stalling speed was 75 miles per hour) and out-turn practically all other aircraft. Another was her armament. The P61 had four .50-caliber machine guns contained in a top dorsal turret and four 20-mm cannons in a front belly bulge below her fuselage. The pilot could command all eight guns forward, producing more firepower than any other fighter in the war.

Her crew was a pilot in the front seat, a gunner in the seat directly behind him, and a special observer in the top, third seat. The observer and the duty he performed was what made the P61 especially interesting and deadly. He was the radar observer (RO), reading and interpreting the instruments receiving signals from a radar device mounted in the long blunt nonmetallic nose of the fuselage.

Radar was something new in World War II. It was this secret that allowed the P61 with her spiderlike outline to see in the dark and find her enemy.

Perhaps those spiderlike lines and the black finish were the main contributors to the P61's arachnoid name. But like the deadly spider, the fighter also had a lethal bite with her four 20-mm cannons. Any enemy plane caught in her radar web stood little chance for escape.

Army engineers worked fast, starting January 9, and by the thirteenth had completed an airstrip built of pierced-steel planking (PSP) on the sand and just 100 yards inland from the waters of Lingayen Gulf. This was to be the new temporary home of the 547th Night Fighter Squadron.

By January 1945, what few bad points existing in the P61 from her original concept had practically all been designed out. True, an occasional minor fire developed in an air filter from exhaust heat on hydraulic oils dripping through small leaks, but they always self-extinguished, causing no damage or real concern. Actually, the P61 with all its power and sophisticated equipment had no nasty habits as far as her pilots were concerned.

In fact, the plane was so good, the veteran pilots of the 547th checked out new pilots with a favorite maneuver that had demonstrated time and time again the true characteristics of the P61. At a high altitude, one engine would intentionally be feathered and the plane turned or rolled in the direction of the dead engine.

Normally, most aircraft would flip on the dead engine side, placing the craft in a deadly spin to earth. The good engine of the P61 always pulled her safely into any position desired. No longer was this procedure used solely to demonstrate the P61's favorable flight characteristics. Rather, it tested the quality of the pilot. As one pilot reported, "It required nerves of steel, cool calm temperament, and faith in American engineering."

Night flying, of course, was dangerous business. The P61's radar had an effective range equal only to its flying altitude above the ground. It was imperative, therefore, for the Black Widows to maintain close control with one another to avoid midair collisions.

The 547th Night Fighter Squadron was composed of some sixteen P61s. The unit was granted tremendous latitude and freedom, which enabled them to perform services of air cover for U.S. PT boat squadrons, Royal Australian Navy coastal patrol vessels, and U.S. Navy patrol aircraft throughout the China Sea area. All of this activity occurred at night or during extremely unfavorable flying conditions when day fighters were grounded.

The Allied invasion of Luzon was about to produce a new hunting field and additional admiration from various elements of the Army for the 547th. With their air power virtually nonexistent, the Japanese Imperial Army took to the roads mostly at night. It was only then, so the Japanese thought, that their convoys and troops would be safe from American aerial attack. But the Black Widows were about to change all that.

Actually, the 547th fell under the direct control of the 86th Fighter Wing, which was a subordinate unit of the U.S. Fifth Air Force. By January 1945, however, the 547th had so demonstrated his unique role and was so unlike the normal day fighter organizations in capability, experience, and format, that the commanding officer of the 86th Fighter Wing exercised very little command over the night fighter unit. The 547th basically operated as an independent entity, planning its own missions, assembling its own intelligence, coordinating its activities through its own liaison, and stood by for particular "alert" calls from any Armed Forces unit that might need them.

This unorthodox and independent method of conducting operations was endorsed by the 86th Fighter Wing mainly because there was no one on their staff who was completely familiar with the night fighter capabilities. Night flying and especially night fighting were still too new.

The personnel of the 547th were just as unique as the equipment they flew. Highly motivated and creative in both officer and enlisted ranks, over 90 percent were handpicked and screened carefully before acceptance. By January, 30 percent of the pilots were on their second or third combat tour. Some had even flown with the RAF and RCAF in Europe. Interestingly, the official record states that the pilots of the 547th were the "old men" in the Air Force. Their average age was twenty-six to thirty.

You had better get down on your knees and pray. Dammit, don't fake it. I mean . . . *pray!* And I want you to swear an oath before God . . . swear you'll die fighting rather than let any harm come to those POWs!

—Lieutenant Colonel Henry A. Mucci, January 1945

On January 16 rumors prevailed around Sixth Army headquarters that the Rangers were going to be assigned their first mission on Luzon.

Suddenly, as it always happens during combat operations, it was no longer a rumor. A reconnaissance patrol consisting of three officers, nine enlisted men, one Filipino guide, and one radar technical, all under the command of Captain Arthur Simons of B Company, boarded two PT boats and headed out into Lingayen Gulf for a little dot on the map known as Santiago Island.

Santiago, Sixth Army G2 (intelligence) believed, was ideally situated for a radar station that could detect enemy planes should the Japanese attempt to approach Lingayen Gulf from Formosa. The Rangers were cautioned that they might find over 4,000 imperial soldiers on Santiago.

At 2200 hours (10:00 P.M.), the Ranger patrol disembarked from the PTs and began to row their rubber boats toward what they had been told was Santiago. Unfortunately, someone had made a mistake, for they were dropped near Saipar Island, some two and a half miles from their destination. When the error was finally discovered, the patrol had to row their tiny boats for two more hours.

Once on Santiago, the Rangers split into two smaller units and soon learned from the excited residents they encountered that there were no Japanese left on the island. All the enemy apparently had pulled out for the mainland the day before. Captain Simons located a suitable spot for the radar station and the Rangers returned to make their report to Colonel Mucci.

Wanting to insure the security of the island, Sixth Army headquarters then requested that Mucci furnish two companies, which were to draw rations and prepare for a twenty-day stay on Santiago. Naturally, all the Ranger company commanders rushed to volunteer. But Captain Simons was senior by date of rank and having already accomplished the reconnaissance mission was rightfully entitled to the assignment. At 1730 hours (5:30 P.M.) on January 19, B and E companies departed Ranger headquarters for an uneventful trip aboard an LSM.

When they landed with a bulldozer, a truck, and a jeep, the natives greeted them with a joyous welcome. No one, obviously, had expected to see so many Americans and such interesting equipment on their small island. After the wild reception, the Rangers got down to serious business and by January 21 the radar station was operational.

As luck would have it, the Santiago mission was to eliminate B and E companies from participating in one of the most dramatic and rewarding assignments ever placed upon a Ranger battalion in World War II.

Around 1500 hours (3:00 P.M.) on the sixteenth, a complement of Imperial Army soldiers, accompanied by several engineers, passed by POW Camp Cabanatuan and stopped to check Cabu bridge to be sure that the Filipinos had not been up to their sabotage tricks again.

The Japanese were now making good use of the major artery connecting Cabanatuan City and Bongabon for their troop movement north. Cabu bridge must remain open and support both armor and trucks until after February 2, at which time imperial headquarters figured the withdrawal to the mountains would be complete.

On the sixteenth, the soldiers were also looking for a good

bivouac area, and they found it along the northeast side of the Cabu, where large trees and bamboo thickets provided ample camouflage for troops and vehicles.

The POW compound, a mile to the south, was considered much too conspicuous for a large contingent of transient troops. True, small units could stay at the compound, but the Cabu bivouac area provided safety in dispersement as well as protection for the valuable bridge.

Shortly after the Rangers settled in their new base, a few Filipinos from a nearby barrio entered the camp with gifts of fresh papaya, bananas, and young coconuts. They asked if there was a doctor among the Americans, explaining that a woman in their village was about to give birth. In the confusion of the Allied invasion, the local midwife had disappeared.

Naturally, Captain James Fisher jumped at the opportunity and, accompanied by Staff Sergeant John Nelson of the doctor's medical detachment, followed the Filipinos to the barrio.

In a nipa hut on the night of January 20, by the flickering light from a coconut oil lamp, "Captain Jim" helped the young Filipina give birth to her first child. With gratitude, the new mother bestowed the best honor possible to the American captain by requesting him to be the godfather for her child.

A few days later, Jimmy Fisher stood in a church built of bamboo cradling the infant in his arms. While Lieutenant Colonel Mucci and another officer assisted, a Filipino priest performed the baptismal service. Afterward, a smiling Captain Fisher announced to the priest, "This is the new generation of Filipinos—those who must build a free Philippines."

The Rangers, of course, seized upon the chance to tease the "godfather." Did their doctor "overcharge the patient"?

Captain Jim took it all in good stride, remarking that, due to his usual absentmindedness, he had forgotten to issue the bill.

At Pangatian a strange series of events began to unfold in POW Camp Cabantuan beginning January 6, three days before the Allied invasion of Luzon.

In the early morning hours of the sixth, the POWs were awakened by a tremendous amount of activity on the Japanese side of the compound. By noon, the guards had packed up and pulled out of the camp, leaving their quarters deserted except for a few soldiers who were sick and unable to travel. Other than those Japanese, the POWs were left practically unguarded for the next several days. Naturally, discussions began about the possibility of making an escape attempt.

The Allied prisoners remaining at Cabanatuan now totaled between 518 and 520; a combination of U.S. Army, Marine, Navy, and civilian personnel, plus a few British and Norwegian civilians, British Army and Navy, and Dutch Army men.

Their physical condition had continued to deteriorate, some were without limbs and more than 50 percent could not even walk. Actually, fewer than fifty men were strong enough to walk out of the camp. Their only chance for escape would be to evade the Japanese soldiers long enough to make it safely to nearby Filipino villages.

If a breakout was attempted, they calculated that probably the guards would shoot half of the men before the fences were cleared. Only about ten should expect to survive once other imperial soldiers were called in to hunt them down. A final argument against the wisdom of a break was the revenge expected upon those left behind. None wished to gamble 500 lives against the slight possibility that ten might successfully escape.

On January 7 and 8, a few more Japanese soldiers drifted into the camp but on the ninth, when the shelling began at Lingayen, those troops also took off, leaving about twenty armed guards at the compound. Generally, these Japanese remained to themselves and, except for the sentries at the towers and front gate, all stayed under cover inside their barracks.

On January 12, the prisoners came up with a bold plan. They had noticed that the remaining livestock had been transferred inside the compound from the large buildings on the opposite side of the south fence. The Japanese placed the animals in a corral just across the center road on their side of the camp.

If escape was impossible, the POWs decided that at least they could face whatever the future held on a full stomach. Teams of fifteen, the strongest of them all, volunteered to make a daring attempt to crawl through the fence, cross the center road, and raid the corral. Success, they felt, would be based mostly on the apathetic attitude of those new guards.

The POW "slaughter team" waited until dark, slipped through the single fence row, and dashed toward their selected target—a Brahma steer. In seconds, like a pack of hungry dogs, the team was upon the steer, slicing away with crude knives made from scrap metal and bamboo. The beast was butchered on the spot, inspected by Lieutenant (Doctor) Herb Ott, and every bit of the carcass carried to the POW area where cooks had already begun the fires. Those cooks had learned many months ago how to make a piece of meat or bone last a long time. That night, the prisoners enjoyed a real meal of meat. For most of the men, it was the first meat they had tasted since the Americans' retreat into Bataan in December 1941—1,120 days before.

Several Japanese guards had watched the slaughter with a peculiar fascination, but seemed uninterested in the entire affair. The POWs knew that if they had tried such an act a month before, while the regular guards were present, everyone would have been shot.

As a result of their desperate action, by January 23, the POW medical staff reported that the majority of men were now gaining weight and strength.

But more imperial soldiers began to arrive, bringing the contingent of guards to over 100, and the nipa barracks on the enemy side of camp were continually filled with troops moving in one day and out the next. Even though the condition of the POWs was beginning to improve, thanks to the meat, it now was impossible for anyone to consider another raid on the Japanese livestock, much less a complete escape.

During those many months in captivity, at least 50 percent of the POWs had attempted to carry on some semblance of military custom and tradition. A certain percent simply said to hell with military tradition, figuring such behavior ridiculous when basic survival was difficult enough.

Some officers actually managed to maintain records of "good deeds," valor, and misconduct. When that large number of POWs left Cabanatuan in late 1944, the records were turned over to the remaining men for safekeeping.

A few "courts-martial" were even held and recorded on scraps of paper for processing should they ever be liberated. The trials ranged from realistic proceedings against officers and men accused of stealing food from fellow prisoners or accepting favors from the Japanese, to the absurd. One starving man was tried (by the offended) for stealing and eating his officer's pet cat, which had (unfortunately for the cat) slipped into the compound through the barbed wire.

Other men, like Sergeant Abie Abraham, continued to keep records of deaths. The doctors maintained logs of diseases, the effects of malnutrition, and the treatment conducted, mostly without drugs and under the most adverse medical conditions.

Square-jawed Colonel James Duckworth, the Bataan hospital commander who first gained the respect of a Japanese tank commander the day of Bataan's surrender, and later the respect of even the cruel Camp O'Donnell commandants, suddenly was shifted from another prison in late 1944 to Cabanatuan.

Colonel Duckworth and a total of about twelve lieutenant colonels and majors composed the high-ranking staff at the camp by January 1945. As the days drifted by they began a serious campaign to gather and file all the records. Then the records were hidden in various places about the camp while everyone waited for the Japanese—or the Allies—to decide their fate.

At 1900 hours (7:00 P.M.), January 25, Battalion Commander Tomeo Oyabu called his Imperial Army unit to a halt at the crossroads just east of Cabanatuan City.

Oyabu had orders to stop at this small suburb known as Sangitan and receive final instructions for his march. Now he would learn if his unit must proceed north to San Jose or northeast past the POW camp to Bongabon.

Divisional Commander Naotake figured that there were entirely too many security leaks at the Imperial Army provincial headquarters in Cabanatuan City to issue such orders until the units were on the move. With the Americans advancing steadily from the west and increasing guerrilla activity throughout Nueva Ecija, the Japanese intended to exercise every possible precaution to keep their troop movements secret from the nosy Filipinos.

Cabanatuan City was the hub of imperial troop movements and Divisional Commander Naotake found himself in complete frustration trying to handle it all plus preparing the city for a delaying defense against the Americans.

General Yamashita left Naotake five battalion-size units, plus the division headquarters unit, to serve as a rear guard in Nueva Ecija while the main body of the army positioned itself in northern Luzon. But Naotake must also cope with the many logistical problems of other units, not under his command, filtering through Cabanatuan as they proceeded north.

To delay the front of American forces, Naotake had orders to hold all main highways running south to north through Neuva Ecija for another week until the last of Yamashita's troops safely evacuated the Manila area. In essence, the Naotake command was expendable.

Without air reconnaissance the Japanese could not determine accurately just where the major strike of the Americans would come. Cabanatuan City, of course, must be held since it sat dead center to the wave of advancing American units. Gapan, fifteen miles to the south, could be sacrificed, for soon all Imperial forces scheduled for the northern withdrawal should be safely through Cabanatuan City. There would be no need to hold Gapan.

San Jose, twenty-five miles north of Cabanatuan City, and Bongabon, twenty miles east, must be held to the last man. Therefore, Naotake decided that the primary defense should be placed equally at Cabanatuan City and San Jose. Bongabon (farthest from the Americans) would be of secondary concern.

Battalion Commander Oyabu's unit, consisting of a little over 800 men, had rested all day in Cabanatuan City while Naotake decided where to send them. The word finally came for Oyabu to move to Sangitan at dark. Now, either the twenty-five miles to San Jose or twenty miles to Bongabon would be an easy one-night march for the battalion.

Since its beginning, the Imperial Army had lacked the motorized equipment enjoyed by Western militaries. To overcome this problem the Japanese foot soldier had received extensive training to build his resistance and endurance. As early as boot camp the soldiers were trained with a twenty-five-mile march, often beginning before daybreak and ending with each man being required to run laps around a parade field. The marching exercise continued, even increased, through advance training assignments, and carried over to other post assignments.

With uniforms that seldom fit (and usually in deplorable condition), the little soldiers' marching stamina had amazed Western observers for years before the war. Carrying his heavy ten-pound rifle, ammunition, bayonet, canteen, first-aid packet, and his own food rations, a fully trained Japanese soldier could easily cover thirty-five miles a day on a cupful of rice, perhaps flavored with dry seaweed or fish powder.

Commander Oyabu picked up the phone at the crossroads' guard station and gave his code name to the officer on the other end of the line in Cabanatuan City.

"Dokuho 359 . . . Dokuho 359, reporting!"

The voice from Naotake headquarters issued the orders. "Dokuho 359, proceed to San Jose! Follow route through Pinaganaan, Talavera, Baloc . . . highway clear. Small enemy units approaching Guimba. Report to Battalion Commander Inoue at San Jose for coordinated defense. Kinpeidan headquarters now here. Kinpeidan will rest and then proceed to Pangatian prison camp. Kinpeidan will then proceed to Bongabon. Dokuho 359 and Inoue battalion *must* hold San Jose . . ."

Commander Oyabu now had his orders. He had no way of knowing that the San Jose assignment would be cut short.

Around daybreak on January 26, advance reconnaissance units of the U.S. 6th Division, I Corps, occupied the town of Guimba in Nueva Ecija. Within hours, outposts were established another nine miles east along the Licab River.

To the south of Guimba, La Paz fell to the Americans, giving them a solid line, over eighteen miles wide, with the town of Licab in the center. The Allies had moved their wide front some seventy-eight miles east of Sixth Army headquarters and were now ready to launch a major drive toward San Jose on the north and Cabanatuan City to the south.

The push of this big wedge to this time had met with little enemy resistance, but Sixth Army intelligence knew that large enemy forces were waiting for them at both San Jose and Cabanatuan City. They also knew that remnants of enemy units were making good progress, moving at night and resting during the day, as they withdrew north and east.

But General Krueger continued to worry about his overextended line. With his units engaged with the Japanese in the mountains both north and south of the central plains, that front line could be cut off should the enemy make a desperate thrust at his middle from either mountain range.

MacArthur's orders, nonetheless, were unchanged. The drive to Manila must continue with all possible speed. General Krueger calculated that his eastern front troops could take San Jose at the north by January 29 and Cabanatuan City by February 1 at the latest.

Guerrilla Major Robert Lapham's knowledge of the terrain and Filipino activities was invaluable to Sixth Army intelligence section (G2) through early January. Now, with Guimba in Allied hands, the Americans were truly in Lapham's backyard, where he had operated since 1942.

At 1500 hours (3:00 P.M.) on January 26, Colonel Horton White, Sixth Army G2, and his special assistant, Major Frank Rowale, were ready to meet with Bob Lapham and discuss, once again, a subject that had been near all their hearts for a long, long time—the Japanese POW camp at Pangatian, Cabanatuan.

When Sixth Army units entered Nueva Ecija province, Filipino runners reported to Lapham routinely, and their information on the situation near POW Camp Cabanatuan had become increasingly alarming.

G2 was now well advised of Japanese troop movements in and around Cabanatuan City. They knew that the POW camp was being used for resting transient troops and that at least 300 Allied POWs were still in the camp.

Intelligence Chief White, a big man with a calm disposition and a pleasant youthful face, joined Majors Rowale and Lapham at the large map spread over a field table in the G2 tent.

"It's too big a job for the Scouts to handle," Colonel White agreed, "but they can sure help." He turned to Bob Lapham and explained. "Two of our Alamo Scout teams have already had experience raiding a Jap POW camp—admittedly, it was a much smaller one and the Navy delivered them to within a mile of the objective. The teams were commanded by Lieutenants Rounsaville and Nellist. Lieutenant Dove planned and coordinated the entire mission. We'd better get them in on this, Frank."

"They are on their way over here now, sir," Major Rowale replied.

"Excellent." Colonel White nodded. "How many guerrillas can we depend on, Bob?"

Major Bob Lapham pointed to a spot on the map several inches southeast of Guimba. "Captain Eduardo Joson has over a hundred armed men here . . . near Lobong—"

"But that's still more than twenty miles from the stockade," Rowale noted.

"Yes," Lapham continued. "But . . . Joson is a good organizer and knows that country like the back of his hand. He can lead your men to . . . here." Lapham pointed to an area he circled with his finger. "Balangkare and Platero. Captain Juan Pajota has more than 300 armed men you can rely on."

"Well, Colonel—what do you think?" Rowale grinned.

"I think we had better get the Old Man's opinion!" Colonel White replied.

Within a few minutes, Alamo Scout Lieutenants Tom Rounsaville, Bill Nellist, and John Dove arrived to be briefed on the outline plan of G2.

His buddies did not call him the "All-American Boy" because he was from Hollywood or because his weight-lifter physique or physical power aided him in achieving some of the highest ratings in the Alamo Scouts. Nor was the title bestowed upon Lieutenant John M. Dove when he won the Bronze Star after his first mission or the Soldiers' Medal for saving the lives of two other Scouts.

John Dove did not drink or smoke and even refused coffee and tea. He was tough, intelligent, hard-working, and clean-living. It was no wonder that the devotion of his men reached hero worship proportions, for he *was* the ideal of every American boy. But the war in the muggy jungle heat of the South Pacific and the secrecy shrouding Scout operations never allowed the record of heroes' deeds to reach the outside world.

During October 1944, Lieutenant Dove had mapped out the entire rescue plan for thirty-two civilian Javanese being held by the Japanese at Moari in New Guinea. Two Alamo Scout teams were delivered under cover of darkness by Navy PT boats. The raid on the prison camp was a complete success. The entire Japanese garrison was liquidated and the liberated Allied prisoners (including some women and children) were safely aboard the PT boats in thirty minutes. The Scouts did not lose a single man.

One of the two teams Lieutenant Dove selected for that raid was commanded by a twenty-two-year-old veteran parachutist from the 11th Airborne Division, First Lieutenant Thomas Rounsaville. This team consisted of a fascinating assortment of five other men. PFC Frank Fox and Sergeant Harold Hard, both expert shots with the M1 rifle, were big, rugged individuals. PFC Francis Laquier possessed the ability to slip through the night with the quietness of a shadow. To Laquier, hunting came as instinct—an instinct for survival in the wilderness that he and all his American Indian brothers seem to possess. Tech Sergeant Alfred Alfonso, an American-Filipino from Hawaii, was nicknamed "Opu" (fat), but his stocky build did not slow him down. He could move with cat-like precision through the underbrush.

The last member of Rounsaville's team was perhaps one of the most interesting personalities. PFC Rufo Vaquilar had not really volunteered for the Alamo Scouts. He immigrated to California from the Philippines at age fifteen and at the "old age" of thirty-eight did not even expect to end up in the war. But the military had other ideas, and he, like many American-Filipinos, soon found himself drafted and sent to New Guinea. Once he arrived, the Army informed him that he was to try out for the Scouts. Generally, it was believed that these Filipinos could be of tremendous value when the Allied army returned to the Philippines.

Vaquilar prefered to carry the lightweight M1A1 folding stock carbine and a .45 automatic pistol. He had even qualified as an "expert" with the big handgun.

Always relating amusing stories concerning his past adventures (even one about a "run-in" with the law), Vaquilar was, indeed, a colorful character. No one knew if there was any truth to those stories. It didn't make any difference anyway. He was now doing his job as a key member of a special group of men who had elected him to fight with them. That was the only important factor.

The second team was commanded by one of the best shots with the M1 rifle in the Scouts, First Lieutenant William Nellist. Also from the 11th Airborne, twenty-six-year-old Nellist carried his six-foot, two-hundred-pound frame with the speed of a football halfback. His team likewise consisted of two eager and most capable Filipino-Americans—PFC Sabas Asis and Staff Sergeant Thomas Siason.

During the Moari raid, Nellist's team was also composed of PFC Andy Smith, PFC Wilbur Wismer, PFC Gilbert Cox, and Sergeant Galen Kittleson. Other than the Filipinos, twenty-year-old Kittleson was one of the smallest men in the Alamo Scouts. Yet his favorite weapon was the Thompson submachine gun and he was a true artist with the heavy weapon. He could squeeze off single rounds, fire short bursts, or rake an area with thirty or more slugs with the deadly accuracy of a rifle.

It was only logical for Lieutenant Dove to call upon the teams of Nellist and Rounsaville when he received word of the Cabanatuan POW camp assignment.

At long last Major Robert Lapham's dream for an attack on the POW camp was becoming a reality. Everyone was in agreement. The 6th Rangers would be the perfect unit to conduct such an attack—with reconnaissance assistance from the Filipino guerrillas and the Alamo Scouts. The idea was presented to Sixth Army Commanding General Walter Krueger, who listened with attentive enthusiasm.

"When do you wish to execute this?" General Krueger directed his questions to Colonel White.

"We don't have much time left, sir," White answered. "The closer our lines move on Cabanatuan City the shorter the minutes of life run for those prisoners. I would say we make our final plan tomorrow with Colonel Mucci—by noon—and suggest that the Rangers strike at dark on the twenty-ninth. After the twenty-ninth our chances of finding those POWs alive are slim."

General Krueger did not hesitate. "Get Colonel Mucci here for a noon meeting—and keep me posted. It looks risky, but it's a wonderful enterprise. I don't want a lot of casualties with this—and I don't want those POWs dead, either!"

At his headquarters in a small barrio near the POW camp, Captain Juan Pajota unfolded the note from Major Robert Lapham that a runner had delivered. A simple strip of graphing paper about eight inches wide, the note appeared no different from the many others received by Pajota from his American commander during the thirty-three months' campaign against the Japanese. Like most of the directives, this one was handwritten with a soft lead pencil. But this note contained a peculiar, unwritten message behind the written one.

"Captain Pajota, send immediately the 50 land mines in your possession. They are badly needed for a specific mission assigned us. Suggest you bring them personally for additional instructions and orders. *RUSH*. Major Lapham."

The word "Rush" was underlined three times, but this was not what impressed Pajota.

If Major Lapham desired land mines (which had remained concealed since their delivery by U.S. submarines a few months earlier), then there was something of unusual interest about the "mission." If explosives were needed for a simple sabotage job, Lapham would not have requested mines. There was only one logical conclusion. Plans for a major assault or defense were under consideration.

Captain Pajota instructed Sergeant Pacifico Tualla, "Go to Lapham! Tell him we will be on the way with the mines as soon as we can uncover them and load up. I will leave this place before 1200 . . . noon, tomorrow. If you cannot find Lapham at Guimba, then go to Captain Joson at Lobong. Joson will accompany you to Lapham!"

It was almost 2100 hours (9:00 P.M.) on the twenty-sixth when General Walter Krueger decided to get some sleep. As the weary general approached his tent the tall soldier standing guard at a position of parade rest snapped to attention, saluting with an M1 rifle.

General Krueger stopped and looked up into the face of the young man. "Stand at ease!" Krueger said, his voice reflecting fatigue.

The guard relaxed.

"What's your name, Ranger?" Krueger asked the startled soldier, who was unaccustomed to being addressed by three-star generals.

"Proudfit, sir! PFC William Proudfit, 2nd Platoon . . . F Company!"

"How tall are you, Proudfit?"

"Six foot, two and a half inches, sir!" PFC Proudfit barked, staring straight into space.

"Without your boots?"

Proudfit's eyes glanced down quickly at the Sixth United States Army commander and noticed that the general was smiling.

"Yes, sir!"

"Boy!" Krueger exclaimed. "I'm only five foot six. I wish I was as tall as you. Where are you from, son?"

"Des Moines, Iowa, sir!"

"Iowa . . . good place, Iowa. Getting enough to eat, Ranger?"

"Yes, sir!" Proudfit replied.

"You look like it!"

Proudfit's clean-shaven face finally broke into a grin.

General Krueger reached into his shirt pocket and produced a cigar. "Care for a smoke?"

"No, sir! Thank you, sir!"

"No . . . I mean when you're off-duty. Guard change is in a few minutes, isn't it?"

"Yes, sir," Proudfit acknowledged. "But . . . I don't smoke, sir!"

"Hum . . . I see. Well then, get some rest. And, son . . ."

"Yes, sir."

"You men keep up the good job, but don't take any unnecessary chances!"

Proudfit's eyes returned to the general. "Yes, sir! . . . You, too, sir!"

* * *

At 1130 hours (11:30 A.M.) on January 27, Lieutenant Colonel Henry A. Mucci left his battalion headquarters near Calasio and made the two-mile ride to Sixth Army headquarters at Dagupan by jeep.

Naturally, the moment the men learned that their colonel was on the way to G2, rumors began to spread through the Ranger camp with exciting speed. A new mission, everyone knew, was in the making, and the game was to guess what it might be and which company would get the assignment.

By 1150 hours all introductions had been made in the G2 intelligence command tent, and the officers were ready to begin their business. Those present for the hour-long meeting were Sixth Army Intelligence (G2) Chief Colonel Horton White, his assistant, Major Frank Rowale, guerrilla commander Major Robert Lapham and Alamo Scout Lieutenants John Dove, Thomas Rounsaville, and William Nellist, and, of course, Lieutenant Colonel Mucci.

Colonel White began. "Colonel Mucci, your Rangers are needed for an important mission. We want you to hit a large Jap POW camp and set our boys free. This is a tough one. Your men are the best-qualified to pull the job off! I'm going to turn most of this meeting over to Major Rowale."

Mucci received the news calmly but with a big grin and then lit his pipe.

It had already been decided that First Lieutenant John Dove would serve as liaison between the two Scout teams selected for the mission (Rounsaville's and Nellist's teams). In this capacity, Lieutenant Dove was to attach himself to the Rangers and move with them.

As the meeting progressed, every known detail concerning the current Japanese troop movements and the enemy situation at POW Camp Cabanatuan and Cabanatuan City was discussed at great length.

The Rangers, Colonel Mucci was told, must make a cross-country march, attack the camp at night, liberate the Allied prisoners, and return safely with them to American lines. Just how to accomplish this was left entirely up to him.

The selection of the two Scout teams was based on their prior experience in raiding a Japanese prison compound. Since Lieutenant Dove had done most of the planning for that mission, it made sense to attach him to the Rangers. Mucci and his officers could exchange ideas with Dove while on the march.

But the successful Alamo Scout raid had been conducted under entirely different conditions. Their raid, being of smaller scale, had required fewer men. The mission was carried out in jungle territory, and the Scouts had the advantage of being delivered and picked up by PT boats.

This new mission was far more complex. The Scouts and Rangers must walk almost thirty miles through practically open country in the central plains—and all of that country, once they left Guimba, was still in the hands of the Japanese. Enemy garrison troops at POW Camp Cabanatuan were estimated to be over 200 in number. Japanese troops of, perhaps, battalion strength were camping from time to time at Cabu bridge, which was only a mile from the POW compound. At Cabanatuan City, only three or four miles south of the compound, enemy forces estimated to be of division strength were gathering and could be expected to move northeast along the road that ran in front of the compound. Japanese tanks were known to be at all these locations, yet they were moving after dark along the roads leading north and east from Cabanatuan City.

To make the situation even more hazardous, Mucci was informed that the entire mission must remain "top secret." The U.S. Air Force would not be told of the mission unless the Rangers requested emergency air cover.

Upon hearing this, Colonel Mucci removed the pipe from his mouth and stared at the dark-complected Major Rowale. "Then we will maintain radio silence unless an emergency exists?"

"Yes, Colonel," Rowale replied, his brown eyes showing no emotion. "Unless it is an extreme emergency or you are forced to make a change in plans. The entire mission is so delicate we can't even risk transporting your men by any kind of vehicle. One tip to the Japs, and I'm afraid you'll find nothing but dead American prisoners when you arrive at the camp."

"And the tanks! You think there are tanks in the camp?" Mucci expressed the concern felt by everyone present. Foot soldiers fighting off tanks, especially while trying to carry sick men, presented a very dangerous situation.

"Well . . . we have good reason to believe there are tanks in the camp," Rowale answered. "Major Lapham's guerrillas report that at least two tanks were hidden in or around two metal buildings . . ." Major Rowale paused and handed Colonel Mucci a six-by-twelve-inch aerial photograph of the POW camp area.

"You see this spot . . . here, at the center of the compound to the right of the camp road?"

"Is this the best photo you have?" Mucci exclaimed as he squinted his eyes to study a two-by-two-inch section on the photo that was the camp.

"I'm afraid so. I have copies for you fellows, also." Major Rowale nodded to the Scout lieutenants. "Now . . . our boys think they see a tank in the shadow of this building. The tank sheds . . . or motor pool section, if you wish . . . are the only metal buildings in the stockade. They are corrugated iron. All the other buildings are bamboo, nipa, and wood . . . except for the chapel over here near the drainage pond. It's concrete or stone, but apparently there's nothing there worth worrying about. Even if there are no tanks in the camp, you must be ready for armor moving up from Cabanatuan City!"

"A few bazookas should do the trick on the tanks in the stockade," Mucci said with assurance. "But, what about this road between Cabanatuan City and Bongabon? You say the road is heavily traveled. We have to secure that road and cross it to hit the camp. If it's traveled continually by armor, even bazookas won't make the job easy!"

Rowale looked up at the calm face of Colonel White. Mucci had just touched on the point that concerned G2 the most. Regardless of the best plans, the entire mission depended on surprise, exact timing and—luck. Luck that enemy traffic on the main highway passing the POW camp would be light enough to permit an attack. And luck that no one would tip off the Japanese that an attack was pending.

"Colonel Mucci," Major Rowale interrupted the brief silence,

"I guess we can't predict how heavy the traffic will be on that road. Major Lapham feels that his guerrillas in the area may have some dope on the subject when you arrive in the camp area. The guerrillas infiltrated the staff of the Philippine Constabulary operating out of Cabanatuan City long ago. They know a great deal about the troop movement. But . . . of course, if your raid is already under way and the Filipinos learn of a Jap unit moving up . . . it may be too late for them to warn you."

"I'll plan accordingly," Mucci stated.

"I'm sure you will, sir," Rowale continued. "But, to ease your mind a little . . . you'll definitely have air cover for your return trip once you request it, and the Black Widow Night Fighters will be out on the prowl between now and the time the mission is over. They don't know about all this, yet, but they are covering every major road and giving the Japs hell each night. We'll tell them to stay clear of the camp . . . unless you radio that you need them at the last minute."

"How about the weather?" Mucci asked.

"Looks good!" Colonel White answered. "Should be dry and warm with scattered medium to high clouds on the twenty-ninth and thirtieth. And . . . you'll have a full moon."

Mucci grinned. "And what about our advance units out of Guimba?"

Colonel White shifted his large frame on the field stool. "We will coordinate this with the 6th Division . . . the 1st and 20th regiments. You fellows can identify yourselves by two green flares. We hope, Colonel, that your walk back won't be so long as the one going over. Our lines should move up a few miles during your absence."

"I'll need more than one company," Mucci said. "With Bravo and Echo companies on that island . . . Santiago, I'll take Charley company and probably a platoon from Fox company . . ."

"Well . . . you'll have some good help, Colonel," Major Lapham injected as he tilted his old campaign hat back from his forehead. "When you step off from Guimba some of my guerrillas will take you to Joson . . . Captain Eduardo Joson's headquarters down near Lobong. He has over a hundred armed men who can serve as your flank guards and guide every trail between Guimba and Pajota's area . . . needless to say, Pajota knows every inch of his territory. He was even based at that compound before the Japs invaded. He'll bring you up to date on the Jap situation when you arrive. These Filipinos have fought a long, hard war, Colonel. It's been mostly hit and run . . . attack and hide. It's cost them their homes and many have lost members of their family. So they are looking for a chance to even the score . . . they are excellent fighters. The villagers will want to feed your men in every barrio you enter. You can trust every one of them except . . . the Huks."

Mucci frowned. "What about those Huks?"

Major Lapham rubbed his pointed chin. "Well, originally we got along with the Huks. At least we tolerated one another. They were killing Japs just like we were—and lots of Japs. But for the last year my men and the Huks have been tangling—"

"It's all political, you know," Major Rowale interrupted. "The Filipinos have been fighting amongst themselves over who's going to run the country after the war."

"Leave the Huks to my men, if you can," Lapham suggested. "Joson and Pajota know how to handle them. They'll know where the Huks are. If anything, the Huks will probably just want to get in on the act. They know that the officers under me are commissioned in the United States Army—that my guerrillas are sworn members of our U.S. Army—at least most of them are. The Huks resent that fact."

When Mucci had all the information he felt he needed he stood up and said, "Okay . . . you say this is to be done on the twenty-ninth. That doesn't give us much time."

"Tomorrow at dawn," Rowale replied. "You'll truck to Guimba and then move out when you are ready. The Scouts will leave tonight and establish contact with this fellow Pajota. They'll reconnoiter the area and be ready to report to you when you arrive in the morning of the twenty-ninth."

Mucci looked at the three tall Alamo Scouts. "Will that give you fellows enough time to get all the dope we'll need? You'll need to travel all night and part of the day, just to get there!"

"We hope so, sir!" Lieutenant Nellist replied. "We'll do our damnedest!"

"Then," Mucci stated, "we'll strike after dark on the twenty-ninth! Just be sure we have that air cover coming back!"

Shortly after noon on the twenty-seventh, Sergeant Pacifico Tuallo arrived at Sixth Army Headquarters with his message for Major Lapham.

When he reported that Captain Pajota would be on the way with the requested land mines, Tuallo was informed to get some rest and prepare for a new assignment.

At dusk, the sergeant must return to Platero and tell Pajota to "keep the mines and prepare all squadrons to be ready to assist the Americans who will attack the POW camp at Pangatian!"

A runner had already departed for Platero with the same message. But Sergeant Tuallo would have the honor of leading the Alamo Scouts cross-country to find Pajota.

Not long after he finished lunch on January 27, Tech Sergeant Norton Most sat at his radio post and stared dreamily out at the waves that rolled onto the dark sandy beaches of Santiago Island.

Life for Sergeant Most and the members of B and E companies had been relatively dull for the last few days, but they could not afford to drop their guard for one minute. The Rangers remained at the alert for a possible Japanese commando attack on the radar station. The radio teams worked in shifts, ready to relay an emergency warning should enemy planes approach over the China Sea.

Suddenly, Norton Most's radio came alive and he began to rapidly record the coded message from battalion headquarters on Luzon. The message was for Sergeant Most. He now had orders to return immediately to Ranger headquarters and join a "special mission" assigned the Rangers. Most knew that there must be something especially important about that mission, else another radioman could fill the position.

Sergeant Most spent the next several hours journeying back to Calasio and, once at battalion headquarters, learned the details of the special mission.

The battalion's communication officer, Lieutenant Smith, informed Norton Most of the plans for the raid, and the two men reviewed the technical requirements surrounding the assignment. The new, lightweight SCR 694 radios would be put to test under difficult conditions. But the SCR 694 was designed for such purposes. Lieutenant Smith was pleased that his entire communications section had volunteered for the mission. From them all, he selected Sergeant Most, Tech 5 William A. Lawyer, and Tech 4 George R. Disrud to actually go on the raid. Tech 4 Disrud, like Norton Most, was a qualified radio "operator." If Most were killed, Disrud could take over.

The rest of the men in the communications section were scheduled to operate relay stations.

The radiomen, now, could try to get a few hours' sleep before the mission.

Japanese Battalion Dokuho 359 Commander Tomeo Oyabu strained to hear his new orders coming in on the static-filled radiophone. It was 1700 (5:00 P.M.) January 27.

Commander Oyabu glanced at his map. According to new orders, he could not return by the same march route his unit had traveled from Cabanatuan City to San Jose less than thirty hours before. Now, he must move twenty-two miles southeast to Bongabon, then another twenty-five miles back south to Naotake headquarters at Cabanatuan.

It was too late to pull his men from their positions and move to Bongabon before daylight, he explained to Naotake. Oyabu requested permission to wait until dark the next day. If they traveled at night they could make the south side of Bongabon by dawn the twenty-ninth. Then they could continue the night of the thirtieth and reach Cabanatuan City the morning of the thirty-first. This way his battalion would not be caught on the highway during daylight hours by American planes.

Commander Oyabu continued to present his idea by phone. Dokuho 359 requested permission to bivouac at Prison Camp Pangatian the night of January 30.

Naotake headquarters realized that the Oyabu battalion could easily make the four-mile march from the POW camp to Cabanatuan City in perhaps an hour, but that idea presented another problem. There were already too many troops scheduled for rest at the POW camp.

"No! Dokuho 359. You must reach the vicinity of Cabu River before the morning of January 30. Kinpeidan headquarters unit is now resting at Camp Pangatian. Kinpeidan will depart Pangatian camp at 8:00 P.M. January 30 for Bongabon. The road must be open for Kinpeidan movement. Suggest you bivouac in the vicinity of Cabu River. At 9:00 P.M. road will clear . . . depart Cabu River at 9:00 P.M. for Cabanatuan City."

Battalion Commander Oyabu, like all good Japanese officers, did not question the final orders. If his Dokuho 359 Battalion must pull out and march over forty miles to the Cabu River, they would do it. His men could rest all day along the banks of the Cabu and be in excellent condition to continue the remaining four miles to aid in the defense of Cabanatuan City.

Oyabu's battalion simply had to wait for that headquarters unit to pass over Cabu bridge on their journey northeast from the POW camp. He could then cross and head south to Cabanatuan.

American forces were still at least three or four days away from Cabanatuan City, the POW camp, and Cabu bridge. At least, that was what Dokuho 359 believed.

When Lieutenant Colonel Henry Mucci returned to his Ranger base it was midafternoon of the twenty-seventh. He immediately informed Captain Robert Prince of the details of the mission, instructing him to prepare his C Company and advise F Company Commander First Lieutenant John F. Murphy to get his 2nd Platoon ready.

"My wonderful Captain Prince," as Mucci was later to describe his C Company commander, would be second in command (under Mucci) and responsible for most of the plans and organizing the mission.

Colonel Mucci planned to hold an "officers call" and stated that he would address the troops scheduled for the raid later in the day. Then he retired to his tent to get his own affairs in order.

Within a few minutes, F Company's first sergeant visited Mucci.

"Hi, kid! What's on your mind?" The colonel greeted the wiry little Sergeant Charles Bosard.

"You know what's on my mind! I want to go on this mission!"

"No, kid—not this one!"

"Colonel . . ."

"No!" Mucci snapped. "And dammit, that's final. Your 2nd Platoon sergeants will be enough NCOs."

"I'm the kind of man you need to pull this thing off, and you know it!" Bosard continued.

"No—you're too valuable. I don't want you shot up!" Mucci looked at Bosard and the sergeant noticed the colonel's eyes were misty. "I don't want anyone shot up," Mucci added in a quieter tone. "If we don't come back, where would F Company get another good first sergeant like you, kid?"

"Goddammit, Colonel! I trained these men. They're my boys as much as yours. If you're their father, I'm their mother. I deserve to go with them!"

Mucci grinned one of his big broad grins. "You want to be my bodyguard? If you go, you'll have to stay close to me. I want to keep an eye on your ass the whole time—else, you'll be in there with your knife cutting up some Jap and getting yourself shot up."

"I don't give a damn what you assign me . . . just let me—"

"Okay . . . Okay!" Mucci began to laugh. "You can go! Now, get the hell out of here and get your fellows ready. Remind Prince I'm going to give a little talk in a few minutes!"

"Yes, *sir!*" Bosard replied.

"Dammit, don't 'sir' me! You call me 'sir' on this mission and I'll . . ."

Before midnight another twenty-five officers, NCOs, and men approached Colonel Mucci hoping to persuade him to take them along on the raid. Each received the same story from the Ranger commander, who had become increasingly emotional at the overwhelming numbers of volunteers. They were all good men, he told them, but he could not take everyone. There would be other missions. Their time would come.

Nonetheless, A Company First Sergeant Ned Hedrick, Staff Sergeant Richard Moore of F Company, and Sergeant Harry Killough of E Company managed, somehow, to change his mind.

The battalion executive officer, Major Garrett, tried to convince Mucci to stay behind, insisting it would be wiser to send him instead. That discussion did not last long. Lieutenant Colonel Mucci had made his final selections and he was going to lead his troops. Nothing and no one would change that decision.

The Rangers of Company C, Company F (2nd Platoon), medics, radio operators—everyone scheduled for the raid—assembled in front of the battalion headquarters to hear what Colonel Mucci had to say.

Colonel Mucci studied the excited faces of his men and began his speech in an unusually calm tone. "As you know by now, we have been given a tough but rewarding assignment. We're going to hit a Jap POW stockade and free a few hundred of our boys the Nips have held for almost three years . . ."

A few whistles and muffled "wows!" came from the men.

"All those prisoners," Mucci continued, "are sick and dying. They are what's left of our troops who held out on Bataan and Corregidor . . . and if we don't free them now, you can bet they'll be killed by the Japs before our front reaches their area.

"We'll be behind enemy lines the entire trip, but we'll have Filipino guerrillas to guide us and help with our mission.

"You fellows are the eight ball company . . . you are really behind that eight ball now! This isn't going to be easy. Nothing has been easy so far, but this is a most dangerous assignment.

"If you feel lucky . . . you're welcome to come along. If not . . . I promise no one . . . repeat, *no one,* will ever say one word to you about your decision to stay back. Naturally, I think married men should stay home for this one, but it's up to you to decide.

"Before you make that decision to come along you had better listen some more. This mission is top secret! Other than the guerrillas and a few Alamo Scouts, we'll be alone and on our own. Our Air Force doesn't know about this mission yet, so we'll need to avoid our boys as much as the Japs. The flyboys may mistake us for Japs. But—we'll have air cover on the return trip."

Now Mucci began to speak louder, the words rolling fast with dramatic impact. "We'll have to attack at night so the darkness can help cover our withdrawal. And we are going to jump that stockade right between two big Jap forces, which will be only a few miles away. There are over 150 Japs in the camp itself!

"Use your knives when you get inside if you need to! We want no Americans in that camp killed, especially by our own bullets!

"You're going to bring out every God damned man even if you have to carry them out on your back!

"Those prisoners will probably be confused and scared. Some may not wish to leave. Remember what they have endured over those long months with the Japs. You will be gentle with those prisoners, but if they refuse to leave, kick 'em out if you must—but get them out *alive!*

"You'll be carrying extra rations besides your three-day packets—extra chocolate. I don't want to see any of you guys eating that stuff. It's for the POWs you release . . . OK!?

"Before daybreak we'll be trucked about seventy-five miles northwest of here to a town called Guimba. Near there, we'll meet the first guerrilla army that will serve as our escort . . . and from there we walk through Jap country, all the way . . . no sleep . . . then we attack and walk back!

"Jungle greens will be the uniform, and soft caps. No helmets this time. They make too much noise. Those who wish to carry an extra .45 can do so. You might need 'em for close-in fighting.

"Now! One last thing. I don't want any damned atheists—any nonreligious men to go on this mission. We are going to gather around the chaplain in a few minutes. You are all going to church if you plan to go on this raid!

"You had better get down on your knees and pray. Dammit, don't fake it. I mean—*pray!* And I want you to swear an oath before God . . . swear you'll die fighting rather than let any harm come to those POWs!"

Colonel Mucci exercised an abrupt about face and disappeared inside his command tent, leaving his men practically spellbound. Everyone went "to church" and swore that oath, and no one requested his name be scratched from the mission.

After Colonel Mucci's speech, First Lieutenant John W. Lueddeke assembled his five-man team—Unit F of the 832nd Signal Service

Battalion. But the men were disappointed to learn that only three of them could go on the mission.

"Okay, men. That's the dope as I know it," Lieutenant Lueddeke said. "This is for volunteers only."

All five men raised their hands.

"Well, I thought so."

The lieutenant removed the liner from his helmet and dropped five small folded pieces of notebook paper into the steel pot. "Weiner, you shouldn't go anyway. But to keep this fair, you can draw in the lottery if you wish."

PFC Morris Weiner cursed his bad luck under his breath. He had fallen off a truck a few days before and broken his finger.

"Ready to draw? Look for the marked paper and then show it to me!" Lueddeke instructed.

"Darn, I lose!" PFC George Woodruff exclaimed as he held up a blank paper. "I'll see you lucky bums later."

The "winners" were Tech 4 Frank J. Goetzheimer, PFC Robert C. Lautman, and PFC Wilber B. Goen.

Twenty-year-old PFC Lautman at five foot seven inches and 140 pounds was not the smallest man in Unit F. In fact, he was a good two inches taller than his tough little comrade, Tech 4 Frank Goetzheimer.

What Frank Goetzheimer lacked in physical stature, he made up with energy, photographic skill, and determination. He was already "jump qualified" having successfully completed the rugged paratrooper school. With a boyish face, twenty-two-year-old Goetzheimer, the "little fellow with the big name," unfortunately had the biggest load of equipment to carry. His ten-pound 35-mm Eyemo Bell and Howell movie camera, plus ten rolls of movie film at five pounds each and the weight of his web equipment with a .45 automatic pistol, was almost equal to half his body weight.

"What are you taking this time, Bob?" Goetzheimer asked PFC Lautman as the men prepared for the mission.

"The Rolie," the reply came as Robert Lautman buckled his pistol belt from which hung a .38-caliber police special revolver. He had traded his heavy .45 service automatic long before to a Navy friend for the revolver.

The little 2.25-inch twin-lens camera Lautman planned to take was usually preferred over the standard but heavier four-by-five Speed Graphic for tough assignments where great distances must be covered on foot. PFC Wilber Goen, nonetheless, planned to carry the Speed Graphic.

Late in the afternoon of January 27, the first section of Japanese Kinpeidan unit, consisting of approximately fifty men, had boarded two troop transport trucks, pulled out of Cabanatuan City, and proceeded to the crossroads at Sangitan suburbs. There they turned northeast and headed directly to their destination— POW Camp Cabanatuan at Pangatian.

Along the road, they passed the bulk of their unit, some 125 men, who were marching to the camp.

By 2100 hours (9:00 P.M.), the entire Kinpeidan headquarters unit had bedded down in their transient quarters area inside the compound with orders from Naotake command to remain in the camp until after dark, January 30.

For these imperial soldiers the next few days would be easy duty. The detachment of about seventy-five guards at the stockade must continue as sentries, unassisted by any transient troops.

The presence of this headquarters group at POW Camp Cabanatuan was the very reason why Battalion Commander Tomeo Oyabu and his Dokuho 359 unit were ordered to proceed to the Cabu River and bivouac there.

Naotake command did not wish Dokuho 359 and the Kinpeidan unit to merge either at the camp or along the road, and they would not. But fate was about to merge the two Japanese units in a common destiny.

At dark on January 27, Alamo Scout Lieutenants Tom Rounsaville and Bill Nellist shook hands with their friend, First Lieutenant John Dove, the "all-American boy."

"Take care of Mucci and the Rangers, Johnny," Lieutenant Nellist said with a teasing grin.

"You fellows stay out of trouble. I'll see you in a couple of days," Dove replied.

Tom Rounsaville turned to look at the two Scout teams, who were chatting together and adjusting rifle slings. "We haven't lost a man yet."

"And, we're not going to lose anyone on the mission either," Nellist added with cool confidence.

Rounsaville tossed the M1 to his back, forcing his left arm through the loop in its sling. "How many Japs did G2 say are in that camp?"

"About 200—give or take a few," Dove answered, "and at least a division at Cabanatuan City."

"Well," Rounsaville replied, "with thirteen Scouts and 100 Rangers—that should be a fair fight!"

By 1900 hours (7:00 P.M.) the two Scout teams, guided by Pajota's Sergeant Pacifico Tuallo and several other Filipino guerrillas, left Guimba for their twenty-four-mile cross-country march to Platero.

For this mission, First Lieutenant Tom Rounsaville's team consisted of Sergeant Harold Hard, PFC Franklin Fox, the colorful Filipino-American Rufo Vaquilar, Hawaiian-Filipino PFC Alfred "Opu" Alfonso, and American Indian PFC Francis Laquier.

First Lieutenant Bill Nellist's team was composed of his two Filipino-American members, PFC Tom Siason and PFC Sabas Asis. PFCs Gilbert Cox, Wilbur Wismer, and Andrew Smith, and Sergeant Galen Kittleson, the Tommy gun expert, completed the group. Perhaps by modern standards the equipment carried on the mission by the photography unit, radiomen, Rangers, and Scouts seems primitive, yet it all was the best available at the time and far superior to anything the Japanese on Luzon possessed.

All the Scouts dressed in their faded green battle fatigues with baggy pants and soft caps were literally a walking arsenal. Each carried a .45 automatic pistol and extra magazines of ammunition, a double-edged wide-blade trench knife, a few hand grenades, and two or four bandoliers of ammunition for their rifles. The Filipino members carried their preferred lightweight M1A1 folding stock carbines, and Sergeant Kittleson, as usual, lugged his Thompson submachine gun.

The deadly nature of their work and several months of dangerous missions behind enemy lines had produced thirteen young men who began this mission with the very seriousness of it all etched in their faces.

As individuals, each was quite capable of carrying out the assignment alone should anything happen to the other team members.

True, the Scout operations before Luzon had been mostly in the jungles and usually during the hours of darkness. Now, they must depend on the Filipino guerrillas to guide them through open enemy-held country during daylight and darkness without being detected. They must cover almost thirty miles on foot, set up plans with Captain Juan Pajota, reconnoiter the camp area, and be ready with detailed information and suggestions when Colonel Mucci arrived with his Rangers the morning of the twenty-ninth. The Scouts would have only about thirty-five hours to accomplish their part of the mission.

By 2000 hours (8:00 P.M.) on the twenty-seventh, the two Scout teams were deep within Japanese territory.

Captain Pajota waited for the Scouts at Balangkare, a few miles north of Platero, well advised by the bamboo telegraph that moved ahead of the Americans. When he met them at dawn on the twenty-eighth, Pajota was not disappointed.

The new generation of Americans, these giants who had come to liberate his country, were everything Pajota had hoped for. The Alamo Scouts (which, of course, he had never heard of before January 26) were tough, intelligent individuals. Most of all, they were dead serious about their assignment and interested in his opinions. He would never forget their names or personalities.

When Lieutenant Colonel Mucci entered his battalion surgeon's tent he found Doctor James Fisher busy checking and rechecking a large assortment of medical equipment. It was almost midnight.

Captain Fisher hardly noticed his visitor, hesitating only a moment to scratch at his close-chopped black hair, then continued to stuff surgical instruments into canvas bags that simply could hold no more.

"What are you doing, Jimmy?" Colonel Mucci finally inquired.

"Got to finish getting these aid satchels ready. I understand the guerrillas have a doctor. Maybe he can use some of our excess equipment."

Mucci watched as Captain Fisher searched through a large wooden trunk.

"Now . . . where in hell did I put those forceps?"

"Is that it on the table?" Mucci asked.

"Yeah! Just where I left them, I guess."

Captain Fisher spread a web belt on the table and began to fumble with the two hooks of a trench knife sheath, and he attempted to attach the weapon.

"Where do you think you are going with that, Jimmy?"

"Why . . . with my men, of course."

"Oh no! No, Jimmy. Not you." Mucci shook his head. "I heard you had some fool notion about going. This will be too tough a mission . . . and, surgeons, especially good ones, are hard to come by in the Philippines!"

Fisher's face flushed. "Colonel, you are taking over a hundred men a long way—"

"Yes, and how many of your medics?" Mucci tried to change the subject.

"Four."

"Who are they?"

"Sergeant Johnny Nelson, Corporal Martin Estesen, Corporal Bernie Haynes, and Corporal Bob Ramsey." Fisher continued, determined to make his point. "And they are good . . . really experts. But suppose some of our boys get hit bad. My medics can't be expected to perform surgery out there under a banana tree or in some nipa hut—but I can! If any of our boys are hit real bad, their chances of making it back to our lines alive are next to impossible—you know that. What are you going to do, Colonel? Leave a trail of dying men all the way back? Our medics can care for serious wounds, maybe even more, but you won't have time for anyone but a qualified surgeon to do fast work."

Lieutenant Colonel Mucci stood silent for a moment, his unlit pipe protruding from the corner of his mouth. He reached up slowly, grasped the bowl, and pointed the stem at Captain Fisher. "You said yourself that the Filipinos have a doctor."

"Good," Fisher replied. "But you can't expect him to follow you about the country."

"All right, Jimmy. I guess there is no way of talking you out of it, is there. But I'm telling you now . . . you are not getting anywhere near that camp when we attack!"

Captain Bob Prince waited until he was alone in his tent, the night of the twenty-seventh, to remove his boots and carefully unroll the heavy army socks. Now he could soak and doctor his blistered feet without anyone noticing the dangerous condition. Those blisters must remain his secret, or else Mucci or Captain Fisher might confine him. Nothing, certainly not blistered, miserable feet was going to hold Bob Prince back from the mission. He planned to carry some GI foot powder in the deep pockets of those baggy green combat fatigues. Somehow, he would make the march over to the POW camp and worry about walking back later.

Before him, on a blanket, lay the necessary tools of war of a Ranger company commander—a .45 automatic pistol in its shoulder holster, web belt with canteen, first-aid packet, pouches with extra .45-caliber shells in their magazines, and the trench knife. Next to that assortment of equipment was his M1 rifle, two bandoliers of clip ammunition (with two packs of cigarettes crammed in one bandolier pocket), several flares, a "Very" flare pistol, and a compass.

By his side lay the aerial photo of the camp area and the topological map of Nueva Ecija province.

Actually, the map that Colonel Mucci and Captain Prince were to rely on was constructed from three separate maps, carefully assembled by Sixth Army's G2 section. It consisted of quadrangles "Zaragoza 335711, Cabanatuan 335711, and Papaya 3457111."

With contour intervals indicated at twenty feet and a scale of one to 50,000 (one inch equaled 50,000 actual inches on the ground), it represented the best that the military had printed in 1944.

It appeared to be extremely accurate. Towns, roads, trails, rice ponds, swamps, rivers, streams, bridges, barrios—everything seemed perfect.

But Captain Prince had noticed that the map indicated the area directly across from POW Camp Cabanatuan to be heavily wooded, yet the aerial photograph taken a few days before showed that same area to be open grassland, dotted with rice ponds.

This would mean that the Rangers must expect little or no concealment while they crossed that last mile to the camp. It might also indicate that the beautiful map had other critical errors.

10

God bless Ameereka.

—Barrio Platero Reception Committee,
January 29, 1945

Shortly before daybreak, at 0500 hours, on January 28, 1945, a small convoy of six-by-six trucks, two jeeps, and a command staff car containing 122 members of the United States Sixth Army Rangers left Calasio. Within a few minutes they were at the Sixth Army headquarters area near Dagupan.

During the short stop at Dagupan, four members of Combat Photo Unit F, 832nd Signal Service Battalion, climbed aboard while a number of Rangers loaded several bazookas, rockets, anti-tank rifle grenades, and additional ammunition.

In less than twenty minutes the convoy was on the move again, proceeding to Guimba, seventy-five miles away. For the next hour and a half, as the vehicles bounced and jerked along the narrow, bomb-cratered highway, some Rangers actually managed to get a few minutes' sleep. Practically none had slept the night before.

At 0715, the convoy arrived at Guimba, and Major Robert Lapham was on hand to greet them. While the Rangers adjusted equipment and checked their weapons, Lapham introduced Colonel Mucci to the Filipino guerrillas who would guide them to Captain Eduardo Joson's headquarters at Lobong.

The men were allowed three hours' rest, then a hot lunch, and another hour's rest before Lapham bid them farewell and "good luck." Bob Lapham wanted to accompany Mucci, but G2 considered his knowledge of the country, which forward units of Sixth Army were preparing to cross, much too valuable to gamble his life now. After all, Lapham had already served his country far beyond what could be expected of any man. Mucci would be in good hands, Lapham knew, with Joson and Pajota.

The Rangers now drew a two-day supply of "K" combat rations (food) and added the cans to the weight they must lug on the long march.

As Mucci had instructed, uniforms were the usual faded green combat fatigues and soft cap. No rank or insignia were worn. By now each man was familiar with the faces of his buddies, their ranks, squads, and nicknames. Automatic weapons were prescribed according to particular assignment, but riflemen had a personal choice of the M1 or M1 carbine. The weapon section men carried BARs instead of light machine guns. Most noncommissioned officers carried a Tommygun and at least one .45 pistol. Captain Prince and Lieutenant Murphy carried both an M1 and a .45, but Captain Jimmy Fisher and Lieutenant Colonel Mucci wore only a .45. The other lieutenants, including Communications Officer Clifford K. Smith and Combat Photo Unit F Commander John W. Lueddeke, carried M1s and .45s, and all medics either a carbine or M1 plus a .45. A number of the men, following Mucci's suggestion, wore two or more .45 pistols. Every man had at least two bandoliers of ammunition, the large trench knife, and at least two hand or rifle grenades.

A dull-olive-colored four-door command staff car bumped to a halt beneath the shade of a large tree about a mile southeast of Guimba. In the backseat of the canvas-topped vehicle sat radio operator Tech 4th Class James M. Irvine, and before him, mounted to the rear of the front seat, was an SCR 284 field radio, which would serve as the base communication link between Sixth Army and Mucci's Rangers during the mission. Here, James Irvine must remain awake and alert for two days to be ready should Mucci be forced to break radio silence prematurely with a message for help or a change in plans.

The communications section was in complete agreement. If Sergeant Norton Most flashed a message back to Guimba, "hand" key rather than voice transmission would be used. Realizing they must operate on the outer limits of their radio's capabilities, the commo men did not wish to take a chance with voice transmission. The human voice could become completely distorted or saturated with static during a crucial message. A modified version of Morse code, dots and dashes, clicks or pauses would be used. Various code letters had been specially designated for the mission. The combination "BZ," for example, meant "mission accomplished." With the exception of the new code, everything else was to be routine.

What worried Tech 4 James Irvine, though, was that he had had less than four hours' sleep the night before. It would not be easy to stay awake during the hot days and balmy evenings ahead. But Irvine had had an idea. Instead of wearing his soft fatigue cap, he brought along his steel helmet. He believed that if sleep conquered him his head would fall forward, the helmet striking the metal case of the radio. The alarm system should work, but Irvine had no way of knowing that the number of hours he must remain alert would exceed the period of time for which everyone planned.

At 1400 hours (2:00 P.M.) Colonel Mucci and his men left Irvine in the radio car and began the first leg of their march to Lobong.

After leaving Guimba the Rangers, now on foot, proceeded two miles due east along a main road, then swung south of the town of Consuelo, through two and three-fourths miles of flat grassland, until they reached the banks of the Licab River.

Their Filipino guides knew just where to cross the river. Even though the water was less than knee deep, sloshing along through a thick bamboo forest and more grassland with wet boots made for very uncomfortable walking.

After another quarter mile the guides called a halt. The front of the Ranger single-file line suddenly was in the presence of some 100 armed Filipinos.

The natives were clad in a variety of uniforms, ranging from old

USAFFE khaki to the simple clothes of rice farmers. The Rangers had reached Barrio Lobong—the headquarters of guerrilla Captain Eduardo Joson.

As planned, Captain Joson and eighty of his armed soldiers joined the Rangers, and the combined force, now totaling 200, departed Lobong at 1830 hours (6:30 P.M.). Joson explained that he must leave twenty armed men to protect his headquarters from possible Huk attack.

With the exception of a few who would guide Mucci to Balang-kare, the guerrillas were dispatched far out on both flanks. Neither Huks nor Japanese would be able to ambush the force without warning.

When the group entered a heavy forest east of Lobong, they were well over six miles into enemy territory.

Nine miles south of Guimba, near the town of Licab, Corporal Vance O. Kiser of F Company and a detail of four other Rangers erected a radio relay station camp. Complete with antenna wire strung in tree limbs, three pup tents, an SCR 694 radio and hand-crank generator, the equipment and activity of the American team was too much for the curious and hospitable Filipinos.

A few minutes after the camp was operational, at about 1800 hours (6:00 P.M.), excited natives from a nearby barrio began to arrive with fresh eggs, fruit, and a chicken. In return, the Rangers traded their rations. Everyone was delighted with the exchange— the Americans glad to give up the tasteless canned goods for "real" food, and the Filipinos happy to receive such fancy gifts. Not only did the villagers love the processed food, they planned to put the empty cans to good use as well.

The existence of this Licab radio station was most important. If reception difficulties occurred between Guimba and Colonel Mucci, the Licab station was now ready to serve as relay transmitter for either group.

It was well after dark by the time the Rangers completed five and a half miles from Lobong and left the thick forest. Now they entered flat land and chest-tall grass. They halted for a ten-minute break in a bamboo thicket about one-half mile south of the town of Baloc.

Before them, stretching at least another 200 yards, was more open grass country through which cut the National Highway connecting Cabanatuan City and Talavera to the south and San Jose in the north. These were the first of two major roads the Rangers must cross. G2 had emphatically warned Mucci that both arteries might be heavily traveled by Imperial Army troops at night. G2 was correct. The sounds from heavy vehicles moving north on the road could easily be heard by the Rangers as they crouched in small groups concealed by the bamboo.

"What do you think, kid?" Colonel Mucci asked as he crawled up next to First Sergeant Charles Bosard.

"You said I'm supposed to be your bodyguard and I haven't seen you since we left Guimba!"

Sergeant Bosard knew very well where Mucci had been during the march—everywhere. The battalion commander was like a "mother hen" moving up and down the column of his men all afternoon, covering almost twice the distance everyone else had while exercising constant control and issuing words of encouragement.

"We're going to have to leapfrog that road—one at a time—if we're going to get across safely tonight. Look at that!" Bosard pointed to a Japanese tank sitting ominously in the moonlight off to the side of the road about 100 yards to their north. "Looks like they are guarding something . . . or waiting for someone," the sergeant added.

"Yeah, I know," Mucci replied. "I saw the tank a few minutes ago. Prince says the map indicates that there is a ravine and a small bridge near the tank. The Nips may be guarding the bridge— or just taking a break. Prince thinks we should go through the ravine and dash, one at a time, through the field on the other side for that bunch of trees over there. I agree. It's our only chance to make it without being spotted on the road. If we try to cross anywhere else we can be easily seen by either that tank or any other Jap coming up the road."

"Yes, sir," Bosard replied.

"Good! Spread the word back! We'll start crawling through this grass for the ravine. See you in the woods!"

Corporal James B. Herrick of C Company clutched his M1 rifle as he crawled through the high grass toward the ravine on the west side of the National Highway. Several Rangers had already slipped through the shallow gully that ran under the bridge where the Japanese tank stood guard.

As Corporal Herrick moved closer to the bridge he could not only see the tank but clearly hear the voices of its unsuspecting crew.

Now he was directly under the bridge, his heart pounding so loud he feared the enemy would hear it. His right hand moved to the left pocket of the fatigue jacket and pressed against his chest. In that pocket he carried something he read each day—a small New Testament Bible his mother had given him.

Slowly, cautiously, Herrick crawled into the grass on the other side of the road and continued to creep along for another fifty yards. Then, crouching low, he sprang forward to run for the trees a mile away on the moonlit horizon.

It required over an hour for all the Rangers and Captain Joson's men to cross the National Highway, but they managed to do it without so much as a single notice by the enemy tank crew.

After they had regrouped and Colonel Mucci had assured himself that everyone was accounted for, they started northeast through the woods toward the Talavera River, carefully avoiding villages and their noisy dogs.

Imperial Army Divisional Commander Naotake realized his situation in Cabanatuan City was rapidly becoming critical. A review of the field intelligence reports indicated that the advancing American forces would be in a position to strike at his city by February 2—maybe even twenty-four hours earlier. One of his five battalions, Inoue, was under attack by forward U.S. units at San Jose, and Commander Oyabu's Dokuho 359 Battalion was on the move somewhere between Bongabon and the Cabu River.

Naotake figured that if he could get all his battalions to the city in time his total holding force of over 6,000 combat troops could easily hold the Americans beyond that February 2 date.

The task of holding the western suburbs of Cabanatuan he assigned to two battalions—Nimomija and Muta. The Matsumoto Battalion was to hold the outskirts on the north, but to effectively accomplish this mission Matsumoto must have reinforcements. It was at this area that Naotake expected the major blow to come from the Allies.

Around 9:00 P.M., January 28, Naotake headquarters radioed Commander Inoue to withdraw from San Jose, as Oyabu had done earlier, and retreat via the fastest route to Cabanatuan City. The only possible route would take Inoue through Baloc and Talavera. If those men made it, they could link with Matsumoto at the northern perimeter.

But Naotake was realistic. They knew it was unlikely that Inoue could arrive unscratched. Somewhere along the National Highway, as his men passed other units heading north, the Americans would surely catch him.

Therefore, the only real hope for reinforcements lay with a complete and successful movement of Oyabu's Dokuho 359 Battalion, which, by now, was well on its way, but at a safer distance east of the National Highway.

If Cabanatuan City were to be held, Oyabu must reach the Cabu River and be ready to move into position with Matsumoto before midnight, January 30.

A few minutes before midnight on January 28, the Rangers reached the banks of the Talavera River, traveled parallel to its waters upstream a mile, and then began their crossing. They had marched over three miles from the National Highway—fifteen miles since leaving Guimba.

With the exception of a five- to ten-minute break each hour, and the frightening wait at the National Highway, there had been no other rest. But the Rangers' spirits were extremely high. So it is with most elite units assigned a mission. The usual "bitching" and complaining often experienced in other foot soldier units simply did not exist in the Rangers or Alamo Scouts. These men were basically volunteers, trained to perfection. They thrived on such assignments. One man later described the march to this point by stating, "Everyone was excited—as if we were going on a Sunday picnic!"

The men all knew C Company's Staff Sergeant Lester Malone loved to tease, and the big Oklahoma farm boy was often the brunt of jokes, himself. As soon as the Talavera was crossed, one of the Rangers noticed that Sergeant Malone had been unusually quiet for the last mile or so.

"Hey, Twister!" the Ranger called to the sergeant. "What's the matter with you? The old cowboy getting tired? How do you feel?"

"I feel great!" Malone replied. "I feel like nothing in the world can hurt old Twister!"

"Well—that's what worried us," another Ranger said. "We weren't sure cowboys could walk this far."

"I tell you what," Malone responded in his heavy western drawl. "You give me your address—don't you all forget, now! And I'll go see the wives of anyone who gets shot up!"

After the Talavera, the Rangers followed Joson's men through another heavy forest for three miles, then spread their single-file line as they entered more open grassland.

As they began slipping through the tall grass the front troops suddenly heard a loud thudlike noise, and they fell forward, releasing the safeties of their weapons. Seeing the front men drop, everyone immediately dove for cover.

For a few moments there was no sound other than the warm evening breeze rustling the tall cogon grass. Then there came another loud thud—and a third. Rifles, BARs, and Tommyguns swung from one point to another, ready to fire, but nothing could be seen in the moonlit field.

Several more minutes passed before a voice broke the silence. "It's *birds!* Big dead birds falling!"

Something had killed the birds in flight. They never discovered the cause, but an act of nature had produced some very anxious moments.

The men were on their feet again and after a mile reached the Rizal Highway, the second and last major road they must cross.

Again, enemy traffic was heavy as a steady stream of vehicles moved out from the town of Luna heading north. And, as before, Japanese tanks were waiting at various points off the highway, spaced several hundred yards apart.

The Rangers waited for a break in the traffic flow, then, using their leapfrog technique, they crossed the road one at a time and dashed another mile through grass to the cover of trees.

Gasping for breath, First Sergeant Charles Bosard sank to his knees and rolled over next to the trunk of a large tree for a few seconds' rest. To his surprise, he discovered he was next to Colonel Mucci.

"Boy! That was a close one," Mucci panted.

"Sure . . . was."

Colonel Mucci began to think aloud. "You know . . . those guard towers at the stockade . . ."

"Yes . . . what about them?"

"I've been thinking . . . we may have to do a knifing job on the Japs in the towers before our boys can crawl in close. You'll have to do it, kid. It'll take someone small . . . good . . . nerves of steel. That's you, kid . . . you'll have to do it!"

Sergeant Bosard stared at the colonel without answering.

Mucci sat silent, then, shaking his head, he said, "No! No, forget it, kid. That would be downright suicide. We'll have to think of some other way."

The Rangers now traveled east a mile and a half, forded the Morcon River, continued east for a mile, turned south along a dirt road another mile, then southeast into more open, flat country. It was almost dawn, January 29. They had but three miles left to travel to the rendezvous with the Alamo Scouts—Balangkare. Twenty-four hours had elapsed since they left their battalion headquarters. They had walked twenty-two miles and POW Camp Cabanatuan was yet another five miles from Balangkare.

The Rangers were tired, but this was not what worried Colonel Mucci. He planned for his men to rest until dusk in either Balangkare or Platero. The matter that concerned him most was the report the Alamo Scouts would give on the Japanese troop movement near their target destination. Had the Scouts obtained all the knowledge necessary? Or, for that matter, had they even reached their objective? Were they still alive?

Since the late hours of January 27 and throughout the twenty-eighth, the bamboo telegraph moved the "alert mobilization" orders of Captain Juan Pajota and his squadron commanders to almost every town and barrio in eastern Neuva Ecija. "Mobilize at once . . . squadron commanders move to meet at Platero . . . prepare for combined action . . . we will help Americans with major assault . . . seventy-five men needed at Balangkare by daybreak."

From the Sierra Madre Mountains, from Bakero and Bagong Sikat in the north, came First Lieutenant Juanito Quitives and his Squadron 200 with over 100 men and First Lieutenant Regino Bobila's Squadron 202, consisting of over 100 men.

From the area of Macatbong and Cabu, Lieutenants F. Bernardo and Ricardo Mendoza brought their 100-man Squadron 201A, and 430 men of Squadron 201 followed First Lieutenant Jose Hipolito to their designated assembly point.

One hundred and fifteen men of Lieutenant Villariuman's Squadron 203 and another 130 men of Squadron 204 assembled near Manacnac, only two miles northeast of the POW Camp.

Squadron 211's thirty-six men with Lieutenant Toribio Paulino moved from the south toward Platero and Balangkare. And around Platero the twenty men of headquarters company began preparations for some very special guests. In all, more than 1,000 Filipino guerrillas, sworn members of the United States Army, mobilized to the orders of their commander.

Some of these men moved cross-country in large squads, traveling first south, then north, then southwest, producing confusion for anyone trying to learn their true destination. Others traveled alone. From the isolated farms, small towns, barrios, and secret command post camps they came, most walking, a few riding carabaos or small horses.

Only about 5 percent, mostly officers and NCOs who had served with the USAFFE in 1941 through 1942, wore khaki uniforms. About one-third were armed with rifles (both U.S. and captured Japanese weapons), U.S. carbines and .45-caliber automatic pistols. The rest carried only their bolos. A few had their round, U.S. World War I–type helmet or army soft fatigue caps. The majority wore their native buri hat. They were a motley-looking bunch of fierce fighters dedicated to serving the United States and ridding their country of the Japanese for good.

At exactly 0600 (6:00 A.M.), January 29, Lieutenant Colonel Henry Mucci and his Rangers arrived at the outskirts of the small barrio of Balangkare. There, in a grove of trees bordering a rice field on the northwest edge of the village, they found Alamo Scout Lieutenants Tom Rounsaville and Bill Nellist waiting for them. Everyone was relieved to learn each group had experienced little difficulty during the last thirty hours and had completed the journey undetected by the Japanese. The Scouts reported that their two teams had arrived at Captain Pajota's headquarters without incident and had been working since the previous afternoon with Pajota's intelligence officer, First Lieutenant Carlos Tombo, gathering as much information as humanly possible. Some of the Scouts were still out on reconnaisance patrol, covering the many trails that zig-zagged from Balangkare to Platero, from Platero to the main road in front of the POW camp. They had traveled the Pampanga River banks north and south, the rice fields across from the camp, and even circled the camp itself, but at a safe distance. What they revealed to Mucci was very disheartening.

There simply had not been sufficient time to gather all the data required to plan a raid on the stockade. The terrain at the camp area was much too flat and open for anyone to get close enough to procure accurate information on the number of enemy troops and their activity there. But even more distressing was the news that for the last twenty-four hours the main road in front of the camp had been heavily traveled by Japanese forces heading north. At least, 200 or 300 Japanese were bivouacked along the northeast bank of the Cabu River a mile north of the camp, and Pajota's men reported that at least a division of Japanese were at Cabanatuan City, less than four miles to the south.

The Scouts, of course, had not been to the big city. There was enough to worry about in the immediate area.

Mucci was obviously upset and disappointed. Unless the situation changed for the better he knew he might be forced to postpone the raid. He now demanded more detailed information on the garrison and the enemy troops stationed there. Even if the road was heavily traveled at night he might order the raid to go on as scheduled regardless of the risk. But before that decision could be made, they needed a complete description of the camp.

While Colonel Mucci, his officers, and the Scouts discussed their hazardous and frustrating situation, a group of Filipinos approached the grove of trees by a trail leading out from the barrio. One of the men was riding bareback on a horse about the size of an American pony. The rider was dressed in a faded khaki uniform and fatigue cap with no rank or insignia. A .45 automatic pistol hung from a web belt, and over his left shoulder was slung a U.S. M1 carbine.

When the group reached a point about twenty-five yards from the Americans, the rider dismounted and, flanked by two other men, walked directly up to the Ranger commander.

"Lieutenant Colonel Mucci?" the little Filipino inquired.

"Yes. I'm Mucci."

The Filipino snapped to attention and saluted. "Sir! I am Captain Juan Pajota. Welcome to Balangkare!"

After a brief exchange of introductions, Pajota was invited to sit down and join the meeting. Mucci immediately informed him, "We plan to attack that POW camp tonight—at dusk!"

Pajota stared into Mucci's face, trying to determine if the colonel was serious. After a moment, he could control himself no longer. "Sir! Are you committing suicide!?"

Mucci's narrow eyes flashed at the comment, which bordered on disrespect. He glared at the Filipino. "Of course not!"

"Well, sir," Pajota tried to explain his bluntness, "you must know, already, the enemy situation from your Alamo Scouts. My own scouts have been reporting to me every hour. Another Jap unit is approaching Cabu bridge from the north—battalion size. If they stay at Cabu River there will be over 1,000 Japs at that place."

Pajota's serious face warped with a frown. "This is a very tough assignment you have been given. There are hundreds of Japs in the camp—and tanks. And maybe 500 POWs. Only a few POWs can walk. They must be carried if you are going to take them out. But—I have a plan for the prisoners. My men are organizing a team of carabao carts for you to use to move the POWs . . ."

Mucci, still irritated by the "suicide" comment, listened, nonetheless, without interrupting.

"Allow me to show you, sir . . . this map." Pajota produced from his shirt the operations map he had so carefully constructed during the long resistance campaign. He began to unfold it and added, "I have wanted to attack this camp for a long time. I was ordered not to do it even though Major Lapham and I had plans for a successful raid."

Colonel Mucci glanced at the Filipino's map and, with his natural diplomatic ability, recognized the opportunity to melt the icy atmosphere that had held since the beginning of the meeting. "Where did you graduate, Captain . . . West Point? That's a very good map!"

As usual, the colonel's insight into human nature paid off, and Pajota grinned with pride. "No, sir. I was trained only by General MacArthur's USAFFE."

At that time Colonel Mucci showed Pajota a sketch of the camp drawn from the aerial photograph and his large topography map. Of course, Pajota knew most of the camp's features by heart, having once been stationed there. But he had never seen such a beautiful map as the one of the colonel now unfolded. He noticed at once that some of the towns' names on the Rangers' map were misspelled, but it did not seem polite or necessary to call anyone's attention to the errors.

Colonel Mucci then began to outline his general plan for the attack, explaining that all his Rangers and Scouts would be required to handle the assault on the camp. Captain Joson's eighty men were to set up a roadblock south of the camp. Several Rangers from F Company with bazookas would assist at that position.

"How many armed men do you have here?" Colonel Mucci directed his question to Pajota.

The guerrilla leader replied with the truth. At least the figure he gave represented the number in the immediate area. "Ninety men with weapons and 160 unarmed men." Since Mucci had not inquired about the total number serving under Pajota, the complete strength was not revealed. Pajota had suspicions that his squadrons would be assigned to a holding action along the road somewhere, but to this point was not sure just where. There was no sense committing more men than Mucci needed.

Pajota also did not reveal that he had four old water-cooled .30-caliber machine guns, hoping the Rangers would turn over more such weapons for his use. To his surprise, the Rangers had no machine guns. They did give his men some additional ammunition, and a bazooka.

Now Pajota learned of his assignment. His armed soldiers must hold the Japanese camped across the Cabu River from crossing the highway bridge and reinforcing the imperial troops at the stockade. The unarmed Filipinos would assist the Rangers by moving the POWs from the Pampanga River area. They would also serve as runners, litter bearers, and carabao cart drivers. Pajota assured Mucci that he could muster at least 400 unarmed men to help in and around Platero. But he still did not reveal that he had decided to assign Squadrons 200 and 202 to be in reserve near Joson's roadblock and Squadrons 203 and 204 to positions near Manacnac behind the Japanese at Cabu bridge. Most of the men in these "ghost" squadrons were armed.

Colonel Mucci was full of questions for Pajota.

"What's the distance from here to Platero?" he asked.

"Five kilometers—about two and one-half miles," Pajota replied.

"And from Platero to the Pampanga River?"

"One kilometer—about one-half mile, sir."

"And from the Pampanga to the front gate of the camp?"

"More than four kilometers—two miles, sir, depending on what route you elect to take."

"The front gate to your position at Cabu bridge—how far?"

"About a mile, sir."

"Good!" Mucci nodded. It all checked with the distances indicated on his large map.

"Captain Joson!"

"Sir."

"You will form your roadblock at this spot near the road—800 yards southwest from the camp. You are to stop all enemy traffic from 1930 hours, on—understand?" Mucci pointed to his map.

"Yes, sir," Captain Joson replied.

On and on the meeting went, Mucci shooting questions between puffs on his pipe, stopping now and then to think, then snapping orders while everyone listened. The staff was told that he would announce his final decision later, after the Scouts reported back and everyone assembled in Platero. There would still be time to either proceed with the raid or postpone it.

In the meantime, both Pajota's and Joson's men must undergo an orientation on the use of the bazooka. Most of the Rangers could try to rest in the shade for the day.

While Mucci and his staff met with the guerrilla leaders at Balangkare a new unit of Japanese troops settled down in the bamboo groves on the east side of the Cabu River only three miles away.

It was 0730 (7:30 A.M.) and Pajota's scouts accurately predicted the arrival of Battalion Commander Tomeo Oyabu and his Dokuho 359 unit.

Oyabu was pleasantly surprised when he discovered that a force of over 300 soldiers was already camped in the woods along both sides of the highway on that east bank of the river. He was especially delighted to learn that these men were from a variety of units, including remnants of a tank company, complete with four tanks and a truck with a mounted machine gun at its cab top.

These fragment units were commanded by four junior officers who had no orders other than to retreat north the next night and attempt to link with General Yamashita's main defense group.

But the young tank officer expressed concern to Oyabu. All his vehicles were low on fuel and he doubted if they could make it any farther than Bongabon. He had not yet decided where to make his stand against the Americans.

Oyabu solved his dilemma. He immediately assumed command of everyone in the area and issued his own orders. They all would rest for another day and then move to the defense of Cabanatuan City—not Bongabon—at 9:00 PM., January 30.

Oyabu's battalion, Dokuho 359, now consisted of a little more than 1,175 men.

One mile south of the bivouacked Oyabu Battalion, the 175-man Kinpeidan headquarters unit continued their rest at POW Camp Cabanatuan.

Other than curiosity, they had little interest in the Allied POWs inside the barbed-wire fence across the camp road. Nor did they have much to do with the ninety-five guards at the camp. To the men of Kinpeidan headquarters, those Japanese, Koreans, and Formosans assigned to guard the prisoners were beneath the dignity of the regular Imperial Army.

Kinpeidan's men were mainly interested in resting and leaving the area just as soon as their orders indicated they should. Everyone could hear the big American guns thundering in the distance. The thought of having to wait until the next night was not an easy one to sleep on.

At Balangkare, the day wore on for the Rangers, who were finding it difficult to catnap due to the tremendous excitement and hospitality of the Filipinos.

C Company's PFC Mariano Garde, of Mexican descent, was, despite the generous gifts of fresh fruit, a little disappointed. He had tried his Spanish out on several Filipinos only to learn that no one spoke the language.

"What the hell is this?" Garde complained to his buddy as he shifted his heavy BAR from one shoulder to another. "Spain ruled this country for hundreds of years and not one soul around here speaks Spanish!"

A few hundred yards away, Staff Sergeant August Stern and other members of C Company's special weapons section began to train the guerrillas in the use of the bazooka.

The Filipinos were impressed with the peculiar-looking pipe the Americans called a bazooka yet found it difficult to believe that its little rocket actually could yield as much destructive power as Stern said it would. They laughed when the sergeant cautioned that "fire comes out both ends" of the tube.

What gave Sergeant August Stern his laugh for the day was when he discovered Captain Bob Prince admiring an egg and trying to decide how it should be prepared. It was the first real egg the C Company commander had seen in a long time, and Stern would never forget the look on the young captain's face when he was told to "poke a hole in the point and suck everything out!"

Little Tech 4th Class Frank Goetzheimer was disgusted, and his buddies of Combat Photo Unit F were almost equally frustrated.

"What's the matter, Frank?" PFC Bob Lautman asked his friend. "You look like you just discovered your Bell and Howell got busted."

"It might as well be broken," Goetzheimer replied. "Those fellows never stopped long enough on the way over here for me to get even a single foot of film. Now they say they are positive the raid will be after dark. Hell! We can't get any shots in the dark with our equipment."

"Yeah! I know. I don't think Goen got many shots on the march. I know I didn't. We're beginning to get some good ones now, though. But . . . you're right. If Mucci pulls this thing off after dark, we'll just be spectators."

At age twenty-four, C Company commander Captain Robert Prince was, indeed, a remarkable young man.

There had never been a mission during his short military career like the one now facing his men. Even if he was a soldier by profession, he would not have had the benefit of studying how to conduct a raid on an enemy POW camp right in the middle of hostile forces on the move. No such action had ever been attempted in the history of the United States Army.

Nor did Captain Prince even have the advantage of seeing one of those many "war movies" flooding the entertainment market in the States. Regardless of how corny those productions were, millions of people back home were enjoying them and learning how movie star commandos planned make-believe attacks.

Colonel Mucci had placed the responsibility for the Rangers' breaking into the camp completely upon Captain Prince. The plan must be his own, original and perfect. One mistake, one miscalculation, one man failing to carry out an assigned job, and everything could fail. And if it failed, Bob Prince knew there was no second chance—all the Rangers and POWs would be dead.

He realized that even in failure, they could inflict heavy causalties on the Japanese, but this was not positive thinking. Prince understood his orders perfectly. No American, especially a POW, was to die. To insure this, every fanatical Japanese in the camp must be killed quickly.

Colonel Mucci, with his decision to turn the bulk of the planning over to his "wonderful Captain Prince," had selected the right man. Prince, above all, was not reckless. He was an intelligent, cool-nerved, positive-thinking individual who went about his work with the calm disposition of a college professor preparing a lecture. If there were a problem during the raid it would not come from poor planning. A problem could only arise from an improbable accident.

Copies of the POW camp's design had been distributed to all officers. They and their NCOs must study every detail of the camp and be ready to add or subtract points as information became available from either Pajota's men or the Alamo Scouts.

Now Captain Prince, sleeves rolled to the upper arm, his fatigue cap pushed far back on his head, was ready to coordinate plans with Captain Pajota.

It was agreed that the guerrillas would provide the perimeter security around both Balangkare and Platero and continue this protection until after the raid. They discussed the matter of evacuating the civilians not involved in some support effort and the problems concerning the carabao carts and food preparation for approximately 650 men.

Prince also passed on a message to Pajota from Colonel Mucci. All dogs in the area of Platero and barrios on the attack route were to be tied and muzzled and chickens penned up in order to avoid any alarm being sounded by nervous animals as strangers (the Americans) passed by.

Pajota stated that he had already ordered his executive officer,

Captain Luis De La Cruz, to inform the villagers to keep their dogs inside.

An evacuation plan, of Pajota's design, was also ready for execution. Civilians residing along the attack route, primarily at Calawagan and Comunal (population, less than 100), were to move southwest of Platero. Later, the people of Cabu, near the bridge, were to pull out one family at a time, southeast for Macatbong. And those few in Pangatian, next to the POW camp, were to move southeast to the Sierra Madre Mountains.

At 1600 hours (4:00 P.M.), Sergeant Norton Most was given orders to break radio silence and send Guimba base the message, "Request air cover along planned withdraw route, commencing 1900 hours." Sergeant Most tapped out the message and, as planned, received no acknowledgement. The message was expected by Tech 4th Class James Irvine at his radio in the command staff car near Guimba and the Sixth Army members who waited there with him. The message simply meant everything was proceeding on schedule.

A few minutes later the Rangers divided into two groups, and, flanked by Captain Joson's men on one side and Captain Pajota's men on the other, the force left Balangkare for the two-and-one-half-mile walk to Platero.

About halfway the march came to a halt. The Alamo Scouts were assembled off the trail under several large trees and were ready to report on the results of their day's reconnaisance.

Despite their several hours' rest and good spirits, the Rangers looked exhausted. Green uniforms were caked with dust and sweat, perspiration soaked their soft caps and trickled down from close-cut hair. A two-day growth of beard was now clearly visible on most of the men.

Colonel Mucci, his fatigue shirt sleeves rolled up almost to the armpits and beads of perspiration covering his high forehead directly under the narrow brim of his cap, sat down to listen to the Scouts.

The Scouts were an even sadder sight to behold. Their loose fatigues, completely soaked with sweat, had turned almost a brownish black from dust and mud. And again, their report was very disheartening. They confirmed what Pajota's men had been revealing all day—200 Japanese soldiers were in the POW camp, at least 800 to 1,000 Japanese were camped near Cabu bridge, and even worse, an enemy unit estimated to be of division strength was beginning to make its way northeast toward Bongabon along the main highway. No one knew for sure just how many Japanese troops remained in Cabanatuan City: at least 7,000.

It was the large unit on the move that caused Colonel Mucci to make a major decision. The raid must be postponed.

Sergeant Norton Most and the communications men set up their SCR 694 radio and as the generator operator began to turn the hand crank, the message was tapped out: "New developments . . . twenty-four-hour delay!"

Actually, almost everyone along that trail to Platero breathed a sigh of relief. The risk of executing the raid while a Japanese division passed by was much too great to guarantee any success and a full night's rest would certainly be most welcome.

Tech 4 James Irvine lifted his steel helmet momentarily to scratch his curly black hair. Not counting the sleepless night before the Rangers' departure he had now been awake for thirty-five hours at his radio post in the staff car near Guimba.

His radio came alive with the message, startling him with the shock of an alarm clock on a rainy morning. Quickly, he scribbled out the coded words on a standard yellow message sheet. "New developments . . . twenty-four-hour delay."

This time, Irvine tapped out a reply: "Message acknowledged." Then he relayed the information to the temporary Sixth Army headquarters at nearby Guimba.

Within a few minutes, Mucci's message reached General Walter Krueger. His face creased by deep lines of worry, the Sixth Army commander muttered to an aide, "I wonder if I sent those boys on too rough a mission this time."

There was always something disquieting about a typical combat radio message. By necessity, these could not be too detailed. But even years of experience with these brief, blunt words could not ease the anxiety of a good commander.

General Krueger did not sleep that night. He paced the floor of his tent, studying maps of Nueva Ecija. He instructed his staff to notify him immediately in case of another radio message from Colonel Mucci.

It was almost dark when the front ranks of the Rangers entered the small hamlet of Platero. The column halted suddenly, causing the men behind the first line to bunch up, then fan out some twenty-five yards on both flanks.

"What the hell is going on? Why is everybody slowing down?" PFC Bill Proudfit, a tall Iowan just past his twenty-fifth birthday, asked Tech 5 Patrick Marquis.

The older man paused. "Well, I'll be—take a look at that! Looks like we got ourselves some kind of reception."

"Wow!" another Ranger exclaimed. "Look at all them girls! Reckon they're for us?"

What had caused the Rangers to stop in their tracks was a reception committee composed of twenty girls ranging in age from fifteen to twenty-three. The Filipinos were neatly lined in two straight rows blocking the main dirt road that led into Platero. Each girl held a bouquet of bright-colored flowers and around their necks hung leis of sweet-smelling white sampaguita blossoms. They were all dressed in white, some wearing short-sleeved, long-skirted "Traje de Bodas," while others wore a modified "Maria Clara" with long skirts and long sleeves sloping down in bell-shaped form to the elbows. A few even wore the exotic "Balintawak" with its wide, flat, winglike sleeves reaching from the elbow and extending high above each shoulder. The natives' costumes represented the very best formal dress owned in the family.

Some girls had their long black hair fixed eloquently atop the head in Spanish style. Yet, for others, it simply hung straight to the shoulders or down to the center of the back.

Prewar school principal Louis De La Cruz, now executive officer and captain in Pajota's army, had specially selected the girls for their beauty and talent from a number of nearby barrios, as well as Platero.

It was twilight and the beautiful picture of the contrast of white dresses, brown skin, and shiny black hair became etched in the minds of all the Rangers. And what happened next was something the Americans would never forget.

As the four Combat Photo men, thirteen Alamo Scouts, and 121 rugged, footsore Rangers moved closer to the "reception committee," the girls, with heavy accents, began to sing:

> God bless Ameereka
> Land dat I love
> Stan beside her, and guide her
> Thru de night with a light from aboved.
> From de mountain—to de preere . . .

The choral welcome was only the beginning for the Rangers, who soon discovered that the entire barrio was preparing a feast in their honor.

Meanwhile, Joson's and Pajota's men circled Platero with a perimeter of defense so tight that not even a lizard could pass through unnoticed.

Groups of two to six Americans were assigned separate homes for dinner and while dispersement was organized, a tremendous noise of squealing pigs and squawking chickens cut through the singing and laughter. The Rangers were, again, impressed and moved. The Filipinos, who they knew were short of food, were killing their prize livestock for the evening meal. It would do no good to try to politely refuse the generous hospitality, for custom dictated that the very best in food be given a visitor, even if the gesture resulted in the host going without for days.

PFC Bill Proudfit was in for another unusual reception. On the way to his assigned "home" he was confronted by an elderly white man who promptly introduced himself as "Mister Bill Beedle . . . formerly of the United States Army!"

Shocked to find an American in the little barrio so far from a major city, Proudfit, naturally, had a number of questions. Mr. Beedle, he learned, was a veteran of the Spanish-American War, had married a Filipino and settled down in Platero "over forty years ago to raise a family." He had escaped the Japanese roundup of American civilians after the 1941 invasion and explained, "at age sixty-one, I couldn't do the Japs no harm, anyway!"

The two men were thrilled to discover that both were from

Iowa. They would have much to discuss the next day, before the raid.

Proudfit then entered the home of Genaro Bernardo and Loureana Saulo, where he was treated at a "table with silverware and all." Next, another surprise.

The family rolled out an old upright piano, which they had hidden behind bamboo mats since the Japanese invasion.

"We have been waiting for the Americans to return," Bernardo said. "Our country can have music again!"

The family's two daughters took turns at the piano and even knew a few of Proudfit's special requests.

At 0100 hours (1:00 A.M.) January 30, Lieutenants Tom Rounsaville and Bill Nellist met with their liaison, John Dove, in Platero. A few minutes later they and Lieutenant Tombo, with several of Pajota's men, slipped out of the barrio, crossed the Pampanga River, and crawled toward the main road and the POW camp.

By 0300 (3:00 A.M.), they were all back in Platero and reported to Captain Price and Colonel Mucci. There was no change in the enemy activity. Japanese troops were still moving along the road in small units. But there seemed to be none entering the POW camp.

At 0600 (6:00 A.M.), the tall barbed-wire gates of POW Camp Cabanatuan swung open to allow a small contingent of imperial soldiers to enter.

These men, mostly clerical personnel released by Naotake from Cabanatuan City, were the last of the Kinpeidan unit. Their arrival brought the total number of headquarter personnel in the camp's transient area to 210.

With them they carried the final movement orders for the entire Kinpeidan unit. Tonight, no later than 8:00 P.M., they must pull out of the stockade, clear Cabu bridge, and proceed north to Bongabon.

As soon as their unit cleared the bridge, Commander Oyabu's

Battalion Dokuho 359 would know it was time to move out to Cabanatuan City.

The full Japanese division that departed San Leonardo on the twenty-ninth had filtered through Cabanatuan City on the twenty-ninth and was now well past the Cabu River. By 8:00 A.M. they would be at Bongabon, some eighteen miles to the northeast.

Naotake planned no further troop dispatching out of Cabanatuan for the thirtieth. Every soldier remaining there must prepare for the city's defense while they waited for Oyabu and Dokuho 359.

Mucci's men were treated to another royal meal as breakfasts of eggs, pork, coffee, and fresh fruit were prepared by the Filipinos in Platero shortly after daybreak on the thirtieth.

At 0930 (9:30 A.M.), Colonel Mucci held an "officers call," including Captains Joson and Pajota and some of their staff. The purpose of this early meeting was to outline to the Alamo Scouts the exact information the Rangers needed to complete their plan.

"I want to know," Mucci began, "just how many Japs are in that camp—where they are and what they're doing! What buildings are holding the tanks—what's the distance from the front gate to those tank sheds! How is the main gate secured? How many gates are there? Are all the guard towers occupied? I don't care how you get all this dope, but we must have it by this afternoon!"

Mucci then turned to Captain Pajota. "Captain . . . I want your men to tell me *exactly* how many Japs are at that Cabu River. And you can show Captain Prince the best approach to the camp. As far as you are concerned, there is no change in the original plan. Your men will hold the bridge . . . Captain Joson will hold the road to the south!"

By 0915 hours the Alamo Scouts with Lieutenant Tombo had left Platero, and Captain Pajota invited the other officers to join him at a barrio home where they could continue their planning away from the curious eyes of the villagers.

The place Pajota selected for the meeting was a large nipa house, constructed mostly of thatched grass, bamboo, and wood.

As Captain Bob Prince climbed the wooden steps and entered the home, he noticed that the floor was made of strips of bamboo spaced about an eighth of an inch apart and nailed to a wooden frame.

Sitting upon a blanket on the floor, in one corner, was an attractive young mother peacefully nursing her child. The girl smiled widely and nodded welcome to her unusual visitors. The two American company commanders, Captain Prince and First Lieutenant John Murphy, unaccustomed to seeing a bare breast, modestly turned their heads and blushed.

Sensing something may be wrong, the mother spoke to Captain De La Cruz in Tagalong. A brief exchange in the Filipino language followed between De La Cruz and Pajota, and the girl raised one hand to cover her loud giggle.

"What did you tell her?" Lieutenant Murphy, his face still brilliant red, asked Captain De La Cruz.

The Filipino smiled. "I told her that in America, babies are fed the milk of a cow . . . from bottles. She thinks that is very funny. She is embarrassed that she did not know such a thing!"

A meeting to plan death—and life—began with the backs of the Americans turned to the mother and child.

11

If any Japs pass, it will be over our dead bodies. We will all be dead!

—Captain Juan Pajota, January 30, 1945

It was past noon on January 30, and though Captain Pajota's scouts had reported hourly on the enemy activity near Cabu bridge, nothing had been heard from Lieutenants Nellist and Rounsaville and the Alamo Scouts. However, Mucci was not worried. He knew he had given them an almost impossible assignment and did not expect a report for another hour or so.

While Colonel Mucci's officers and high-ranking NCOs continued to discuss various assault ideas, the Rangers catnapped in the shade, cleaned their weapons, or amused themselves by talking with those Filipinos who spoke some words of English.

First Sergeant Bosard even found time to enter a few lines in his small diary.

"Jan. 29–30 '45. Filipinos so happy to see us. They sang God Bless America and touched us to see what Americans feel like. Marched 29 miles so far."

On the barrio's perimeter, Tech 5 Patrick Marquis chatted with several guerrilla soldiers and attempted to learn some Tagalog. One young Filipino remained unusually silent, his eyes fixed on the three Army .45 pistols that hung in brown leather holsters from Marquis's web belt.

The sergeant finally confronted the young man.

"What's your name? Do you speak English?"

"Private Godofredo Monsod, Jr., sir—of Lieutenant Quitives's Squadron 200!" The Filipino answered in almost flawless English.

"How old are you, Monsod?"

"Eighteen, sir!"

"You don't have a weapon—a gun?"

"No, sir. I will kill the Japanese with my bolo! My father was provincial commander of the Constabulary in Cabanatuan City. The Japanese made him acting governor of Nueva Ecija. But— they discovered he supported the Americans and took him to Fort Santiago at Manila. No one returns from that place. My father did not return. The Japanese executed my father!"

Marquis slowly unhooked two holsters containing the heavy pistols. "Here—now you can settle the score on a more even basis!" he said as he handed the weapons to Private Monsod.

Captain Juan Pajota and the men of his command had received generous and expert medical attention during their thirty-two-month campaign against the Japanese from many brave doctors of Cabanatuan City who risked their lives to treat the guerrillas. Five of these daring men were Antanio De Guzman, Nicholas De Guzman, Pedro Jimenez, Eli Ballesteros, and Juan Lazaro. In most cases, the wives of other members of the family were either physicians or qualified nurses. Each would have been shot or beheaded by the Japanese had their activities been discovered.

Late in the campaign, on December 1, 1944, Pajota's "General Order Number 42" enlisted another doctor, Carlos Nuguid Layug, and assigned him "Commanding Officer, Medical Company."

Doctor Layug was a large man for a Filipino, well over six feet tall. In fact, when the Rangers met him in Platero the evening of January 29, they first thought he was Chinese.

But Layug was pure Filipino, graduating from the University of Santo Tomas in 1937. After training at Camp Murphy Medical Field Service School, he enlisted in the USAFFE Medical Corps in

1941. That move took him to Bataan, yet he survived the Death March and Camp O'Donnell. Then, assisted by his wife, Julita, he set up a medical practice in Manila. Before long, the Japanese told Layug that he was to be the "official doctor" at a sugar plantation where alcohol was manufactured.

Considering this appointment to be "collaboration" with the enemy, Carlos Layug and his family fled to the central plains of Luzon and eventually settled in the Balangkare-Platero area to wait out the war while doing what they could for local villagers with limited medicines and equipment.

Naturally, Captain James Fisher was ecstatic when he and Doctor Layug met and began to discuss mutual problems surrounding combat field surgery. Layug was especially appreciative and thrilled with the gifts of extra surgical tools Jimmy Fisher turned over to him.

Then they began the necessary plans for establishing a temporary field hospital to be ready for any casualties resulting from the raid.

Carlos Layug suggested the barrio schoolhouse would be ideal, and during the day of the thirtieth, the two doctors, assisted by Fisher's medical corpsmen and several Filipinos, converted the one-level wood building into an emergency hospital.

Blankets were nailed over the windows so treatment could be performed without the light attracting unwanted attention. Oil lanterns were hung and placed in strategic places, and heavy wooden desks were arranged to serve as operating tables. Next, clean sheets and blankets, donated by Platero's citizens, were stacked, and bandages, blood plasma canisters, medicines, and surgical instruments were neatly laid out. By midafternoon the hospital was ready for patients everyone prayed would never arrive.

Then there was time for Jimmy Fisher and Carlos Layug to discuss the future. Once the war was over, Doctor Fisher promised, Layug would have more medicines and equipment than he could possibly dream of. Sixth Army medical sections would see to that, Fisher assured.

* * *

While the doctors were occupied with their emergency field hospital, Captain Pajota summoned Lieutenant San Pedro and instructed him to distribute the fifty land mines. All would be issued, for the guerrilla leader was concerned about the condition of the explosives. In the tropics, mildew and corrosion often left such mechanical explosives undependable.

Twenty mines were to be given to Lieutenant Bobila and ten to Lieutenant Quitives for use on the main road near the point Mucci had designated for Captain Joson's roadblock.

Twenty mines were to be saved for Pajota's roadblock at Cabu bridge.

Now Pajota turned his attention to logistical problems. Runners were dispatched to see how the men were coming along with their assignment to have carabao carts in position along the Pampanga River. Second Lieutenant San Pedro and part of Squadron 201A were given the job of guiding the Rangers from the Pampanga to the camp, and several guerrilla NCOs were placed in charge of the preparation of food in Platero to be ready for the liberated POWs and Rangers during the withdrawal.

By 1400 hours (2:00 P.M.), the Alamo Scouts still had not reported back to Platero, and Colonel Mucci was becoming impatient and concerned. Less than five hours remained until dark and every minute of that time was needed by Captain Prince to work out his final plan of attack and review it with the men.

But less than three miles away, the Scouts were very busy. They had circled the camp several times, crawling and creeping through the grassy fields that surrounded the stockade. Darting from tree to tree, bush to bush, gully to bamboo grove, they had investigated the entire area from the camp northeast to Cabu Bridge and southwest a mile, and the flat rice land from the highway in front of the stockade to the banks of the Pampanga.

Nonetheless, the Scout team leaders felt that no one had been near enough to the camp to determine with certainty all the information Mucci needed. There was only one way to obtain that final data. Someone must get close to the front gate without being detected by the Japanese guards.

Alamo Scout team leader First Lieutenant Bill Nellist was not a foolish individual driven by dramatic psychological motivation. Like all the Scouts, he was only a soldier well trained to do a special job in the Army—a job that often required him to take more chances than the average man.

Before noon on the thirtieth, Nellist discussed an idea with Lieutenant Tom Rounsaville. There was a small nipa hut in the field directly in front of the POW camp's front gate, less than 400 yards northwest of the highway. Apparently the little house was abandoned.

Lieutenant Nellist proposed that if someone could position himself in that hut, he would have an excellent vantage point from which to study the front of the camp, traffic on the road, and the field to the rear of the hut through which the Rangers must travel and position themselves for the attack. Bill Nellist volunteered to try his idea and so did Filipino-American PFC Rufo Vaquilar. This sort of job was just what Vaquilar had been craving and Lieutenant Rounsaville agreed to release him from his team for Nellist's use.

Now the problem was how to get to the nipa hut without attracting the attention of the Japanese. Vaquilar had the solution. Runners were sent back to Platero with a peculiar request. They needed, at once, two Filipino straw buri hats, two colorful shirts, and two pairs of trousers. One outfit must be the largest size in the barrio.

When a runner returned with the clothing, he received a special reward. Vaquilar traded his M1A1 carbine for the man's .45 pistol.

As Rufo Vaquilar slipped the native clothes over his fatigues and replaced his soft cap with the straw bun, he crammed both his own .45 and the new pistol into his belt, under the shirt. "Now I'm comfortable," he said to Nellist. "I feel like I'm back home in California!"

Lieutenant Nellist also struggled into the clothes and discovered that, by some miracle, the straw hat fit perfectly. Inside his shirt, he placed the aerial photograph of the camp area and a notebook. With great effort, he managed to slip his M1 rifle under the clothes with the barrel extending down along one leg. It would cause him to walk with a limp, but otherwise, the trick should work.

The two Scouts in their disguise entered the highway some 600 yards southeast of the camp and began to walk northeast, Vaquilar 100 yards ahead of Nellist. In this manner, from a distance, the enemy guards at the camp would be unable to recognize the drastic difference in size between the little Filipino and Nellist's huge six-foot, two-hundred-pound frame.

As Nellist came to the south edge of the stockade fence, he turned northwest, stepped into the highway drainage ditch, and began to cross the field to the hut. Vaquilar continued along the road until he was almost even with the camp's front gate, then he, too, turned and crossed the field. Once inside the empty home, the two men congratulated each other. Thus far, the plan had worked. No one at the camp was the least bit suspicious of their activities.

Bill Nellist removed his rifle and set the front of the barrel on the bamboo frame of an open window facing the stockade. To be an expert shot one must be proficient at judging distances, and Nellist still held the record as one of the best marksmen in the Scouts. Placing his cheek next to the rifle stock, he aimed through its "peep" sight, moved the elevation adjustment up, then back to the usual battle sight setting of 250 yards.

"I would say I am exactly 350 yards from the gate," he said to Vaquilar.

Next, Nellist removed the eight-by-twelve-inch aerial photograph of the camp and, with a pencil, began to mark or circle different areas on the photo.

"Number one is definitely the tank shed. It's the metal building—but I don't see any tanks. It must be a 300-yard run from the gate to the shed."

"I do not see any tanks, also," Vaquilar replied.

Nellist then drew a diagram of the camp to correspond with the photo and listed the numbers he had made with a comment for each one on a sheet of paper. He even suggested correct firing elevations for the nipa barracks containing the enemy troops.

Within a few minutes, PFC Franklin Fox climbed into the nipa hut, soon to be followed by PFC Gilbert Cox and Sergeant Harold Hard. They had crawled all the way from the Pampanga River to approach the rear of the hut.

"What the hell you guys think this is, a convention?!" Nellist whispered, "Where are the rest of the fellows?"

"We are all spread out about 300 yards up and down the road," Fox answered. "Some are checking out the crossing at the Pampanga."

"Well, here!" Nellist said, "Make yourselves useful. Get these notes back to Mucci before he blows a fuse—and you guys get lost! This place is too crowded. The Japs will see us sure as hell!"

F Company commander First Lieutenant John F. Murphy was a likeable young officer but not exactly what anyone would classify as a typical military type. Although he was an excellent marksman, the men often noticed that Murphy carried his M1 about as if it were a toy. Lieutenant Murphy had been a football star at Notre Dame during his college years and, as with most of the men, was in the Rangers only because he wanted to serve his country in the most effective way possible.

"A dream of a man," as one of his NCOs later described him, Murphy did not need to "order" people. "Men just did things for him because they knew it must be done, and because they loved him."

"What's up?" Murphy asked with the usual friendly college-boy grin spread on his long face as he entered the house in Platero. Captain Prince was beginning another officers call.

"We have the first complete report back from the Scouts," Prince answered. "It's 1430 (2:30 P.M.). We don't have much time left, so let's get started on this!"

The Scout report confirmed some of the things already known from the aerial photo and topographical map. The stockade sat on practically level ground, though its rear section was somewhat elevated above the front. The front of the camp ran 600 yards east and west along the highway and its depth was approximately 800 yards. All the Allied POWs were contained in a section on the northeast corner along the highway and were separated from the rest of the stockade by a single barbed-wire fence, six feet high.

Additional details now available from the Alamo Scouts and Pajota's men provided what Prince basically needed.

The entire stockade was enclosed with three rows of barbed-wire fence, four feet apart, standing some eight to ten feet tall. A dirt road ran perpendicular from the highway and front gate to a seldom-used rear gate.

"There are three guard towers about twelve feet in height, here, here, and here." Prince pointed to his diagram and watched as each officer marked points at the main gate, the northeast corner, and the southeast corner of his sketch. "There are normally two Jap sentries in each tower with a machine gun—but the southeast tower is empty now. Don't take any chances! It may not be empty after dark."

"What about the front gate?" platoon commander First Lieutenant Melville R. Schmidt asked.

"The front gate is barbed wire on a wood frame, eight feet tall. It splits open from the middle—either inward or outward. Must be about twenty feet if fully opened. It's secured by one heavy padlock, three and a half feet from . . . the . . . ground. Now, how in the hell did they know that?" Prince puzzled as he read those last few words of Nellist's report. Then he continued.

"The gate is guarded by a senry who stands in a well-protected shelter, at the inside, right of the gate . . . just next to a wooden guardhouse. There are at least two Japs in the guardhouse."

"Where are the tank shed and communications center located?" platoon commander First Lieutenant William J. O'Connell asked.

"Here . . . and here." Prince pointed to the right center of the camp where Nellist had marked number "1" and number "4" on his sketch. "A single-row barbed-wire fence about six feet in height separates different areas inside the stockade and runs down the center road. The rear guard quarters are these buildings between the southeast corner and the rear gate, next to the center road. There are two pillboxes along this east fence running north and south—just outside the fence. They are elevated and protected by sandbags and logs. Each has three occupants with a machine gun. The Jap enlisted men's quarters are in the southeast section . . . and directly across from them . . . across the camp's center road, are the Jap transient quarters. These buildings up near the front gate . . . near the commo section and tank shed must hold officers and men of the main guard body."

"How about those tanks . . . how many?" Lieutenant O'Connell asked.

"That's a good question. Apparently, the Scouts haven't seen any tanks around the shed . . . but they may be concealed. There's supposed to be two, maybe four, in there somewhere. There are two large trucks partly concealed by another metal shed, though." Prince paused to get his breath. "There are between 200 and 275 Japs in the compound! Traffic has been light along the main road . . . so, this may be a lucky break. It's obvious, gentlemen . . . we'll need to isolate the POW section by hitting the Jap quarters and tank shed . . . and hold the Japs in the rear of the camp. If any of the Japs fight their way forward, they'll catch us before we evacuate the POWs—and we'll be goners! Now . . . all of your fire should be effective. The buildings are nipa . . . bamboo and wood. Our fire should tear right through that stuff!"

While Captain Prince continued his meeting with his staff in Platero, Lieutenant Bill Nellist and PFC Rufo Vaquilar were becoming concerned that their position in the nipa hut across from the POW camp might be discovered as the day wore on.

At 1600 hours (4:00 P.M.), Nellist turned away from the open window to rest his eyes from the strain of staring at the stockade.

Vaquilar suddenly pulled at his sleeve. "Look!" the Filipino whispered as he pointed to the southwest corner of the camp.

In the center of the highway, shuffling in wooden sandals toward the main gate, was a young Filipino lady dressed in typical barrio clothes. She seemed to be in no rush at all.

"I thought the guerrillas told all the civilians to stay off this road today!" Lieutenant Nellist said as he joined Vaquilar at the window. "What's she doing out there?"

"Don't know."

The girl stopped at the gate and began to talk with a guard. It seemed as if the conversation lasted a full three or four minutes.

The Japanese soldier handed the girl something, which she shoved inside her blouse, and then she turned and continued casually up the road toward Cabu.

"What do you suppose that's all about?" Nellist asked. "Would it be normal for a young gal to walk up to a Jap, alone?"

"I do not think so," Vaquilar replied.

The two Scouts stared at each other, each with the same questions written in the expression on his face. Had the girl told the Japanese soldier something important? Why *would* a Filipina gamble her safety to confront a Japanese soldier? Did the soldier hand her money for information?

PFC Vaquilar moved toward the open rear door of their nipa hut.

"Where are you going?" Lieutenant Nellist barked.

"I will go to the gate, myself! If the Japs are tipped off, there will be lots of action in that place by now. If not . . . everything will be peaceful."

"I can't cover you . . . if they go for you, I can't shoot. You know that! I could pick off the God damned Nips in the tower, and several at the gate. But, if I fire, it'll blow the whole mission." Nellist knew Vaquilar was well aware of the consequences, but he had to give the man a chance to change his mind.

The Filipino smiled. "Do not worry, my friend. Rufo Vaquilar knows how to do this. If they grab me they will think only that I am a guerrilla. They cannot know I am an American. And . . ." Vaquilar pulled up his shirt, exposing the handles of his two pistols, "ten or twelve of them will not live long enough to think that I am anything!"

With that remark, PFC Rufo Vaquilar jumped to the ground and began his walk to the camp, moving in a wide arc to the south, then up to the highway.

Lieutenant Nellist braced his M1 on the window frame. Beads of perspiration formed on his forehead and trickled in small streams down his cheeks. And the question continued to race through his mind—would he . . . could he allow himself to fire on the Japanese if they discovered Vaquilar's true identity?

Vaquilar, meanwhile, began a walk up the highway to the front gate, his hands clasped nonchalantly behind his back, the two big automatics hidden beneath the bright-colored shirt. As he neared the gate, he turned and stared into the face of the Japanese sentry, raised one hand to tip his hat, then bowed slightly while his eyes searched as far as he could see beyond the enemy soldier.

The guard frowned at Vaquilar with a puzzled look, but said nothing.

Vaquilar then continued up the road until well out of sight of the camp, then turned left to cross the field to the nipa hut. "I do not know what the girl said to them," he reported calmly to Nellist, "but everything seems normal in that place."

Lieutenant Nellist let out a deep sigh of relief.

In a minute, PFC Franklin Fox was back with them in the hut. "What on earth are you guys doing?" he asked. "We thought Rufo had decided to tackle the camp by himself!"

"Never mind!" Nellist responded. "Get back to Mucci and tell him everything is quiet up here. We're going to stay in this spot until after dark. If there's any change, one of us will report back in time. Otherwise, we'll see them when they get here!"

The Scouts never learned the truth about the girl who caused them so much concern. Actually, she was helping the guerrillas. A former vendor of fruit to the stockade guards, she, like Vaquilar, had approached the gate to get, not give, information. The girl promised to bring the sentry some fresh fruit for a deposit in cash. Instead of returning, she reported directly to Pajota's men.

It is not easy to ride a carabao. Their girth is so great the strain on one's thighs is painful, and at every stride the whole skin seems to slide about as if it were detachable from the flesh. The huge, round body affords no opportunity for any hand grip, and the only way a rider can maintain his position is to balance himself in some rhythm with the motion of the beast.

A few years of constant practice had developed the necessary skill for Pascual and Aquilar. By the age of eleven, the two boys had mastered the art of riding the carabaos, and with their short legs and a touch of the hand, could command the peaceful animals in any way they desired.

On dry land or in shallow rice paddies the carabao is really no problem for such experienced riders. But approach a pond or stream and that presents a different situation. Carabaos are, after all, water buffalo, and the sight of water would lead them straight for a long swim regardless of the desires of the rider.

On the afternoon of the thirtieth, Pascual and Aguilar were no ordinary farm boys. They were now guerrillas serving directly under Captain Pajota in the "intelligence section."

They, like most young boys riding carabaos in and out of the barrios, along the roads, and past the rows of fence around POW Camp Cabanatuan, were familiar sights to both the Japanese guards and the POWs. The Japanese usually ignored them until a playful game of tossing stones to the POWs got out of hand. Then the boys were driven off by shouts and threats.

That afternoon, the stone game began near the east fence and as a small group of POWs picked up the rocks to toss them back they noticed something unusual. Some of the stones were wrapped with pieces of paper, tied tightly with strands of grass.

The POWs removed the paper and turned to toss the rocks back across the fence. But the boys had casually moved on toward the highway, waving to the guards in the east corner tower.

Once inside their barracks, the POWs unfolded the paper.

"Listen to this," one man whispered. "It says, 'be ready to go out anytime'!"

"Yeah! Mine says the same thing. Wonder what it means?"

"Probably just something the kids dreamed up!"

"I don't think so," another argued. "Mine says, 'Be alert for . . .' I can't make out the last word."

The notes were torn into tiny bits and distributed equally to four men. Once they were outside, the small pieces were scattered and covered carefully with dirt. The messages were generally discounted as having no important meaning.

Meanwhile, Pascual and Aquilar had proceeded down the high-

This photo was given to Lieutenant Hilado by guards who had helped her smuggle medicines into POW Camp O'Donnell in August 1942. It is inscribed on the reverse "To Miss Hilado. Thank you and good-by. We will pray for your good luck."
(Courtesy of J. H. Hilado, R.N.)

Filipino guerrilla spy Nurse Josefa Hilado (standing at center) with Dr. and Mrs. R. Atienza and several Japanese Imperial Army prison guards at Capas Red Cross Center near POW Camp O'Donnell in August 1942. The guards didn't know that the truck contained hidden stores of quinine, which were smuggled into the camp later that day.
(Courtesy of J. H. Hilado, R.N.)

One of the Japanese guards at Camp O'Donnell presented this photo of himself to Lieutenant Hilado as a gift in August 1942.
(Courtesy of J. H. Hilado, R.N.)

American POWs on the steps of the Camp O'Donnell Red Cross headquarters in August 1942, with their Japanese guards and Lieutenant Hilado (center) *(Courtesy of J. H. Hilado, R. N.)*

U.S.-educated Imperial Army colonel S. Aoyagi stands next to the POW Camp O'Donnell cemetery monument erected by his "Public Relations" group in late September 1942; the cemetery held the remains of over 38,000 Filipinos and 2,000 Americans who died at O'Donnell from beatings, starvation, disease, and execution. Dedicated "To the memory of gallant Filipino soldiers who died here," the monument was intended as a pacification effort directed at surviving Filipinos released by the Japanese. Colonel Aoyagi's program was a failure. *(Courtesy of J. H. Hilado, R.N.)*

American guerrilla colonel Bernard Anderson prepares to meet a U.S. supply submarine in 1944. "They built the nucleus of a guerrilla command which gained them a well-deserved place in the history of unconventional war." *(Courtesy of Colonel Anderson)*

American guerrilla major Robert Lapham in
January 1945. "There was a certain charisma
about these men which attracted the Filipinos in
magnetic fashion." *(U.S. Army photo)*

Lieutenant Colonel Henry A. Mucci
possessed a natural ability to
motivate people. *(U.S. Army photo)*

Lieutenant General Walter
Krueger, commander of the
U.S. Sixth Army, in 1945.
Having come up through the
ranks, he could appreciate
the hardships the soldiers
endured in both training and
combat. *(U.S. Army photo)*

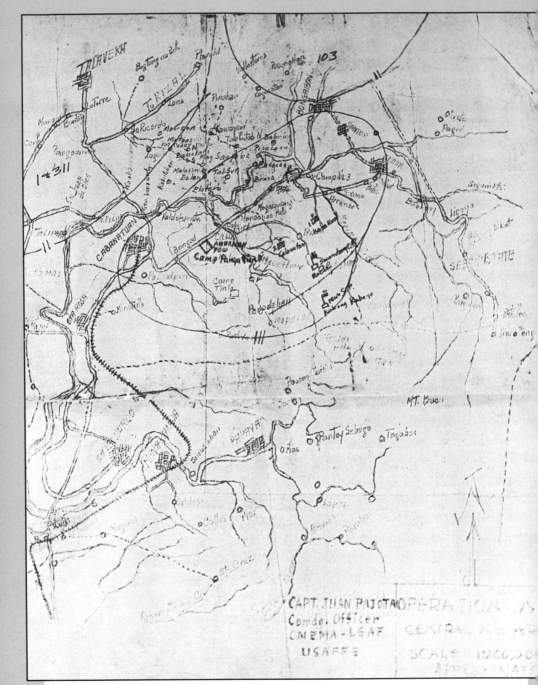

Captain Pajota's operations map.

Rangers cross the
Pampanga River over a
sand bar less than two
hours before the raid on
January 30, 1945.
(U.S. Army photo)

They were the kind of
soldiers everyone liked
(left to right): Tech 5
Francis "Father" Schilli,
Corporal Roy Sweezy, and
an unidentified Ranger,
taken a few weeks before
the raid. *(Courtesy of
Francis Schilli)*

One of Captain Pajota's squadrons crosses the Pampanga River en route to Cabu Bridge about six o'clock on January 30, 1945. Note the wide variety of equipment and weapons and the "medic" carrying a bamboo pole (just entering the water on the left bank). *(U.S. Army photo)*

Jimmy Fisher cradling an infant in his arms in a Luzon church built of bamboo. *(U.S. Army photo)*

Captain Robert Prince, C Company commander, Sixth Rangers (left), with Colonel Horton White, Sixth Army G2. *(U.S. Army photo)*

Only hours into their freedom, the Allied column takes a break. *(U.S. Army photo)*

Alamo Scout Team leaders a few weeks before the raid on POW Camp Cabanatuan (left to right): Lieutenant William Nellist, Lieutenant Thomas Rounsaville, Lieutenant Robert Sumner, and Lieutenant John Dove. *(U.S. Army photo)*

Juan Pajota—seen as a major in February 1946— had become known as a determined, daring, yet cautious leader. *(Courtesy of Juan Pajota)*

Staff Sergeant John Crowe, "Hard to Get" radar operator Lieutenant Bonnie Rucks and pilot Lieutenant Kenneth Schrieber, and Colonel R. L. Johnson (left to right) in 1945. *(U.S. Air Force photo)*

With a small elite unit like the Scouts, one's value could never be doubted: (front, left to right) PFC Wilbur Wismer and Lieutenant William Nellist; (back, left to right) PFC Galen Kittleson, PFC Tom Siason, and PFC Andrew Smith. *(U.S. Army photo)*

They were a motley-looking bunch of fierce fighters dedicated to serving the United States and ridding their country of the Japanese for good: some of Captain Juan Pajota's "boys"; Sergeant Benigno Barca is on the left. *(U.S. Army photo)*

Some of the Sixth Army Alamo Scouts who participated in the raid, photographed on February 1, 1945: (standing, left to right) PFC Gilbert Cox, PFC Wilbur Wismer, Sergeant Harold Hard, PFC Andrew Smith, and PFC Francis Laquier; (kneeling, left to right) PFC Galen Kittleson, PFC Rufo Vaquilar, Lieutenant William Nellist, Lieutenant Thomas Rounsaville, and PFC Franklin Fox. *(U.S. Army photo)*

Men of the Sixth Rangers discuss the raid while a former POW looks on, January 31, 1945. *(U.S. Army photo)*

The last photo taken of Captain James Fisher, M.D. (foreground, hand on belt), chatting with Captain Bob Prince about three hours before the raid on January 30, 1945. *(U.S. Army photo)*

An enlarged photo of the POW camp gives a clear view of the tank shed area (#1) and communication area (#4), which was also a Japanese troop section. Zigzag defense trenches are directly above #4. *(U.S. Army photo)*

The original air photo of POW Camp Cabanatuan used to plan the raid, with Lieutenant Nellist's marks still visible. The tank shed area is indicated #1, #4 is the communication area and guard towers; the creek bed through which F Company passed to reach the rear of the camp is in the upper left. Captain Prince folded the photo, creating a crease line through the center (left to right). *(U.S. Army photo/courtesy of Robert Prince)*

The original radio message sent January 30, 1945, to T/4 James Irvine at Guimba by Staff Sergeant Norton Most from Platero. It reads: "Mission accomplished—Starting back—Leaving some with friends." Note that the time was corrected from the civilian "11:03 P.M." to military time, "2303 hours." *(Courtesy Norton Most)*

"Nagisit law wa–law wa," also known as the "Hard to Get": a P61 Black Widow of the 547th Night Fighter Squadron, January 1945. *(U.S. Air Force photo)*

A Cabanatuan prison hut constructed of bamboo and nipa. *(U.S. Army photo)*

Liberated POWs alongside one of the carabao carts as the column rests near Sibul on the morning of January 31, 1945. *(U.S. Army photo)*

Alamo Scout Team leaders Lieutenant William Nellist (left) and Lieutenant Tom Rounsaville after their return from the raid, February 1945. *(U.S. Army photo)*

One of the first photos of liberated POWs taken by Combat Photo Unit F, taken northwest of Balangkare just after dawn on January 31, 1945. *(U.S. Army photo)*

Lieutenant General Walter Krueger (back to camera) awards the Bronze Star to Wilbur B. Goen, Unit F, 832nd Signal Service Battalion, after the raid; Frank J. Goetzheimer, also of the 832nd, is on the right. Goen was killed in action a few weeks later. *(U.S. Army photo)*

Major Juan Pajota with the author in Manila, 1976. *(Author photo)*

Lieutenant Colonel Henry A. Mucci, several hours after the raid. *(U.S. Army photo)*

During a rare interview in 1976 at a secret location near Manila, Commander Luis Taruc, founder and leader of the HUKBALAHAP, answers the author's questions about World War II Huk guerrilla activity. Originally a socialist group, the Huks evolved into the Communist New People's Army (NPA) after Commander Taruc surrendered to the Philippine government. *(Author photo)*

A group of Rangers and Alamo Scouts was selected to visit the States after the raid to assist in a bond drive. This photo was taken in the Oval Office in early March 1945, a few weeks before President Roosevelt's death. (left to right) Sergeant Robert Anderson, Staff Sergeant Clifton Harris, Staff Sergeant Theodore Richardson, PFC Leland Provencher, Sergeant Harold Hard (Scouts); PFC Leroy Myerhoff, PFC Carlton Dietzel, PFC Charles Swain, Staff Sergeant William Butler, Lieutenant Melville Schmidt, Captain Robert Prince, Sergeant Gilbert Cox (Rangers). *(U.S. Army photo)*

Dr. Captain James C. Fisher Memorial Park, on the outskirts of Barrio Balangkare, where Captain James Fisher and Corporal Roy Sweezy were originally buried, in February 1945. Today the area is rice land. *(Courtesy of Juan Pajota)*

A 1976 photo of Captain James Fisher Memorial in the center of Barrio Balangkare, designed so that those who had helped the Americans would have a place to dry their rice. *(Author photo)*

Patches worn by men of the two elite combat units. *(Author photo)*

way for a few hundred yards and stopped to rest while their animals grazed.

Then they mounted and started back up the road, passing in front of the camp until they reached the Cabu River. From there they followed the south bank until the point where it fed into the Pampanga, crossed, and proceeded directly into Barrio Platero.

Their report to Pajota confirmed what the Alamo Scouts had said. One guard tower, the southeast one in the rear of the camp, was unoccupied.

It was now 1620 hours (4:20 P.M.) and everything at the stockade seemed quiet.

Shortly before Captain Pajota's young carabao riders reported to their commander, Captain Bob Prince had worked out the last details for his plan of attack on the POW camp.

In their final meeting, all noncommissioned officers were brought in to be sure each understood his assignment completely. Prince, after first outlining the plan, had left the organization of particular phases to each junior officer. Now it was time to review the attack plan in its entirety, giving everyone the opportunity to question anything they did not understand. Colonel Mucci had reviewed the plan and, making a few comments and changes of his own, issued his approval. The raid was to begin shortly after 1930 hours (7:30 P.M.), but everyone was expected to be in position for attack at "1930, sharp!"

Above all, the element of surprise was stressed. Exact timing would yield that advantage.

Captain Joson was told, again, that he would be given a six-man bazooka team under the command of Staff Sergeant James O. White of F Company. Joson's men must form a wedge-shaped roadblock 800 yards southwest of the camp along the highway. They, along with the bazooka team and several other Rangers from F Company, must stop all enemy traffic at this safe point south of the camp beginning at 1930 hours.

The extra bazookas under Ranger control, Colonel Mucci believed, were essential at the Joson position since this point might take the brunt of a large Japanese force moving out of Cabanatuan City. If the raid and evacuation of POWs required a full thirty minutes, as expected, enemy troops would easily have time to muster in the city and charge down those three miles of open road to reinforce the stockade.

Still unknown to Mucci, Pajota's Squadrons 200 and 202, with a combined strength of almost 200 armed men, were already in position some 400 yards north of the road behind the point where Joson would make his stand. Squadrons 200 and 202 must stand ready to move up to help Joson or swing northeast to assist Pajota—whoever most needed their fire power.

Captain Pajota's orders, likewise, remained unchanged. He was to engage the enemy camped on the northeast side of the Cabu River and keep them from crossing the bridge and reinforcing the guards at the stockade or attacking the Rangers as they withdrew. In order to accomplish this, Pajota must gain complete surprise on the Japanese and hold until the Rangers and POWs were safely across the Pampanga River. His signal to disengage would be a second red flare fired in the air by Captain Prince. The first flare would indicate that the Rangers were ready to withdraw from the camp.

Once that second red flare was fired, Pajota could withdraw southeast to lure the Japanese in the opposite direction from the retreating Allied column. He had decided that there was no need to reveal that his squadrons had four machine guns. The Rangers would have no use for the heavy weapons during the assault on the camp, but the guerrillas certainly needed them. For even though the strength of the Japanese at Cabu bridge was now well known, Pajota had been given only one bazooka. He planned to use a combined force of less than 200 men to hold the river front and bridge. If the automatic weapons and bazooka did not stop the enemy, if the land mines failed, then the combat could quickly become hand to hand.

Colonel Mucci emphasized that he wanted all phone lines cut along the highway both northeast and southwest of the camp. Pajota instructed Lieutenant Regino Bobila to cut the wire at a telephone pole at 1800 hours (6:00 P.M.) near a trail that led from the highway to Bangad. Since this spot was over 1,000 yards southwest of the camp, the Japanese would not suspect that the action had anything to do with an assault on their stockade. The guerrillas were always cutting the lines anyway, just to annoy the enemy.

However, at 1915 hours, only a few minutes before the raid was to begin, First Lieutenant Carlos Tombo would cut the phone line at the south, but this time the sabotage must be closer to the camp—150 yards from the southwest corner of the stockade. Lieutenant R. Mendoza and Sergeant Ciraco Matias would cut the lines, about the same time, 150 yards to the north of the camp.

Pajota was not the only commander worried about his assignment at Cabu bridge. Colonel Mucci worried about just how well a guerrilla army, accustomed to hit-and-run attacks, could stand in a prolonged direct engagement with an enemy force superior in numbers. What would be the course of action remaining if Pajota's men were overpowered at the bridge, or if his men broke and fled to the hills?

Mucci, at one point in the meeting, revealed those troubled thoughts. "Captain Pajota, you *must* hold at that bridge!"

Pajota responded without hestitation, "We will hold, sir. If any Japs pass, it will be over our dead bodies. We will all be dead!"

On that solemn note, the meeting continued.

"Murf," Captain Prince addressed First Lieutenant John Murphy, "your men understand their assignment?"

"Completely, sir," Murphy replied.

First Lieutenant Murphy's men, less those assigned to assist Captain Joson at the roadblock, were given the mission of liquidating the enemy guards at the rear entrance to the camp and preventing the Japanese from moving up into the POW section. The 2nd Platoon of F Company must move along the east side of the camp leaving squads to destroy the guard tower at the highway (northeast corner), the two "pillboxes" along the east fence, and the supposedly unoccupied guard tower at the southeast corner. The men must also cut a large hole in the east fence near the rear of the camp for an emergency escape route if needed by C Company, which would enter by the front gate and move down the center of the stockade.

"We should have good cover with the help of that creek bed which runs along the east side," Murphy said. "At least, until we get to the back corner. Circling behind the back fence will be the most critical move. It will take the longest time."

"Now," Prince went on, "everyone understands that the signal for the attack to begin will come from Murphy's men at the rear of the stockade! When they begin firing, we'll launch our attack through the front gate! This goes for you, also, Captain Pajota." Prince glanced at the guerrilla commander. "No one is to fire a shot until Lieutenant Murphy's men open up!"

Pajota nodded. He understood.

"When Murphy's men commence firing, I'll shoot up one red flare. I hope it's not necessary. Everyone should be too busy to see it, but I'll fire it, anyway."

Then Prince began to review the plans for the main assault—the break into the camp. With F Company taking care of the northeast corner guard tower, "pillboxes," and rear guard tower, the concentration of activity for C Company would be the main gate and POW section.

Using the concept of Ranger organization, Prince and Mucci planned C Company's assault in two basic waves of attack. The first wave would be launched by the 1st Platoon's three sections. The second, by the 2nd Platoon's three sections.

The 1st Platoon, under First Lieutenant William J. O'Connell, would attack the main gate, using its two assault sections and its special weapons section.

The first assault section, led by Staff Sergeant Preston N. Jensen, would rush the main gate and break in as its members killed the gate guards and gate tower guards. As they jumped into action, the second assault section, under Tech 4 Homer E. Britzius, would move quickly across the highway and fire through the right front fence to cover the entry of the first section and the special weapons section, which would follow at the heels of the first section. Just as soon as the first section and weapons section were inside, the second section would lift its fire, move into the camp behind the weapons section, and open fire, again, on the enemy on the right side to keep them pinned down and away from the POWs on the left side. By this time, the first section and weapons section with the bazookas were expected to be at the middle of the camp, firing on the tank sheds and enemy troops on the right center and right rear area.

After the entire 1st Platoon had passed through the gate, the 2nd Platoon under Lieutenant Melville R. Schmidt would move in. Their basic assignments were to open the POW area, start the prisoners out, and set up supporting fire toward the left rear of the camp.

To accomplish this, Lieutenant Schmidt's first assault section under Staff Sergeant Clifton R. Harris would charge through the open gate and force entry through the POW gate. Some of the Rangers would move rapidly to the rear of the POW area and open fire on the Japanese already under fire from F Company, positioned outside the fence.

The 2nd Platoon's second assault section under Staff Sergeant William R. Butler would move into the camp, down the center road, and thwart any enemy attempt to reach the POWs.

The weapons section under Staff Sergeant August T. Stern would be held in reserve in or behind the ditch across the highway from the camp. Remaining there with them would be medics, Alamo Scouts, the Combat Photo men (whose cameras were useless in the dark), and a number of Filipino guerrillas. All of these "reserve" men would assist and direct the rescued POWs through the main gate to the waiting carabao carts at the Pampanga River.

When all the POWs were clear of the stockade, Captain Prince would fire another red flare as a signal for the Rangers to withdraw. Just as soon as everyone had reached the Pampanga River and crossed, Prince would fire the last flare for Pajota to disengage at the bridge and withdraw southeast. Once certain he had outdistanced the Japanese, Pajota's forces were to double back to protect the retreating Allied column's rear.

Captain Pajota now had another suggestion. He stated to Colonel Mucci that it had been the observation of his men during the last few weeks that whenever American planes flew over the camp the Japanese became terribly upset and nervous, keeping their eyes on the sky sometimes for several minutes after the planes passed.

"Ask your planes to fly over," Pajota recommended. "No shoot—no bombs. Just fly over a few minutes before your attack!"

Mucci considered the idea a few minutes. It was time to notify Sixth Army that he would need air cover by daybreak, anyway. Perhaps Pajota's idea had some merit and might provide needed distraction those final minutes before the assault.

Sergeant Norton Most had his radio set up and ready near the schoolhouse "hospital." It was 1635 hours (4:35 P.M.). The Rangers would leave for the raid in twenty-five minutes, and Sergeant Most doubted seriously, considering Army red tape, if any plane could be scrambled and reach the camp before dark.

In Barrio Pangatian, nine-year-old Florencio Santiago stood on the bamboo steps of the small nipa hut he called home and stared in the direction of the narrow bridge that crossed the slow-moving, muddy waters of the Cabu River.

Somewhere on the opposite side of the Cabu, he knew, Japanese soldiers were camped waiting until after dark to move along the highway as they had done each night during the last month.

But there must be something special about tonight, he thought. Why else would Pajota's men send word for the villagers to evacuate into the mountains? Was Pajota going to actually attack those Japanese? Surely not! There were too many Japanese there and Pajota had no tanks.

Florencio heard his mother call. It was time to join his parents and his brother for the long walk east to the mountains.

He turned and looked in the opposite direction of Cabu bridge and could see the top of one of the guard towers at the POW camp some 400 yards away. And then his thoughts raced to the Americans in that stockade. He and the other children of his barrio had often given food to those prisoners—whenever the Japanese guards would allow. He had even learned a few words of American slang during the last year and a half.

The Americans were always happy to see him. Now, he wondered if they would still be there to joke with him when everyone returned from the mountains.

"Hurry, Florencio! We go now!" he heard his mother call again.

And he joined his family to begin the two-mile journey to the Sierra Madre.

There can be no question about the outstanding courage of all Filipino guerrillas. But one group, the Huks, had its own agenda, which often conflicted with U.S. aims.

It was not that the Huks wanted to be on the opposite side from the guerrillas who were controlled, influenced, and supported by the United States. Nor was it the Huks' goal to war with the Americans. To the contrary, Luis Taruc and his Huk followers never ceased their fight to drive the Japanese from the Philippines and welcomed all help in this regard.

But once it became evident to Taruc that the Huks' own hard-earned victories against the Japanese were essentially ignored by the Americans, everything changed. The Huk leader wanted MacArthur to recognize his group as a strong popular movement. The Allies were labeling them all as communist. Only those Filipinos working directly with the Americans were receiving credit for the resistance struggle. In October 1944, despite Taruc's repeated demands, only the USAFFE guerrillas were receiving modern arms and supplies from American submarines.

From then on, friction between the communist faction among the Huks and the much more middle-of-the-road fighters who followed Taruc reached a kindling point. The communists insisted that America must recognize the Huks' strength or their party stood no chance at all of political survival once the war ended. To this end, they must win as many battles as possible against the Japanese—and consequently they must have all modern weapons, even if acquiring them meant destroying other guerrilla units.

Guerillas fighting under Colonel Anderson and Major Lapham soon discovered the danger of two enemies: the Japanese and the Huks.

It was 1645 hours (4:45 P.M.) when Captain Pajota called his staff together in Platero for their last meeting.

"Are the machine guns in place and well camouflaged?" the

guerrilla commander asked as the men gathered around him and squatted on their haunches.

"As you ordered, sir," Squadron 201's commander, First Lieutenant Jose Hipolito, assured him.

"Excellent! We will not place the mines in the road until later—the same with the bomb on the bridge."

"The Japs still have no guards on the bridge," Second Lieutenant Erive advised.

"Good." Pajota nodded. "Our scouts have all reported and the Americans are ready. I will now tell you my alternate plan, should our frontal attack fail. We must remember that the objective is to hold the Japs until all the POWs and Rangers have safely crossed the Pampanga—"

"Sir," one officer interrupted, "the Japs still have their tanks hidden less than a kilometer from the bridge. Do the Americans expect us to stop tanks with machine guns, rifles, and grenades?"

Pajota glared with squinting eyes. "If the bomb on the bridge fails, there are still the land mines in the highway. The tanks must stay on the road to cross the bridge. They cannot climb the high, sandy banks of the river on our side."

"So what!" the officer persisted. "The tanks may cross the bridge—and then?"

"We will stop them with our bodies if necessary!" Pajota replied.

"What do the Americans care? We are only Filipinos—isn't that it?"

"We are soldiers, Lieutenant!" Pajota snapped. "The Americans have given us what we need! Colonel Mucci has given us a bazooka. The bazooka is assigned to Headquarters Company next to the left side of the road, near the bridge. The bazooka will stop tanks. Now—enough! Pay attention to the alternate plan!"

Pajota's eyes studied the faces of each man for a moment. Then he smiled reassuringly and began to explain his plan. "If the Japs manage to cross the bridge before the Rangers complete their job, our entire force will move from the left flank . . ." he began to draw lines in the dirt, lines representing the highway, the river and Cabu bridge ". . . across the road to the right flank by a series of rushes . . . starting with Headquarters Company. At the same time, I will send runners. One will go to Squadrons 203 and 204, which are waiting north at Manacnac. Squadrons 203 and 204 will move south and attack the Japs at the rear. The squadrons should hit the rear of the Japs in five minutes from the time the runner arrives with the order to move!"

Pajota spoke with his usual softness of voice, but with a steady, positive tone, and paused long enough for only those glances into the faces of each officer. It was as if he were taking their pulse.

"And then," he continued, "the other runner will have reached Squadrons 200 and 202, already—who are in reserve behind Captain Joson's roadblock at the south. Lieutenant Quitives and Lieutenant Bobila—you will then move your Squadrons 200 and 202 northeast along the highway to serve as rear guard for the Rangers. The Americans will be moving northwest out of our battle area. The Japs following me southeast will be pinched on all flanks—203 and 204 from the north, 200 and 202 from the south. Our Headquarters Company and Squadron 201A will turn about and fire on the Japs from the east. Squadrons 201 and 211 will cross the highway and attack from the west.

"And then . . ." Pajota erased the lines in the dirt with a sweep of his hand. "And then we will have the Japs encircled!"

The captain stood up slowly. "Any questions?"

There was a moment of silence, but he could read the expression of excitement on all of them. It was time to make the most of their enthusiasm.

"Due to the importance of this mission, I have elected to commit our entire force. Our firepower is good. We have plans for all contingencies. We will destroy the Japs at the bridge!"

"If the alternate plan is not necessary," one lieutenant spoke, "do Squadrons 203 and 204 attack the Japs retreating from the bridge, past Manacnac?"

"No!" Pajota replied. "They are to move only if my message arrives for them to attack with the alternate plan. Now, remember these things: We must gain complete surprise! Once the battle begins you must stay in position until I give the order to withdraw. The Japanese are noisy fighters. They yell to increase morale. In the position they are now—they do not know the area—they will use only one method of fighting. The Americans call it 'Right down the alley'! The Japs will come across that bridge and they will keep coming until they run us over, regardless of how many we kill—unless we kill them all. I have told the American Colonel Mucci that no Japs will pass. When the night is finished . . . there will be no more Jap force at Cabu bridge. We will annihilate them!"

The freedom granted the 547th Night Fighter Squadron by higher headquarters combined with the squadron's willingness to cooperate with non–Air Corps units was about to pay off handsomely. Thanks to that liberty, the barriers of normal military channels could be bypassed as Sixth Army intelligence received the relayed radio request for help from Colonel Mucci's Rangers. A call was, in turn, placed directly to the headquarters of the 547th and Captain Robert Wolfston, Squadron A2, had a brief discussion with his assistant, First Lieutenant Reuben E. Nieves.

"Better get Keyser or the 'Old Man,' quick! It's almost 1700 now," Captain Wolfston said.

The "Old Man," squadron commander Lieutenant Colonel William C. Odell, and his executive officer, Major Francis M. Keyser, listened carefully to the report of the Ranger request.

"Tell operations this should be a max effort!" Colonel Odell instructed. "Dispatch as many as we can get airborne!"

At 1705 hours (5:05 P.M.) Captains Wayne E. Coyle and William C. Behnke studied the request and then began to move with cool precision.

"Who's next on the alert roster?" Captain Behnke asked.

"Lieutenant Schrieber," replied Coyle.

"Okay. Good! Tell him we have a special mission. There will be an Army officer here from Sixth Army HQ in a few minutes, so Schrieber will have a passenger."

There was nothing special about the selection of Schrieber as the pilot for the mission. Those P61s scheduled for routine missions on January 30, 1945, were either already airborne or preparing for takeoff. Lieutenant Kenneth Schrieber was simply the first name on the "standby" pilots list for any emergency that night.

But if there was nothing special about the method of selection, the pilots and crew were, indeed, a special breed of men.

Twenty-six-year-old Kenneth Schrieber, for example, had a proven reputation as a skilled, careful pilot and an alert, inquisitive man with a good sense of humor. His P61 Black Widow was officially known as number 390, however, Schrieber and his radar observer (RO), Second Lieutenant Bonnie Rucks, had nicknamed their plane the "Hard to Get," and a friend in the Seabees had painted a reclining voluptuous nude blonde on the fighter's nose when they were all on Owi Island in New Guinea.

What made the "Hard to Get" a perfect plane to carry a passenger was the fact that the P61 carried only her four 20-mm cannons and lacked the usual .50-caliber machine gun turret on her top. The raised seat normally occupied by the craft's gunner, just behind the pilot, offered good visibility for any observer.

Captain Behnke sat at his field table in the operations office studying a map of central Luzon when Lieutenants Schrieber and Rucks reported for instructions. It was 1713 hours (5:13 P.M.), and Schrieber was already dressed. Both men were armed with .45 caliber automatics in holsters strapped across their chests and snugly nestled beneath the heart.

"What do you have for us, sir?" Lieutenant Schrieber asked as he saluted the captain.

"Sixth Army's got something a little different going on tonight," Captain Behnke replied. "The Rangers are assaulting a Jap POW camp in the Cabanatuan, Cabu area of Nueva Ecija. The camp should be about—here!" The operations officer pointed to a spot on the map along a road connecting two towns. "Sixth Army HQ is furnishing a captain who is supposed to know the exact location. He'll ride with you and help you find it. Now— you actually have two assignments. The Rangers' raid should begin shortly after dark, about 1930 hours. The Ranger CO seems to think that if you could make a couple of low-level passes right at sunset, it might divert the Jap guards' attention from the ground to the sky. That's the first assignment. Second, the guerrillas have assured us that all civilians in the area will be cleared from the highways. Therefore, anything that moves on a main road, other than right in front of that Jap stockade—even a donkey cart—should be considered the enemy. Strafe anything that moves on those roads! If the raid is successful, our boys will be returning to our lines by back trails. It's up to you to give them cover in that camp area. I'll divert as many other fighters as I can to back you up. Any questions?"

Lieutenant Schrieber rubbed his heavy mustache with a fore-finger and glanced up at the tall, slender RO. "How about you, Bonnie?"

Lieutenant Rucks shook his head, no.

"Will we have any radio contact with the Rangers?" Schrieber asked.

"Negative—just with our base, if you need it."

Lieutenant Schrieber's face broke into a smile. "Okay, sir. We're ready!"

"Good luck," Captain Behnke said as the crew of the "Hard to Get" saluted and turned to leave.

At 1725 hours (5:25 P.M.), P61 number 390, the "Hard to Get," her two-man crew, and an Army passenger rolled down the pierced-steel runway, lifted into the evening sky over Lingayen Gulf, turned, and headed east. In a few minutes, she would be over Nueva Ecija province.

In the meantime, the operations officer became alive with ex-citement as Captains Coyle and Behnke set the plans of backup cover for the "Hard to Get" into motion. All available Black Wid-ows in the 547th were turned loose.

Two P61s on defense patrol near Lingayen were radioed and Captain Cecil A. Littlefield and Captain Edwin A. Annis vectored away from their orbit points and rushed toward Nueva Ecija.

At the base, considerable scrambling continued as First Lieu-tenant Richard B. Peterson climbed with his crewmate into their night fighter and took off.

A few minutes later, several more followed, and by 1745 hours (5:45 P.M.), the sky over central Luzon was filled with at least ten Black Widows seeking their prey.

The night sky over a particular area can become a little crowded in short order, and even with radar, the speeds at which the P61s were traveling made navigation extremely dangerous.

But the 547th had perfected a system for such events. While the "Hard to Get" closed in on her target at POW Camp Cabanat-uan, the other aircraft would remain in divided sectors nearby, ready to replace her should she expend her ammunition or en-counter any difficulties.

Every possible avenue to or from Cabanatuan City and its

POW camp would now be covered from the air. No Japanese mechanized equipment in the sky or along the roads would be safe from detection and attack by the deadly Black Widows.

At 1700 hours (5:00 P.M.), January 30, 1945, the force of Army Rangers, Filipino guerrillas, Alamo Scouts, and Unit F's Combat Photographers marched out of Barrio Platero leaving Sergeant Norton Most and his radio crew guarded by several armed villagers. The little army, at this time, totaled almost 375 men. Many of Pajota's squadrons were already in position. All watches had been synchronized.

In a single file, they followed Pajota's "scouts" southwest down a narrow dirt trail, which wound its way for one-half mile through tall cogon grass and bamboo groves to a steep bank at the Pampanga River. There, several guerrillas split from the group and disappeared into the grass. Captain Luis De La Cruz and Lieutenant Padama would direct their men in organizing the carabao carts, which must wait on both sides of the river.

The Filipinos knew where to cross the river at its shallowest point near a long, flat sandbar that split the waters in midstream. The river was narrow here, and only knee deep, but everyone was warned that it ran waist deep in other areas and often 200 yards wide.

As the Rangers and their guides approached the water, the group split into three units. On the left, Captain Pajota and his squadrons moved upstream 100 yards, crossed the river, and proceeded southeast for the Cabu area. On the right, Captain Joson's eighty men, accompanied by Staff Sergeant James White's six-man bazooka team and several other F Company Rangers, moved downstream 100 yards, crossed the river, and started south for the point on the highway where the roadblock would be established.

In the center, the Rangers waded single file into the warm, shallow water, and after fifteen to twenty yards, splashed upon the sandbar. They crossed the twenty-five yards of dark sand, then waded another twenty-five yards to the opposite, sloping bank. There, they entered more cogon grass and even higher Talahib grass.

The men were now well-prepared with the knowledge that their map was incorrect. As Captain Prince had noted from the aerial photograph, the next two miles to the stockade would be mostly flat grassland breaking off into rice fields and shallow ponds with their knee-high dikes. For this first three-fourths mile, though, it would be safe for the men to walk, as the high grass would conceal them from view.

Staff Sergeant John W. Nelson, a six-foot, 170-pound medical corpsman, was heavily weighted by the blood plasma canisters, M1 carbine, .45 pistol, and other combat medical supplies he carried. But this did not worry him. He had become accustomed to being both a medic and a rifleman with the Rangers long ago. His friend and medical detachment commander, Captain Jimmy Fisher, was just behind him, and the doctor, though in excellent physical condition, was not a combat soldier.

Regardless of Colonel Mucci's fussing and arguments and the pleading of all the medics, Jimmy Fisher could not be convinced to stay in Platero. He was going to be with his men wherever they went.

John Nelson was the first sergeant of the medics and, of course, worried with the responsibility of all his men. But he knew his men could take care of themselves very well under fire. Captain Fisher was another matter. Sergeant Nelson reached for the handle of his .45 pistol. A photograph of his wife was under the grips of the automatic. And Nelson began to think how he would stand close to Jimmy Fisher during the raid. He would keep the Japanese away from the doctor, first with his carbine and then with that pistol, if necessary.

For that first one-half mile all the Rangers were in excellent spirits, like a team marching onto a football field for the last big, important game. To most of them, the full impact of the danger that lay ahead had not yet hit.

F Company's first sergeant, Charles Bosard, could only think of how thrilled and proud he was of his men. "There are *my* boys," he whispered to himself over and over again. "They'll do a good job. I trained them. They'll do just fine . . . I know it!"

Captain Robert Prince glanced over his shoulder and noticed Colonel Mucci, as usual, was moving up and down the line, chatting with his Rangers. For a brief moment, Captain Prince realized the pain from his blistered feet, but then his thoughts changed quickly to the critical minutes ahead. He prayed that his plan of attack would work.

Some of the men were teasing Sergeant Lester "Twister" Malone again, and he joked back by reminding a married Ranger that there was not much time left. "Twister" still needed the man's address to "go visit his wife" if he got "all shot up."

PFC Bill Proudfit joined in the fun with a few men in his squad. They were complaining that Colonel Mucci had not given them enough time to become "familiar" with all those young girls who sang "God Bless America." Again, the spirit of the march suggested to Proudfit that they were heading for a Sunday-school picnic. He heard the BAR man behind him say, "I don't *hate* the God damned Japs! We just got to kill 'em, not hate 'em—don't we?"

Another Ranger responded, "Yeah! If you'd been in that camp up there for three years, you'd hate 'em. You'd better shoot that BAR like you hate 'em!"

"Damn! This thing is getting heavy!" a Ranger next to Corporal James Herrick complained as he continued to shift the big BAR from hand to hand.

"Give it to me! I'll lug it for a while," Herrick offered, and the two men exchanged rifles.

It was 1800 hours (6:00 P.M.). Twilight—and the air was warm and still, filled with the fresh, sweet smell of rice hay. The Rangers had covered a mile since leaving the banks of the Pampanga. Before them, stretching to the highway, was nothing but rice fields. Some ponds were completely dry, some muddy, many half-filled with dark, stagnant water. There were no trees, no shrubbery, only a single nipa hut scarcely visible on the horizon a mile away.

Captain Prince gave a waving hand signal and Lieutenant John Murphy with his men of 2nd Platoon, F Company (less the men with Captain Joson), split away from the group and began heading east. Within another one-half mile, before they hit the highway, F Company would be in position to enter the creek bed, which crossed under the road and ran along the east side of the camp.

Bob Prince moved his arms, giving another signal, and Lieutenant William J. O'Connell's 1st Platoon took the front-line position followed by rows of Lieutenant Melville R. Schmidt's 2nd Platoon. Now, the Rangers began to spread apart, their lines moving with a front some thirty to forty yards wide. It would be necessary for them to stay reasonably close together to insure that each squad arrived intact at the highway. If one man was out of place the moment the attack began, the entire plan could fail.

The Rangers walked another 500 yards, but there was no more conversation among the troops. The guard towers of POW Camp Cabanatuan were now visible on the horizon.

Corporal James Herrick shifted the heavy BAR he carried for his buddy and his right had crossed over to grasp at his jacket pocket. His New Testament Bible was still there, over his heart. Herrick marched on, content with the thought that he had read the Bible for an hour before they left Platero.

Captain Prince glanced at Colonel Mucci, who was staring at the distant outline of the stockade. Mucci turned to face Prince, then nodded. The captain gave another hand signal and the Rangers began to drop to their knees. The men must crawl the rest of the way to the highway, almost a mile away.

Captain Juan Pajota's men, with far less distance to travel, began to reach the southwest bank of the Cabu River and squadrons systematically dropped off into positions as the force moved toward the highway and Cabu bridge.

Near the intersection of the Cabu River and the Pampanga, First Lieutenant Jose Hipolito and Squadron 201 entered a grove of bamboo and set up one .30-caliber, water-cooled machine gun. Next to them, Squadron 211 under Lieutenant Toribio Paulino also set up a .30-caliber machine gun. These two squadrons could easily cover the river and the remains of the old "temporary bridge" from their point. This was important because the banks here were not steep. They had been worn down by carabao carts crossing the shallow waters and afforded an easy path for the Japanese to use.

Then part of Squadron 201A under First Lieutenant Bernardo dropped off and set up a BAR on a tripod and a .30-caliber machine gun.

Before the remaining force reached the highway, Headquarters Company established their position with two BARs and the bazooka. From this point, they could easily cover the river and Cabu bridge. An excellent crossfire range would be effected with Lieutenant Erive's men on the right side of the highway. The intersecting point of the crossfire was the bridge, but they also had clear vision up the highway some 200 yards. Most of Squadron 201A and part of Squadron 204, all under Second Lieutenant Erive, had moved into positions on the southeast side of the highway from another staging area and set up defenses on the right side of the bridge. With two BARs, one .30-caliber machine gun, and several Thompson submachine guns, these men were in the best position to rain fire upon the bridge.

Captain Pajota, accompanied by Lieutenant Abad, Corporal Andasan, and Private Sulayao, started to inspect each position. The guerrillas were approaching a small mound of earth that stretched from the Pampanga to the highway. Pajota would make sure that all his automatic weapons were in front where they could swing freely from flank to flank and furnish the most effective field of fire. The men armed with rifles and carbines or pistols were positioned behind the automatic weapons. In the next rank were men armed with bolos and his medical corpsmen, who carried long bamboo poles. The poles were part of a "stretcher" arrangement and were used in the following manner. A blanket or large cloth was tied at the center section of the pole, thus forming a baglike carrier in which a wounded man was placed. Two men, one on each end of the pole, would then raise the bamboo to their shoulders and be on their way. Perhaps the system appeared awkward to Western armies familiar with a flat stretcher with four handles, but actually the ancient method used by the Filipinos was quite effective. The pole, with casualty in the bag, was easy to manage and light to carry. It also granted each "medic" one free hand to swing a bolo or fire a weapon.

For some unknown reason, the Japanese commander, Oyabu, failed to post any guards on either end of Cabu bridge. It was a mistake that would cost him dearly. Some members of Squadrons 201A and 204, who were traveling with Pajota, easily slipped unnoticed across the highway. Others managed to place twenty land mines in the highway southwest of the bridge. The guerrillas had also succeeded in fastening a "time bomb" under the bridge on the northeast (Japanese) end an hour earlier. Pajota's "time bomb," one of several delivered by U.S. submarine, was set to detonate between 7:40 and 7:50 P.M. Since the Rangers planned to be in position at 7:30 and begin their assault on the stockade shortly thereafter, Pajota hoped his bomb would catch the enemy on the bridge and destroy them with the structure.

Every guerrilla knew Dokuho Battalion 359 was across the river. They had spied on the Japanese all day, and now they could easily hear the voices of imperial soldiers as they talked around small campfires. The Filipinos also knew the fires would be extinguished very soon—before complete darkness settled in. But during those last few minutes of light, the Japanese were enjoying a meal.

Pajota had correctly anticipated the Japanese reaction to a surprise attack. Though Imperial Army strategy usually called for a battalion commander like Oyabu to fix a point on a front and launch rapid encircling attacks, this tactic was, of course, primarily effective when the terrain was known. Normally, the encirclement was conducted in the form of a number of attacks at one time, the first coming in a small circle, then, finally, in a frontal attack with the whole battalion weight thrown at that selected point.

Japanese courage, Pajota fully appreciated, was no myth. It might be fanatical, blind courage, but it could not be discounted. The imperial soldier had been trained and was skilled in teamwork, but if that broke down the soldier could become highly nervous and emotional. He was not trained to think as an individual. Without his leaders, the individual soldier's only remaining tactic was suicidal.

For night fighting, the Japanese were specially accustomed to procuring all possible information by carefully reconnoitering an area. If they could not do this, then they usually deliberately exposed men to draw fire, thereby learning of their enemy's whereabouts.

Battalion Commander Oyabu had not reconnoitered the Cabu area. Pajota's men knew he had not. After all, Oyabu and Dokuho 359 had no idea they might engage enemy forces before they reached Cabanatuan City. Also, Oyabu could not employ the encircling tactic because his forces would be attacked from across a river.

Pajota, therefore, was safe with his calculation that the Japanese at Cabu bridge would lack a battle plan. There was only one tactic remaining for them to use. The Japanese would charge upon the bridge and fanatically throw wave upon wave at the Filipinos (as Pajota had assured his men the enemy would do).

But the Cabu bridge was less than 100 feet long. The shallow river, in spots, was narrower than that, for a lack of rain had left the Cabu almost dry in some areas. The true test would come when the Japanese battalion, recovering from a surprise attack, launched its full force upon the bridge or through the river. Either way, if the Japanese succeeded in crossing, only the land mines, a few bazooka rockets, and the "alternate plan" could save Pajota— and the Americans.

It was now 1825 hours (6:25 P.M.). It would be another hour before Pajota, satisfied his men were ready, assumed a position directly behind Squadron 201A and Headquarters Company. It would be another hour and five minutes, he knew, before the Americans were ready outside the POW camp.

In the flat rice fields across the highway from the POW camp, the Rangers continued to crawl and snake their way over small dikes, which formed the rice ponds into almost perfect squares. They had less than one-half mile to crawl.

"CLANG, CLANG . . . CLANG, CLANG . . . !"

Suddenly, a strange, metallic noise came from somewhere in the POW camp.

The sound repeated: "CLANG, CLANG, CLANG." Safeties released as the Rangers shoved their weapons forward, ready to fire. Everyone froze. On each face was etched the same expression. Had they been detected?

"Give me back that damn BAR!" Corporal Herrick heard his buddy whisper. "This is stupid! You've got my BAR and I've got the ammunition!"

The two men quickly exchanged weapons.

"CLANG, CLANG . . . CLANG, CLANG!"

Then, as fast as the noise had begun, it ceased. Everyone's eyes fixed on the area they knew was the front gate. If that noise *was* an alarm, Japanese soldiers would pour out of the camp and charge the field any minute.

Captain Prince rolled over on his back to look at his watch in the faint evening light. It was 6:30. Where was F Company? Had they been spotted by the enemy in the towers? Bob Prince, his heart pounding, turned over and placed the sights of his M1 rifle on the front gate of the stockade.

12

It's okay . . . we're Yanks! . . . Get the hell out of here!

—Sixth U.S. Army Ranger, POW Camp Cabanatuan, January 30, 1945

In the POW compound section of Camp Cabanatuan one of the prisoners, a U.S. Navy man, dropped a two-foot-long pipe from his bony hand. The hunk of iron dangled silently from a leather thong, which connected it to a triangle-shaped gong.

"Is it 1830 or 1900 hours?" the POW asked his buddy.

"How in hell should I know? It's not dark yet—must be 1830. What difference does it make?"

"Difference, mate? Dammit, it makes a lot of difference! Did I sound five bells or six?" the POW shouted.

"I don't remember. Six, I think."

"Well, then, I'm wrong! I should have struck five bells for 1830, not six. Don't you remember anything, mate? Five bells for 6:30 and six bells for 7:00 P.M. I've messed up again!"

"You sure it ain't the other way around?"

The debate between the two Navy POWs was practically a daily occurrence but generally ignored by the other POWs. At 6:30 that night most of the prisoners were wandering about their compound yard or preparing to bed down for the night. When some of the Navy POWs first erected their "bell" during the middle of

1944 and began to strike out the typical half-hour "period of watch," their experience did, for a while, generate curiosity. But none of the prisoners actually ever "stood watch" and by January 30, 1945, even the originators of the system had lost enthusiasm.

In the rice fields one-half mile from the front of the stockade the Rangers were still prone, weapons ready, and unaware that the clanging sound was not an alarm but two U.S. Navy men attempting to hold to a small memory of their days aboard ship.

Captain Prince turned to his side and squinted to read the watch—1835 hours (6:30 P.M.). Less than an hour remained for everyone to be in position. A full five minutes had passed since the last clanging sound. Prince could wait no longer. He raised his arm, palm forward, and swung it down. The Rangers resumed their crawl toward the stockade.

At 1840 hours (6:40 P.M.), Alamo Scout Lieutenant Bill Nellist stood at the back door of his nipa hut in the rice field, 350 yards from the highway and the POW camp's front gate. He had been watching the Rangers crawl toward his position for the last fifteen minutes.

The faint sound of an airplane in the distance caught Nellist's attention, and he turned to look north. The plane's silhouette was easy to recognize. It was an American P61 Black Widow.

"What's that flyboy doing over here?" Lieutenant Nellist whispered to PFC Vaquilar. "I thought this mission was top secret. We're supposed to get air cover on the way back—not now. That guy may think we're Japs and cut loose on us!"

Vaquilar hunched his shoulders. "Don't know. Perhaps we should go to the field and join the Rangers before *they* think we are Japs."

The two Scouts shed their Filipino clothes, leaped out the back of the hut, and began to crawl to the first small rice pond dike. There they lay motionless and watched unnoticed until more than half of the Rangers had passed. Then they turned and began to crawl with Mucci's men toward the highway.

"Hey! Where'd you guys come from?" a Ranger spoke to Nellist.

"We've been waiting for you and Mucci."

"You guys Scouts?"

"Yep," Nellist answered.

"Should have known!" the Ranger replied.

Second Lieutenant Bonnie Rucks's eyes shifted from his radar instrument to the canopy, assuring him that the sky was free of enemy planes. The crew of the P61 "Hard to Get" knew there were only a few Japanese planes left on Luzon, but it would take but one to jeopardize their special mission.

"It's 1845—getting dark out there, Chubby. Where in hell is that camp?" Rucks spoke into the radio to his pilot, Lieutenant Kenneth Schrieber.

"Don't know for sure. We should be close. You got anything to eat? I'm getting hungry," Schrieber replied with a slight laugh, knowing his radar observer loved to tease him about his insatiable appetite.

"I thought so!" came Rucks's reply.

"How about it, Captain?" Kenneth Schrieber leaned back and glanced over his shoulder to the gunner's position where the Army captain sat, a large topographical map spread across his lap.

None of them knew exactly where to look for the camp and the "Hard to Get" had been moving in a large circle, west over Talavera, north to Bongabon, and east to the Sierra Madre Mountain chain for several minutes. Gradually, Lieutenant Schrieber lowered the altitude and tightened his circle, using Bongabon as a vortex.

"We'll find it this round," the captain assured, "if that's Bongabon we're over. Let's follow the highway, now. If we're heading southwest we should approach our target."

"We're heading southwest," Schrieber said. "If we were higher you could probably see Lingayen Gulf far off our right wing on a clear day."

"Good! What's our altitude? Can we take her down a little for a closer look?"

"We're at 1,500 now. How low you want?" Schrieber asked.

"As low as we can get."

"Okay—here we go! Keep your eyes peeled, Bonnie!"

"Roger," the RO responded.

"1,000 . . . 800 . . . 600 . . . 400 . . . 200 feet. Leveling off at 200, boys," Lieutenant Schrieber calmly announced.

"All clear," Bonnie Rucks called into the intercom. "There's a river up ahead and—a bridge."

"That's got to be the Cabu. We're on target!" the captain interrupted.

The big Black Widow roared at treetop level over Cabu bridge, startling the bivouacked Japanese. Suddenly, the "Hard to Get" was over Cabanatuan POW Camp, the plane's wing scarcely 150 feet above the northeast guard tower.

"My God, there she is!" Lieutenant Rucks cried into the microphone, "off our left wing!"

"I can see our boys deploying in the field across the highway— over on our right! They must be almost ready to attack!" the captain yelled.

In seconds the Black Widow was a mile down the road and Lieutenant Schrieber throttled back to slow the fighter. "Did we blow their cover?" he called in a concerned tone.

"Negative! Quite the contrary. We really got the Nips' attention. Let's go back—a little slower. We'll take another look," the captain said.

Lieutenant Schrieber put the "Hard to Get" in a wide, sweeping turn to the west and climbed to 1,000 feet. Then he turned again near Bongabon to head southwest. At 1850 hours (6:50 P.M.), Schrieber lowered his altitude to 500 feet and slowed the big ship to eighty-five miles per hour. In a moment they buzzed over Cabu bridge for a second time and turned left gradually to pass directly over the stockade.

"There are the guard towers," Lieutenant Rucks spoke first. "Look at the Japs duck! Too bad we can't cut loose on 'em. If our boys weren't there, we could blow the whole place to hell!"

"You can see the prisoners out in the yard!" Lieutenant Schrieber stated.

"Yeah! I see 'em," the captain acknowledged.

Lieutenant Kenneth Schrieber fed more rich fuel to the "Hard to Get's" big engines and banked her into another sweeping turn. "Come on," he said. "We got to be sure these roads stay clear."

Inside the POW camp, a tremendous amount of excitement had been generated by the Black Widow's sudden appearance.

"I tell you that plane was ours!" Sergeant Abie Abraham insisted. "I saw American writing on her nose. I could have hit it with a rock!"

"We don't have no plane like that!" another POW argued. "Why would anyone paint a plane black?"

"To fly at night, stupid!"

"It was ours! How long has it been since you saw a Jap plane around here? The slopeheads couldn't build anything like that baby. She's American!"

As darkness enveloped the camp, the arguments diminished and the POWs broke into small groups to return to their quarters.

Doctor Merle McNeal Musselman sat down on the wooden steps to the camp's dispensary and leaned back, staring dreamily into the darkening sky. "Think I'll just sit here awhile and watch the stars come out," he said to a medic sitting next to him. "Tell me some more about the constellations, Sergeant."

The man with Musselman was an authority on the stars, and the two POWs often engaged in conversations on philosophy and the heavens.

Not far away, on the steps of his barracks, Sergeant Abie Abraham started to relate another experience from his days of Army service in Panama to his friend, Bill. "It was a long time ago," Abraham began, "before my assignment to Luzon. The jungles are hot and steamy in Panama—even at night. Not like these mild evenings here in the Central Plains . . ."

Twenty-seven-year-old PFC Eugene Evers had been on duty at the hospital ward all day and the medic was completely exhausted. He left the group of friends who were still debating the identity of the strange black plane and returned to his barracks. There he decided to play some scratched phonograph records as long as his arm had strength to turn the mechanical crank, or until sleep ended his day.

By 1915 hours (7:15 P.M.), Captain Prince and C Company's 1st Platoon had reached the drainage ditch directly across the highway from the front of the stockade. It was dark and the moon had not come up. Yet the glow of a rising full moon yielded enough light for Prince to see his men of the 2nd Platoon at their position in another shallow ditch, ten yards behind. Lying in the field ten yards behind the 2nd Platoon was his "reserve" third line of troops consisting of combat photographers, medics, several Filipino guerrillas, and Alamo Scouts. In fifteen minutes, 1930 hours, F Company was expected to be in position at the rear of the stockade. Prince was convinced that, thus far, none of them had been seen by the enemy. C Company was now ready for that first shot from F Company, which would signal the start of the raid.

While C Company waited at the front of the camp, F Company, 2nd Platoon, made its way cautiously into a muddy creek bed and through a six-foot drainage pipe that passed under the highway. They emerged on the camp's side of the road still concealed in the five-foot-deep creek bed, but they knew that the ditch would become shallower within 200 yards. Those who must travel all the way to the rear of the camp would resort to crawling again at that point. Lieutenant Murphy was leading the first three squads through the ditch. They would be the ones who had the greatest distance to travel—along the east fence, then turning right and crawling to the rear gate area of the camp.

Staff Sergeant Richard Moore, Tech 5 Patrick Marquis, PFC John Pearson, and PFC Gerhard Tiede were in one of the front squads. As they passed the first (northeast) guard tower, they heard a voice cry out in Japanese. Every Ranger in the ditch froze. From their position, heads peeking barely over the edge of the creek bank, they could easily see two enemy sentries in the twelve-foot tower. It was less than fifty yards away. One Japanese soldier had his back turned to the Rangers and was looking out over the POW section. The other guard was staring directly at Moore's squad. The Japanese slowly raised his rifle, as if not certain what he had seen.

"He's pointed that son of a bitch at *us!*" Sergeant Marquis whispered.

"Ssh! He's wearing eyeglasses. Maybe he can't see us," Staff Sergeant Moore replied.

"We'd better blast him while we can!" Marquis suggested.

"*No!* Don't fire!" Moore ordered. "We got a long way to go, yet. Don't shoot! We can't fire until Murf gives the signal. Keep low—keep moving!"

The squad of Rangers crouched lower in the ditch, hugged the right bank and continued. The tower sentry, apparently convinced he had seen nothing important, lowered his rifle.

Staff Sergeant David M. Hey's squad was one of the last of F Company. They took a position on the creek with their weapons aimed at the two northeast tower sentries—and waited.

As the rest of F Company continued along the creek bed, another squad was left at a point only twenty-five yards from the first enemy pillbox. They could see two, possibly three Japanese standing in the "box" next to a machine gun, which was pointed directly at the creek bed. The sentries seemed to be engaged in a casual conversation.

Farther along the fence, less than 150 yards from the stockade's southeast corner, Sergeant Joe Youngblood's squad was left for the second pillbox. Their assignment would be to destroy that machine gun nest, cut a hole in the camp's three fence rows for C Company's emergency escape route, and keep the enemy quarters in the stockade rear sections under fire.

Twenty-five-year-old PFC Bill Proudfit crawled up next to Sergeant Youngblood, set his M1 sights on the pillbox, and glanced around. They were on a small bank of earth that could permit a parallel range of fire to the enemy. Like himself, three other Rangers aimed their M1s and were silently joined by a man with a carbine, one with a BAR, and one with a Thompson submachine gun. With all of that firepower plus their grenades, Proudfit sensed a slight feeling of secure enthusiasm. They should easily pulverize the pillbox and rip apart the nipa barracks less than 100 yards away. PFC Proudfit turned to look at the southeast guard tower.

"You think it's really empty?" Proudfit whispered to Sergeant Youngblood.

"I don't see anyone up there, but we'll shoot it apart anyway," the sergeant replied. "I'm sure Murf and the boys back there have the same idea."

Youngblood attached a grenade launcher to the barrel of his M1, placed four rifle and four hand grenades in front of him, and waited.

At 1925 hours (7:25 P.M.), Lieutenant Murphy, with the remaining squads of F Company, reached positions at the rear of the camp. There, concealed by a ditch that ran along a seldom-used dirt road, the Rangers began to take aim at selected targets—a pillbox at the rear gate and the rear guard quarters inside the stockade. Lieutenant Murphy was concerned with that "empty" southeast guard tower. Murphy instructed one BAR man and three armed with M1s to prepare to "riddle it" with bullets.

Tech 5 Bernard Haynes, the medic assigned to accompany the men to the back of the camp, aimed his automatic carbine at the rear gate pillbox and began to mumble to himself, "I hope to hell this works . . . I hope to hell this works . . ."

Farther west, along the ditch, the last squad prepared for action. It would be their job to maintain the heaviest fire into the barracks at the rear of the camp. Staff Sergeant David Hey crawled through the ditch, checking the positions of his men.

"Dave, I can see the Japs in the barracks windows! See there?" Tech 5 Francis "Father" Schilli pointed his M1 in the direction of one nipa building.

"They're sitting in there in their underwear!" Corporal Roy Sweezy noted as he released the safety on his M1.

Tech 5 Patrick Marquis balanced his rifle on a bank of earth and reached back to open the flap of his pistol holster. It was then that he remembered he had given two .45s to the young Filipino guerrilla. He had only one left.

"Say, what's that!" Pat Marquis whispered to PFC Gerhard Tiede, "what's that sound?"

"I don't hear nothing," Tiede replied. "What kind of sound?"

"I'm not sure. It's . . ." Marquis began to chuckle before he finished his statement.

"What's so God damned funny at a time like this? I'm scared silly."

"Me too!" Marquis confessed. "That sound . . ."

"Yeah?" said Tiede.

"It's my teeth chattering!"

Though total darkness had now settled on the area, dim yellow lights were glowing in the barracks near the rear of the stockade. Occasionally, the red glow of a cigarette could be seen in the darkened buildings. All of the enemy soldiers in that rear area were relaxing, their voices and laughter cutting the still evening air.

1930 hours (7:30 P.M.). Lieutenant John Murphy's men were all in position and ready for the attack. All waited for Murphy to fire that first shot. But Lieutenant Murphy was cautious and uneasy. Pajota's men had assured him that the buildings outside the stockade, behind F Company's positions, were unoccupied. Murphy wanted to be sure of that. He also wanted to be certain that all his men were exactly where they were supposed to be. So he dispatched two men to quickly check on the outside buildings and PFC Peter P. Superak to retrace their approach route and check squad positions. John Murphy would allow fifteen more minutes before firing that first shot.

PFC Superak crawled cautiously around the southeast corner of the camp and began making his way toward the creek bed while his eyes shifted from the ground to the guard tower and back again. It was much too dark, now, to tell if anyone had climbed into the tower. Superak crawled another fifty yards and was beginning to wonder just what had become of the rest of F Company as he entered the creek bed. The gully was only a foot or so deep at this point and as he inched his way along something in front of him moved and his heart seemed to leap into his throat. In a second he was staring into the barrels of four rifles.

"Who is it?" someone whispered.

"Superak!"

"Damn! You scared the hell out of us, Pete! What are you doing sneaking around like that? What's holding up the works?"

"Murf."

"Why? It's past 7:30."

"Yeah," PFC Superak said. "Murf wants to be sure everyone is in position."

"Well—go back and tell the lieutenant everybody's ready but him!"

Superak turned to begin his return crawl to the rear of the camp.

Eight hundred yards southwest of the stockade, along the highway, PFC Thomas Grace and PFC Eugene Dykes of F Company contemplated an idea as they waited with the others in Captain Joson's roadblock formation. All of Joson's men were positioned in ditches on the north side of the highway. Staff Sergeant James White's bazooka team was on the south side, as were several other F Company Rangers. They had set up their roadblock in a "V" alignment with the open end toward Cabanatuan City, so that an approaching enemy could be sucked into a tighter wedge of fire. Everyone with Joson was ready.

What had Grace and Dykes's attention, though, was the row of twenty-foot-tall telephone poles and the sagging wires connecting them along the south side of the highway. PFC Grace stretched his arm and tried to hook one wire with the front sight of his rifle. He could not reach it. Then, jumping as high as possible, he tried again. The wire was still inches from the tip of his barrel. Disgusted with his fruitless effort, he turned to Dykes.

"You reckon anyone thought to cut these wires?" he asked.

"I'm sure Mucci wouldn't forget something like that," Dykes replied.

"Yeah—but suppose he didn't know these lines were here."

"Well—let's cut 'em."

Eugene Dykes set his rifle down and shinnied up the pole.

"Careful!" Grace warned. "They might not be phone lines. They may be hot!"

PFC Dykes produced a pair of wire cutters from his pocket, snipped the two lines, and dropped to the ground.

"Boy! It's really getting dark. The moon will be coming up in a few minutes. Wonder what's holding up the attack?" PFC Grace puzzled.

What Grace and Dykes did not know was that First Lieutenant Carlos Tombo had already cut the phone lines only 150 yards south of the stockade and Lieutenant Mendoza and Sergeant Matias had severed the lines 150 yards from the stockade's northeast corner, all along the highway. The Japanese in POW Camp Cabantuan had been isolated for eighteen minutes. Apparently, the enemy had not yet realized that they were without communication with both Cabanatuan City and Bongabon.

*T*ime: *1940 hours (7:40 P.M.)*. Captain Pajota was now standing calmly in the rice field about 200 yards northwest of the highway and 100 yards behind his Squadron 201A. Directly in front of him were Private Salayao and Lieutenant Abad. To his left stood Corporal Andasan. From this slightly elevated area the guerrilla commander could see past the positions of his men of Headquarters Company, to Cabu bridge.

Across the river, the Japanese had extinguished their campfires but their voices still echoed through the narrow river valley.

Pajota raised his fatigue cap and placed it farther back on his head. His men were now ready for their most important battle of the war. Pajota was content with the thought that, at long last, he would have that one great stand against the hated enemy of his people.

At the rear of the stockade PFC Peter Superak completed his dangerous assignment by reporting back to Lieutenant John Murphy. All the men of F Company were in correct positions, and waiting for the signal to begin the attack.

The minutes crept by, but still John Murphy did not fire the signal shot. He glanced at his watch—1944 hours (7:44 P.M.). There was a coincidence about that next minute. What difference would one more minute make? It was January 30, 1945—1945 hours was, indeed a special time.

At exactly 1945 hours, Lieutenant John Murphy raised his M1 rifle, aimed it at an open window in the nearest enemy barracks, and squeezed the trigger. In the next few seconds, complete pandemonium engulfed the area. The raid on Cabanatuan had begun.

* * *

At the same instant Lieutenant Murphy fired, volleys of rifle, BAR, carbine, and Tommygun fire erupted along the dirt road at the rear of the stockade. In a split second, the Japanese sentries in the pillbox at the rear gate were dead. Several men near the camp's southeast corner turned their weapons on the "empty" guard tower and cut loose with continual bursts.

"Give 'em hell, boys!" Sergeant Joe Youngblood yelled, and the Rangers with him along the stockade's east fence blasted away at the pillbox only thirty-six feet to their front. Then, they too turned their weapons to the "empty" tower.

The bamboo box at the top of the tower splintered into large pieces, which flew wildly into the air. It was a good thing F Company did not ignore the tower, for a lone enemy soldier, killed instantly in a hail of bullets, toppled head first and smashed to the ground with a heavy "thump." The tower had been occupied since late afternoon.

As Youngblood's squad concentrated their fire on the barracks inside the stockade, the sergeant jerked the safety pin free from a hand grenade and tossed it toward the pillbox. The moment the grenade left his hand, he pulled the pin on a second and tossed it at the same target. With a deafening noise, the first grenade exploded just in front of the pillbox. The second one landed inside the box and exploded with a muffled sound, ripping to pieces the bodies of its occupants. They had been killed in the first barrage of the Rangers' fire before returning a single shot.

Then Youngblood's squad held its fire as five men rushed the fences with wire cutters. A gaping hole some fifteen feet wide was quickly cut through all three fence rows. As the wire cutters rushed back to their gully, orange flashes developed at the windows of one large nipa barracks and bullets began to snap over the Rangers' heads and kicked up bits of dirt at their feet. The squad now trained their fire on that building, and in seconds the orange flashes ceased.

As the steady popping sounds from the M1 carbines, the cracking of M1 rifles, the booming of BARs, and the ear-shattering chatter of Tommyguns continued all along the stockade's east and rear fences, Sergeant Youngblood began to launch his rifle grenades. They exploded well inside the camp, tearing large sections from the walls of nipa barracks.

Farther up the creek bed, toward the highway, the other pillbox was destroyed in the same moment and manner as the first. Their occupants never had the opportunity to return a single shot. And at the northeast corner of the stockade, near the highway, Staff Sergeant David Hey and a smaller squad blasted away at the two silhouettes in their corner guard tower. One enemy soldier collapsed to the floor, the sentry with the eyeglasses spun completely around and draped over the rail, his rifle falling to the ground. The Rangers continued to fire into the tower and hunks of wood splintered away from its structure. Automatic weapons fire sliced into the limp form of the Japanese on the rail, ripping him apart at the middle. Both halves of the body finally fell from the tower.

Sergeant Hey's squad, their mission completed, moved toward the highway and headed for the front gate.

The moment F Company's first shots were heard by Captain Robert Prince, waiting in the ditch across from the front of the stockade, he raised his Very pistol and jerked the trigger. The flare went high into the evening sky and burst with a brilliant red glow, illuminating the area for several seconds. As Prince predicted, few Rangers even noticed the flare. Everyone had sprung into action when Lieutenant Murphy fired.

Staff Sergeant James V. Millican aimed his BAR at the enemy sentry standing in the waist-high pillbox at the front gate and squeezed the trigger. Through his sights, Millican could see the top half of the guard disintergrate. Practically every soldier in the ditch had joined the sergeant in firing on that lone Japanese. Millican then turned his automatic rifle on the guard shack, located just inside the gate, and began to fire rapid bursts through its wooden walls. At the same moment, other Rangers opened up with heavy fire directed into the main gate guard tower. Two Japanese soldiers toppled from the tower and fell to the highway near the gate.

Meanwhile, PFC Joseph Lombardo, with deadly accuracy, had

tossed a hand grenade across the highway. It sailed through the fence and into the open window of the guard shack. As it exploded, Lombardo pulled the pin on another grenade and threw it like a football directly into the cloud of smoke that was once the shack. Just following the second explosion, bits of wood and bamboo began to rain down upon the highway.

Less than thirty seconds had elapsed since F Company fired the first shots. All the guard towers, guard shacks, and pillboxes were now neutralized. C Company moved into action.

Staff Sergeant Theodore R. Richardson's job was to open the stockade's front entrance. While others were firing into the guard house and towers, Richardson, Tommygun in hand, charged across the highway and up to the main gate. Using the butt of the submachine gun, he began to frantically smash at the large padlock. In a few seconds, he realized his efforts would be unsuccessful. He drew his .45 automatic pistol and started to point it at the stubborn lock. Next, one of those strange "impossible" things that sometime occur in combat happened.

PFC Leland A. Provencher, carrying a BAR, was directly behind Sergeant Richardson when both Rangers saw a Japanese guard appear on the road inside the camp only thirty feet away. The enemy soldier had his rifle at his shoulder and fired. The bullet missed Richardson, but struck his pistol, knocking it from his hand. PFC Provencher cut loose with his BAR at the same instant Richardson fired his Tommygun from the left hip. The guard's arms flew up and he fell backward, killed instantly. Somehow, Richardson managed to quickly recover his pistol and fired one shot at the lock. It shattered with the impact of the .45 slug.

But before the two men could push the gate open, another figure appeared in the road near the body of the guard.

"What the hell is going on here!?" the man inside the camp called out in English.

For a moment, Richardson and Provencher held their fire, fearing the man might be a POW. Then the figure turned toward the nipa barracks and began to shout in Japanese. He had revealed his true identity. Both Rangers fired another burst from their automatic weapons. The man jerked backward as bullets tore through his body, and he crumpled to the ground.

In the ditch, just as Lieutenant Willian J. O'Connell was about to wave his first assault section into action, he heard the Ranger next to him exclaim with disgust, "Damn! My rifle's jammed." The lieutenant tossed the man his own M1 and pulled his .45 pistol from its holster. The gates were open.

"Now!" Lieutenant O'Connell shouted to Staff Sergeant Preston Jensen. The sergeant and his men sprang from the ditch and rushed for the open gate.

At the same moment, less than twenty-five yards to the right of Jensen's squad, Tech 4 Homer Britzius and the second assault section dashed across the highway and opened up with their covering fire as the first section entered the stockade. Behind the first section, the weapons section of the 1st Platoon prepared to start their charge into the camp. It was 1945:50 hours. The raid had been under way only fifty seconds.

Staff Sergeant Manton Stewart of C Company's weapons section craddled his bazooka under his right arm while the grasp of the left hand tightened on his M1 rifle. His thoughts raced to his little Baptist church in Texas, and he could feel the words come to his lips, "Trust in the Lord . . ."

Up from the ditch Stewart leaped, followed by other members of the weapons section.

"Trust in the Lord . . . 300 yards to go . . . go . . . *go!"*

Out of the corner of his eye he could see bodies of dead Japanese as he charged through the gate. "Stay to the right of the road," he mumbled to himself. Seconds ticked by. Everything depended on his section's bazookas destroying that corrugated metal tank shed before the enemy armor could move against them.

As the Rangers with Stewart entered the stockade, the second assault section at the highway fence lifted their fire, rapidly shifted to the left like the backfield of a football team, and charged in. Fifty yards inside the camp, Tech 4 Homer Britzius signaled for his second section to leave the road and move to the right. They had passed a large drainage pond and spread out to begin spraying the enemy officers' quarters with a continual hail of bullets.

"One hundred yards . . . 100 yards . . ." Manton Stewart, running up the center road, repeated to himself, "200 to go . . . 200 to go! Got to get those tanks!"

Bullets were ricocheting and pinging all around the weapons section as they continued their charge up the camp's center road. Now they could see the orange and red flashes from F Company shooting from outside the fences. Stewart's section was racing time through a crossfire from their own men and the Japanese!

"Two hundred yards!" Stewart puffed, "100 to go . . . 100 to go . . . 250 . . . 250 . . . almost there . . . 50 more to go . . . Lord . . . Lord!" Everywhere was the noise of battle, rifles cracking, BARs pounding, and the burping bark of Tommyguns. But at the moment, the sounds seemed far away, as if he were running desperately in a dream.

"Twenty-five yards to go!" Suddenly, there on his right he could see the metal buildings—the corrugated iron sheds. Less than two minutes had elapsed since the weapons section left the highway. Sergeant Stewart's heart was pounding. He gasped for breath as he dropped to one knee and raised the five-foot bazooka tube to his shoulder. Men were behind him and beside him, firing in several directions, yet his thoughts fixed only on his target. He could feel his legs trembling, not from fear, but from the exhausting dash.

Now he had the first shed in the sights of his bazooka, and he blinked his eyes to clear them of the small rivers of perspiration that flooded from his forehead. The sheds seemed only in outline form. He could not see them clearly, but he knew they must be the target. He was certain he had run 300 yards, and they were the only metal buildings in the area.

Then the sergeant had his confirmation. Two large trucks loaded with Japanese soldiers were preparing to pull away from the sheds. But where were the tanks? They must be in the shed, he thought. Aim for the shed, his brain commanded.

"Range . . . fifty yards! *Ready!*" Sergeant Stewart shouted.

The Ranger behind him shoved the first rocket into the bazooka tube and slapped Stewart on the shoulder. *"Ready!"* the loader replied.

Stewart squeezed the trigger and a bright flame burst from both ends of the tube as the rocket sped toward the target. In less than two seconds, the rocket penetrated the thin metal wall of the building and a tremendous explosion shook the area. The first blast was followed by a secondary explosion, and hunks of metal began to rain to the ground with funny clanking sounds. Stewart's first rocket had hit some type of vehicle inside the shed.

He felt the slap on his shoulder again, turned the bazooka to the next shed, and fired. In a second, the building erupted with a blinding flash. Now, one of the enemy trucks was on fire. The Japanese were spilling out of the vehicles, flames from burning gasoline leaping from some figures as they dove earthward. Other Japanese, escaping the inferno, but illuminated by the holocaust, fell before they could run a few yards. The deadly marksmanship of the Rangers was exterminating most of the Kinpeidan headquarters unit before they could fire a shot.

Sergeant Manton Stewart had the second truck in his sights when he felt the slap on his shoulder again. For a third time, he squeezed the bazooka's trigger. The front half of the truck disintergrated in the rocket's blast.

The sheds, and whatever they contained, were nothing but a smoldering mass of twisted metal. Both trucks, likewise, were an indistinguishable pile of junk, surrounded by dead or dying imperial soldiers of Kinpeidan unit.

Only thirty seconds had elapsed between the first and third rocket blasts. The weapons section had accomplished their mission in less than four minutes from the start of the raid.

Manton Stewart set aside his bazooka, raised his M1 rifle, and began to fire at anything that moved in front of him.

At Cabu bridge, a mile northeast of the stockade, all hell had broken loose the moment Captain Juan Pajota and his guerrillas heard the first shots fired by F Company.

Along the southwest bank of the Cabu, Pajota's squadrons opened fire with a continual barrage directed at the Japanese bivouac area less than 300 yards away. Pajota had succeeded in gaining the element of complete surprise his forces needed.

At the same moment the firing began, a tremendous explosion erupted with a cloud of dust and smoke at the north end of the bridge. The "time bomb" had been detonated. In seconds a light breeze carried the cloud away and the guerrillas nearest the bridge then noticed that something had gone wrong. Only the northern one-fourth of the bridge was destroyed by the explosion. The remaining seventy-five feet on the Filipinos' side was still very much intact. In a minute a runner from Squadron 204 brought the distressing news to Pajota. The guerrilla commander smiled. "Tell Lieutenant Erive to aim his weapons just above the damaged area! The Japs will still charge the bridge from the highway. Tell him not to worry. It is now impossible for the tanks to cross the bridge!" Pajota instructed.

Pajota's eyes narrowed and his smile spread across his face. A smell that excited him had reached his nose—the odor of burning gunpowder.

Suddenly, above the constant chatter of Pajota's four machine guns and the staccato cracking of hundreds of rifles, the shouts of the Japanese could be heard. They were now organizing and returning fire. Four minutes into the battle, the first squad of imperial soldiers emerged from the woods, formed on the highway, and started for the bridge at a fast trot. It was not until they reached the riverbank that they realized the north bridge section was gone. Nothing but a gaping hole filled with broken timbers awaited them, and a hail of bullets from the guerrillas. *"Banzai . . . Banzai!"* the Japanese shouted as they attempted to leap across the hole. Then they were silent. All had been killed.

But in less than a minute, a second squad appeared in the road, and with screams of *"Banzai,"* they charged the bridge. Before they reached the hole, all were dead. It seemed as if the murderous fire from Pajota's squadron might not discourage the Japanese. Behind the second squad, another appeared, and, behind them, yet another. All met the same fate. None succeeded in crossing the destroyed section of the bridge.

Now, screams and shouts from the Japanese developed all along their side of the river. The Filipinos answered by remaining silent and turning their weapons in the direction of their noisy enemy. At the bridge, shouts of *"Banzai"* always began somewhere up the highway and became louder and louder as squads of Oyabu's Dokuho 359 Battalion reached the river. Bodies of Japanese soldiers, falling to ferocious gunfire, began to stack up as they fell upon one another at the bridge. The battle had become a slaughter. In the first bloody minutes, Pajota's men had not used one hand grenade or suffered a single casualty. "Everyone was too busy firing at the Japanese to even think of using grenades."

For some reason, Imperial Army Commander Oyabu had not yet ordered his precious tanks into action. Perhaps he was waiting to learn the true strength of his enemy across the river and their positions. Perhaps he had no intention of wasting them by chancing an approach to a bridge that they no longer could cross. In any case, by the fifth minute of the battle, the tanks still remained concealed in a mango grove less than 300 yards up the highway. But a truck loaded with sixteen troops and a mounted machine gun did pull onto the highway, turned, and started for the bridge. Twenty-five yards short of the bridge a blinding explosion completely demolished the truck, and it burst into flames. The first bazooka rocket fired by Pajota's Headquarters Company had found its mark. The few imperial soldiers who survived the blast leaped clear of the burning wreckage, but were quickly liquidated by guerrilla small-arms fire.

Now, Pajota's bazooka squad aimed their weapon at the tanks, which were clearly visible in the light from the burning truck. A second and a third rocket sped toward the mango grove, and the entire area erupted in an orange fireball. At least two of the tanks were out of action before firing a shot. Squadrons 201A and 204, on the right flank of Pajota's line of defense, raised the elevation of their automatic weapons and began to rake the illuminated mango grove with heavy fire.

At POW Camp Cabanatuan the raid was now into its fourth minute. F Company continued to fire through the east and south fences, receiving only scattered light return fire from the Japanese.

The 1st Platoon of C Company, first and second assault sections and the weapons section, had their enemy pinned down in the stockades right front area. Three Ranger squads were already directing fire toward the rear of the camp, trapping the Japanese in that area in a deadly crossfire with F Company.

The Rangers had achieved complete surprise with their assault and, thus far, the Japanese had been unable to establish any organized resistance whatsoever. By the end of the fourth minute, there were no American casualties.

PFC Leland Provencher reached for his ammo pouch and then slammed another magazine into the BAR. Just as he raised the weapon to fire into a small shed in front of him, the door to the building flew open and a voice called from inside, "Don't shoot! Don't shoot—I'm an American!"

"What the hell you doing on this side of the camp?" Provencher shouted. "I thought all you fellows were on the other side!"

A frail figure shuffled up to PFC Provencher. "I had a premonition," the POW panted, "that something was going to happen tonight. I'm a generator operator. I got permission to go to that generator shed . . . pretended to work on the equipment. Look at this old magazine I was reading!" The POW held up the tattered pages of a *Life* magazine. There was a bullet hole clean through it. "Just missed me a moment ago!" he added.

Provencher nodded. "Head for the main gate! *Quick!*"

The first Allied POW had been liberated.

C Company's 2nd Platoon, led by Lieutenant Melville Schmidt, had moved into action with its second assault section rushing up the camp's center road. This section, with Staff Sergeant William Butler leading the way, joined the Rangers of the 1st Platoon by aiming their fire at both the rear and right (southwest) side of the stockade.

The first assault section of the 2nd Platoon, led by Staff Sergeant Clifton Harris, dashed up the camp road, then turned to break into the POW compound area.

Staff Sergeant "Twister" Malone was the first to reach the gate to the POW area. *"Ya who!"* he yelled as he placed the barrel of his M1 against the lock and pulled the trigger. The padlock shattered with the impact of the .30-caliber bullet, and the big cowboy shoved the gate open.

The moon was up now, bathing the area in a bright glow. A few yards inside, Twister encouraged his first POW. A skeleton of a man stood in the moonlight, his mouth wide open, his sunken eyes staring at Twister.

"It's okay . . . we're Yanks! Get the hell out of here!" Sergeant Twister Malone barked at the POW.

"I can't leave yet," the bewildered man replied, "I've got records hidden. I must take them with me."

"No time! Come on—assemble at the main gate."

Behind Twister, the rest of the 2nd Platoon's first assault section charged into the POW compound.

Ward medic PFC Eugene Evers was sitting on his bamboo bunk, inside the POW camp barracks, listening to his old phonograph records, when he heard the first shots fired by F Company. His immediate thought was that the Japanese had begun to execute his fellow POWs. Evers dove, head first, for the floor.

As the battle continued to rage, the concussion from exploding grenades caused the phonograph needle to jump and skip about the record. Evers had no intention of moving to attempt to stop the machine. Then the form of a big man, carrying a strange-looking weapon, appeared in the open doorway of the barracks. PFC Evers and the other POWs huddled around him let out a gasp. They were sure they had but seconds to live.

"Take it easy, fellows! The Yanks are here!" the big man assured. "Assemble at the main gate . . . you're going home!"

"My God!" Evers exclaimed, "you're not in khaki! We thought you were a Jap. What's that you're carrying?"

"It's a Tommygun—we're Rangers!"

"A what? You're *what?*"

Suddenly, several bullets zinged through the nipa wall just inches from the man in the doorway. The Ranger turned and, from a half crouch, fired a rapid burst across the camp road. "Come on! Let's get out of here!"

Still trying to recover from their shock and confusion, Eugene Evers and his roommates followed the Ranger out of the compound and on to the center road for the main gate. In their empty barracks, the phonograph needle became stuck in a final record groove, and it turned with a whining sound until the spring mechanism finally became unwound.

In the nipa barracks next to the one occupied by PFC Evers, four American POWs fell to their knees and began praying the moment the shooting started. They, too, were sure the Japanese had begun a mass execution. Above the sounds of battle they could hear the shouts from men dashing about the compound.

"Did you fellows hear that?" one of the POWs whispered. "Someone out there said, 'God damn son of a bitch'!"

"God forgive him," another POW answered as he crossed himself with a trembling hand.

"NO . . . *no!* That's English . . . that's English! Those must be Americans out there, not Japs! Those are our boys!"

Before any of the four POWs could say another word two big men leaped in the open door. One was carrying a BAR, the other an M1.

"Come on, fellows—you're free! Assemble at the main gate!" one of the Rangers shouted.

"Hello, Yank, glad to see ya!" a POW responded. "Where's your helmets?"

"Left them at home, Pop! They're too heavy."

Only seconds before F Company started the raid, Sergeant Abie Abraham and his Navy buddy "Bill" were still sitting on the wooden steps to their barracks in the compound exchanging wild stories of bygone days.

"Well," Sergeant Abraham said, "looks like we lived another day—" The first sounds of F Company's shots abruptly cut their conversation.

"The Japs!" Bill shouted, "Oh, my God! They're coming to kill us! Hide . . . quick!" He scampered into his hut and joined other POWs who were already hugging the floor.

Sergeant Abraham stood up. The entire stockade seemed to have erupted in rifle and automatic weapons fire.

"Not me!" the sergeant shouted, "not after all this. I won't die on my knees!"

Abraham fell to the ground, crawled under the barracks and dug into the sort dirt with his hands until he found a club he had carved from narra wood and hidden months ago. He then scampered back to the steps and entered his barracks with only one thought on his mind. He would strike and kill the first Japanese soldier who came through the open door. He would take one of the enemy with him when his time came to die.

"Please don't kill me!" Bill pleaded as Sergeant Abraham entered.

"It's me . . . Abie! Your pal, Abie. Take it easy."

It was then that the voices of Rangers caught Abraham's ear and he turned to see a man with a Tommygun racing toward his barracks.

"We're Americans!" the Ranger was shouting. "Tell everyone to assemble at the main gate!" The Ranger reached the foot of the steps. "Can you walk, Mac?" he asked Abraham.

Sergeant Abie Abraham felt the tears begin to flood his eyes. "Yes. I can walk. You'd better give those other boys a hand. They're real sick. I walked out of Bataan. I reckon I can walk out of this place," he choked.

Lieutenant Merle McNeal Musselman, M.D., and his friend were still engaged in their conversation about the stars while sitting on the camp dispensary steps when the raid began.

Lieutenant Musselman leaped to his feet. Like most of the others, his first thought was that the Japanese had begun a systematic execution of POWs. Then his thoughts were on his patients in the surgical ward a good 200 yards away. He ran as fast as he could to the surgical hut and climbed in. All the beds were empty. A chill ran though his entire body. How could over 100 bed patients disappear so fast? He turned, jumped to the ground, and headed toward the front of the compound.

Bullets were whizzing everywhere. It was now obvious to the doctor that something more than an execution was under way . . . but what? He had covered fifty yards. Suddenly, he was confronted by two large men in strange, muddy green uniforms. One man shoved a rifle barrel into Musselman's stomach.

"Who are *you*?" the man with the rifle demanded.

"I'm Dr. Musselman! Who are you fellows?"

"We're Rangers—"

"What?"

"Rangers! Yanks! Come on—we got this place, pal!"

POW Colonel James Duckworth, M.D., was in a deep sleep when the raid began. Even the explosions and weapons fire did not wake him. But when the first Ranger burst into the hut, the colonel sat up quickly.

"Assemble at the main gate!" the Ranger yelled into the dark room.

"Don't anyone move until I find out what's going on here!" Duckworth ordered.

"Who are you?" the startled Ranger asked.

"I'm *Colonel* Duckworth!"

"Well—Colonel, get your ass out of here! I'll apologize to-morrow!"

POW Edwin Rose was asleep in his barracks when the first shots were fired. The years of confinement at Cabanatuan had all but finished the life of this sixty-year-old Englishman. Weakened by beriberi, dysentery, and malnutrition, eyesight failing, Rose was nothing but a shell of a man. His sense of hearing was prac- tically nonexistent, but as the battle reached a crescendo, he swung from his bamboo bunk and stared into the face of one of his buddies.

"What is that noise?" Rose asked. "I thought I heard shots."

"My God, man," his friend replied, "they are coming to kill us!"

"Who?"

"The bloody Japs! They are shooting up the place."

Rose shuffled toward the open door of the nipa hut.

"Where are your going, Rose?"

"To the latrine . . . dysentery, you know."

"At this time? We'll bloody well be dead in a minute and you're going to the latrine!"

"Ah, what?"

"Dammit, Rose, they are going to kill us!" his friend screamed.

"Then . . . I am going to die comfortable. The Japs must wait until I am done, or kill me there! Cheerio!"

Edwin Rose hobbled down the wooden step, turned and dis- appeared into the night. In just a few moments his friends in the hut heard the voices of Rangers.

"All Americans—head for the main gate!"

The POWs shouted back, "We're not Americans—but we're coming too! *Rose! Rose!* Dammit, Rose . . . come back! The Yanks are here!"

Edwin Rose did not answer.

*T*ime: *1954 hours—nine minutes into the raid.* At the rear of the camp and along the east fences, the men of F Company contin- ued to fire into the Japanese quarters. The enemy's return fire, which had remained light from the beginning, now began to dwindle. Staff Sergeant David Hey's squad had completed their withdrawal to the highway and started circling to the front of the camp to assist with the evacuation of the POWs.

Inside the POW compound area the men of C Company's 2nd Platoon were well under way with the organizing of bewildered, frightened, and sick prisoners for the escape.

Corporal Marvin "Pop" Kinder had one POW by the arm, attemping to help him to the camp's center road. The man pulled back.

"What's wrong?" Kinder asked.

"I've got to get my papers!"

"No time," Kinder replied. "We got to keep moving."

"You don't understand," the POW insisted. "A man ate my cat—an officer's cat! I court-martialed him for that. She was a beautiful cat . . ." The POW began to cry, and Corporal Kinder gently picked him up to carry him toward the gate.

Corporal James Herrick slung his M1 over his shoulder and leaned forward to speak to the POW lying on the bamboo bunk.

"Come on trooper, we got to go now," Herrick spoke softly to the man. "I'll carry you. I've got a Bible. You can read it on the way home—but we got to get out while we can!"

"No . . . I'm going to die," the POW replied between short breaths. "Leave me . . . help the others! I'm going to die anyway. Save yourself!"

Corporal Herrick picked up the man by placing him on his back, grasping the POW's arms in front of his chest, piggyback style. They moved out into the compound yard and through the gate to the center road. About halfway to the main gate, the POW suddenly gasped and became limp. Herrick at first feared the man had been hit by a stray bullet, and quickly but gently sat him on the ground next to a fence post. The Ranger checked the man's pulse. There was no beat. The POW was dead, apparently from a heart attack—fifty feet short of the front gate and freedom.

1955 hours. The raid had been under way ten minutes and PFC Rufo Vaquilar waited impatiently with the other Alamo Scouts in the ditch across from the front gate for the first POWs. With the Scouts were several Filipino guerrillas, the combat photo men, a few medics, and the "reserve" weapons section of C Company.

The full moon, crossed occasionally by high clouds, continued to bathe the stockade with its bright glow. Far down the camp's center road the first POWs, accompanied by a few Rangers, were finally visible to the men waiting in the ditch. Rufo Vaquilar could wait no longer. Drawing both .45s from his belt, he leaped to the road and dashed through the open gateway. Three hundred yards to his front, the first and second assault sections with the bazooka weapons section were still firing on the Japanese in the rear area. He would go join them and help with the POW evacuation later.

At a full run, 150 yards into the stockade, Vaquilar began to pass the silent buildings on his right that once housed the enemy officers. Rufo Vaquilar stopped and turned to face one large nipa structure. From the corner of his eye he had caught a glimpse of something moving in its doorway. A Japanese soldier, his face dripping with blood from a head wound, staggered onto the wooden porch and started to raise his rifle. He pointed it directly at the Alamo Scout.

"Mabuhay!" PFC Vaquilar yelled, and he fired both pistols simultaneously. The recoil of the big hand guns jerked the small Filipino's arms to his nose. Two .45-caliber slugs slammed into the chest of the enemy guard, sending him sprawling off the porch. Rufo Vaquilar then turned to assist the Rangers with the POWs.

1957 hours. Twelve minutes into the raid and still there were no battle casualties among the Americans. POWs, some walking, some being carried by Rangers, were now emerging from the stockade as free men.

Sergeant John Nelson, to this point in time, had succeeded in maintaining a watchful eye on his friend and battalion surgeon, Captain Jimmy Fisher. But the excitement and desire to join in the evacuation was too much for Fisher.

"Hold on, Jimmy! Stay down for a while until they cross the highway," Sergeant Nelson cautioned.

"Let's spread out," Captain Fisher replied. "Move off to my left a little."

Sergeant Nelson reluctantly obeyed and began to jog northeast along the highway until he reached a point about fifty yards from Fisher.

Suddenly, a blinding explosion erupted in the center of the

highway near the front gate. Three seconds later another explosion occurred a few yards from the first—and then a third blast some thirty feet from the second left a small round hole in the road.

"Man down! Man down." Shouts sprang up along the ditch and highway. Several men were caught by the explosions and had collapsed.

"Medic! Over here . . . *man down!*"

Somehow, within the far southwest corner of the stockade, at least one Japanese soldier had escaped the murderous fire of the Rangers and made it to a shallow zig-zag trench. From there a light mortar had been quickly set up and three rounds were fired with pinpoint accuracy toward the front gate, almost 600 yards away. In the process, the enemy's effort was cut short. The distinctive dull "thump" sound of the mortar rounds leaving their launch tubes attracted the attention of the Rangers outside the rear fence. Every member of F Company's squad with Tech 5 Francis "Father" Schilli and Corporal Roy Sweezy turned their weapons in the direction of the mortar's sound and began firing. The mortar fell silent, but its first three rounds had been extremely effective.

On the highway, at the front of the stockade, the good fortune of the Allies had run out. Alamo Scout Alfred "Opu" Alfonso lay near the edge of the road, bleeding profusely from a shell fragment wound in his groin. Corporal Marvin "Pop" Kinder had just turned a POW over to a Filipino and started to go back into the camp for another when the mortars exploded. Kinder was knocked sideways from the concussion but not hit. As he struggled to regain his senses, he noticed Staff Sergeant David Hey reaching for his back.

"What's wrong with you?" Kinder shouted.

"Pop! I think I'm hit. Look at my back! Touch it . . . it's wet!" Hey replied.

Staff Sergeant Hey's back had been pierced by several flakes of road gravel kicked up by the blast, but his wounds were minor.

Corporal Martin T. Estesen had been hit by a small shell fragment. But Estesen was a medic. He ignored his own wound and rushed to administer a shot of morphine to Private Alfonso and bandage the Scout.

Alamo Scout Lieutenants Tom Rounsaville and Bill Nellist were on the highway when one of the mortar shells exploded behind them. Nellist miraculously was unhurt but he saw Rounsaville crumple forward, then rise to his knees.

"Where are you hit?" Lieutenant Nellist yelled as he reached Rounsaville's side.

"In the butt! I'm bleeding." Lieutenant Rounsaville had received a small fragment wound in his buttock.

"Lie down . . . lie down!" Nellist commanded. Bill Nellist quickly drew his large trench knife and sliced a bloody rip in the seat of Rounsaville's fatigue trousers. "I can see a hunk of shrapnel sticking out," Nellist said.

"What the hell are you doing?" Rounsaville barked.

"I'm going to cut it out!"

"Not with *that* God damned knife, you're not!"

"Hold still, Tom! Dammit, hold still!"

Lieutenant Nellist pulled a pair of small wire cutters from his pocket and grasped the protruding metal fragment with the tool. With a quick jerk, he had the fragment removed.

"*Ouch!* Damn you, Nellist," Tom Rounsaville screamed.

"It's all over with, pal—I think you're gonna live. When we get back they can pin the Purple Heart on your ass!"

First Sergeant Charles Bosard shoved his way through the crowd of men on the highway. Most of the wounded were already being carried into the field toward the Pampanga River. Bosard felt a man grab his arm and turned to see Captain Bob Prince.

"You okay?" the captain asked.

"Yes, sir!"

"How many did we lose?" Prince was calm, but the expression of concern on his dusty, sweat-lined face was clearly visible in the moonlight.

"Five or six wounded . . . none killed," Bosard reported.

Sergeant Bosard started to enter the ditch, then froze momentarily. A Ranger was lying on his back in the ditch, with bloody hands clasped at his abdomen.

"Man down . . . here!" Bosard shouted. "Medic . . . medic! Man down!"

Charles Bosard turned to the wounded Ranger. "Where are you hit?" he asked.

"Stomach!" came a weak reply.

Three more Rangers rushed up to Bosard.

"Find Captain Fisher . . . *quick!* This man is hit bad!" Bosard yelled at the figures beside him.

The wounded man raised one hand. "This *is* Captain Fisher!" he managed to say.

"Jimmy! My God! . . . What kind of medicine can we give you?" Sergeant Bosard asked as he dropped to his knees, next to the doctor.

"None! There's no medicine . . . for this wound."

Captain James Fisher had just started onto the highway and was heading for the gate to assist the POWs when one of the mortar rounds exploded in front of him. The concussion had lifted the battalion surgeon into the air and slammed him back into the ditch. A large hunk of the mortar shell had penetrated deep into his stomach area. James Fisher, of course, knew his wound was critical.

Sergeant Bosard gave the doctor a shot of morphine, and, together with PFC Leroy Myerhoff and two Filipinos, carried him two miles to the bank of the Pampanga.

"Stay with him!" Bosard ordered the others when they finally reached the river. "No matter what happens . . . stay with him and get him to Platero!" Bosard turned and started back to the stockade.

Time: 2000 hours (8:00 P.M.). The men at Captain Joson's roadblock continued to glance back up the highway toward the stockade. For fifteen minutes the sounds of the battle at the camp, accompanied by flashes from grenade and rocket explosions, had frustrated the roadblock troops. They wanted desperately to be in that battle.

"I guess if the Nips are coming from Cabanatuan City they should be on this road soon. They must have heard all the shooting by now," PFC Eugene Dykes said.

The brilliant full moon illuminated the highway and the men could see almost a mile in all directions. Suddenly, PFC Thomas Grace pointed his M1 south at Cabanatuan City and began to shout, "Come on you sons of bitches . . . *come on!* We're ready for ya!"

"Are you kidding?" Dykes laughed. "There are over 7,000 Japs in that city! If they come up this road all at once, they'll run right over us! We'd better pray they decide to stay home!"

The roadblock troops waited and wondered—when would the Japanese rush out of the city to reinforce their comrades?

2005 hours (8:05 P.M.). Approximately twelve miles west of Cabanatuan City, above the Rizal Road, a P61 Black Widow from the 547th Night Fighter Squadron turned slowly at 5,000 feet. The pilot began to lower his altitude for a pass along the highway so his radar observer could verify what he thought his equipment told him was moving below.

The RO spoke into the fighter's intercom. "I was right! Sure as hell . . . looks like six trucks . . . no, could be five trucks and a tank."

"Roger," the pilot answered. "Cannon magazines ready!"

The early fears of Imperial Army Command Naotake at Cabanatuan City had just materialized. Their Inoue Battalion, which evacuated San Jose to return to the capital city's defense, had been spotted by the Black Widow's crew.

The RO scanned the moonlit sky in all directions for enemy planes. "No bandits anywhere!" he reported. "You're safe . . . all clear for the approach. Ready . . . left a little! Okay . . . hold her steady! Might as well follow the road . . . steady . . . steady . . ."

The big plane dropped lower and lower. The pilot now had the opportunity to try his "night binoculars," which were mounted on a track above his head and slightly to the left. This recent technological development gave him a visual range five times that which the human eye could see. And, with its optical gun sight, accurate cannon fire was assured. The pilot swung the binoculars into position in front of his face and locked them in place with one hand. He began to align the dots in the instrument with the vehicles below him on the highway.

"Contact! I've got my eyes on them now! You're right . . . trucks and a tank! Stand by . . . we're closing in . . . closer now . . ."

The Black Widow leveled in flight at 500 feet above the highway, her big engines roaring at full throttle. The pilot's hand moved slowly to the twin gun button switches on his control wheel. Then, before the Japanese convoy even saw the fighter, devastating fire from the four 20-mm cannons converged on the vehicles. Immediately, three trucks exploded in flames. The P61 passed over the inferno, banked, and turned for another pass.

"We missed a few. The tank's still moving!" the RO called.

"We'll get 'em this time!" the pilot assured.

The pilot did not need his binoculars in the second pass, for the burning enemy trucks had illuminated the countryside. Again, cannon shells raked the highway, ripping flesh and metal into tangled fragments. Dark smoke billowed from the engine of the tank, and flames now leaped from all the vehicles.

"We'll make one more pass . . . just to be sure," the pilot of the Black Widow announced. "Let's see if we can get some of the infantry!"

The Japanese convoy would never reach Cabanatuan City. The Inoue Battalion had ceased to exist. Now, Naotake could only hope that the Oyabu Dokuho 359 Battalion would arrive from the Cabu River before dawn, as planned. Naotake and the Imperial Command at Cabanatuan City did not know that their expected Dokuho 359 Battalion was rapidly being liquidated at Cabu bridge. With communication lines down, Naotake did not even know that their prisoner of war camp, four miles away at Barrio Pangatian, was under attack. The men with Captain Joson at the roadblock had nothing to worry about. There would be no Japanese reinforcements charging up the highway to challenge them.

*T*ime: *2008 hours (8:08 P.M.).* Twenty-three minutes into the raid, at Cabu bridge, the slaughter of Dokuho 359 continued. No more Japanese squads rushed at the damaged bridge. Now, they only trotted down to the remains of their truck and attempted to return fire at the guerrillas. As fast as one squad was annihilated, another appeared in the highway.

But Captain Pajota had detected something even more reassuring. His enemy seemed to be in a state of total confusion. Not only could the guerrillas hear the shouts of *"Banzai"* from the charging squads along the highway, they could also hear considerable shouting and yelling amongst the Japanese all up and down the river. There was one logical conclusion to draw. Most, or all, of the enemy officers must be dead. The remaining members of Dokuho 359 were in a state of chaos.

Captain Pajota sent Lieutenant Abad forward to check their ammunition supply and casualty count. In a few minutes, Abad returned, his face beaming with excitement.

"Sir," the lieutenant reported, "many Japs dead on the highway at the bridge. Their bodies are three deep!"

Suddenly, two mortar rounds exploded in the field a good hundred yards behind Pajota. He did not turn, but continued to stare at the battle scene on the other side of the bridge. Several more mortar rounds exploded safely behind him.

"And . . . our casualties. How many?" Pajota asked.

"None, sir!"

"None?" Pajota's lips parted in a slight smile.

"None, sir!" Abad repeated.

"And wounded . . . how many serious?"

"None, sir! Only some scratches."

"Our ammunition?"

"The men have plenty, sir!"

Juan Pajota's eyes shifted from the dead and dying Japanese at the truck to the mango grove where one tank was still burning. Could all the tanks be destroyed? Why were they not turning their cannons on his men? These questions raced through the mind of the guerrilla commander with haunting rapidity. Apparently, either the tanks were destroyed or in such damaged condition that they could not be turned to fire across the river. All the tanks had been facing the highway and not the bridge when the attack began. If they were damaged, then the cannons and machine guns were pointing in the wrong direction, completely useless against the Filipinos.

Lieutenant Abad stared into Pajota's calm face and asked, "How long will the Jap commander permit his men to die this way?"

"They are only human," Pajota replied. "But they will keep coming. They know no other way. They believe death is where eternal life begins."

"The same with we Christians, isn't it?"

"The same," Pajota acknowledged, his eyes still fixed on the battle.

"Then . . . *Mabuhay!*" Abad shouted.

Pajota smiled and nodded. "Mabuhay!"

By 2008 hours the Rangers at the stockade had evacuated more than three-fourths of the some 500 POWs.

Sergeant Joe Youngblood's squad had withdrawn from their position on the knoll across from the silent pillbox and were now at the highway, helping with the evacuation. The only men of F Company firing were those at the far southeast corner and along the dirt road at the rear of the camp. They were still receiving only light, scattered fire from the few Japanese alive inside the wire fences.

Most of the POWs had to be carried the two miles through the rice fields and high grass to the Pampanga. There at the river, waiting carabao carts were filled with human cargo for movement to Platero.

Staff Sergeant August Stern, his BAR slung over his shoulder, was carrying one POW piggyback from the highway. He had traveled only a few yards through the muddy terrain when the odor from the area revealed his location. He was wading through the camp's sewage drainage ditch. Stern tripped and toppled forward to his knees in the slime but managed to balance his POW without dropping him. The sergeant staggered to his feet, a flood of profanity pouring from his lips.

"Son," the man on his back said, "I'm Chaplain Kennedy! I'm a Catholic priest!"

"I'm sorry, Father," Sergeant Stern replied.

"That's okay . . . I understand. There's a time and place for everything. I guess this is it!"

At the Pampanga River, most of the loaded carabao carts had crossed to the opposite bank. The remaining POWs must be carried across and placed in empty carts returning from Platero. But many of the Rangers approaching the Pampanga without Filipino guides found themselves wading in knee- to waist-deep, fast-moving water. They had missed the sandbar area, used earlier, by over 100 yards.

Corporal James B. Herrick and PFC Melvin P. Shearer removed

their fatigue jackets and buttoned them over their MI rifles, quickly improvising a stretcher.

"What are you doing?" the POW with them asked. "Why don't you leave me? I can make it now!"

"We're making a stretcher. We're going to carry you across," Herrick replied.

"Boy! You fellows sure are tough!"

"Na," Shearer said, "we ain't tough—just tired, that's all."

*T*ime: *2015 hours (8:15 P.M.).* Thirty minutes into the raid. Thus far, the Americans had suffered no deaths from the battle at the POW camp. Captain Bob Prince completed his second search of the POW compound area of the stockade, convincing himself that all Allied prisoners had been safely evacuated. Prince removed another flare from a canvas pouch, loaded his Very pistol and fired it into the air. The flare burst and burned for several seconds with a brilliant red glow as it floated to the ground. This was the signal for all the Rangers to withdraw from the camp and head for the Pampanga. All the POWs were safely on their way to Platero. But unknown to Lieutenant Colonel Mucci, Captain Prince, or anyone else, there was still one POW somewhere in the camp. Prince had searched the barracks but not, of course, every shadow of the compound.

Various Rangers and Alamo Scouts were to recall that during the entire raid Captain Robert Prince had performed with the cool precision of a well-oiled machine like a "perfect leader." Yet in these final minutes a matter of great concern ate at the young captain. One squad of F Company, at the far rear of the camp, had not returned to the highway. Captain Prince and at least twenty-five other Rangers would wait for them.

At the roadblock, 800 yards southwest of the stockade, the Rangers of F Company's weapons section and Captain Joson's men saw the red flare signal. A few of the Filipinos under Joson were released to return to Platero. Others were assigned to cross the rice fields to the fording area at the Pampanga to assist with any remaining POWs and carabao carts there. The Americans moved up the highway and joined their comrades who were in the final rescue phase near the front gate. The remainder of Joson's command was to stay in position until the second flare was fired.

One mile northeast of the stockade at Cabu bridge, Captain Juan Pajota's men were still heavily engaged with Japanese Battalion Dokuho 359, or rather, what was left of the unit. For thirty-one minutes the Japanese showed no sign of giving up with their suicidal efforts to cross the Cabu.

Private Sulayao, standing near Pajota, pointed to the southern sky. Captain Pajota turned, glancing for a moment at the red flare signal, and then the battle captured his attention again. That first flare made little difference to his squadron's situation. They were to hold until Captain Prince fired the second flare, indicating that all the Rangers and POWs were safely across the Pampanga.

Off to the left Pajota noticed his men of Squadron 211 and 201 suddenly shift their fire to an area across the river near the point where the Cabu intersects the Pampanga. There, twelve Japanese soldiers, clearly visible in the bright moonlight, were dashing from the Pampanga bank toward the Cabu, apparently attempting a flank attack.

The guerrillas' machine guns began a constant chatter and rifles cracked in heavy volleys. Four of the enemy dropped twenty-five yards short of the riverbank, the others charged on through a hail of bullets. Five more toppled over like toy soldiers, their screams masked by the sounds of automatic weapons fire. The last three almost reached the river before they fell.

Captain Pajota's squadrons, to this point, had not suffered one fatal casualty.

The last squad of Lieutenant John Murphy's F Company, which was still at the rear of the stockade, saw Captain Prince's flare and began to withdraw. First, they moved slowly east along the rear fence rows, then turned the corner to proceed some 800 yards to the highway. To this point they had received no enemy fire from inside the stockade. In fact, for almost four minutes before the flare signal, not one shot had been fired at them.

F Company had carried out their assignment with perfection. Apparently all the Japanese along the east and rear fences and inside the rear of the camp were either dead or too seriously wounded to offer any further resistance. During the thirty-minute raid there had really been very little effective resistance from the enemy and none of that was organized. Except for those wounded by the three mortar rounds, and a few others with minor scratches, there were no American battle casualties.

Now six Rangers, the last squad of F Company, began to trot along the east fence rows of the stockade. They had covered about 400 yards when suddenly, bullets began to "pop" over their heads, rip through the grass, and ricochet from numerous spots on the ground. The six men immediately hit the dirt, clutching their rifles and looking for targets as they fell.

"Where in the hell is it coming from?" one Ranger shouted.

"Must be stray shots from that battle up at the bridge!" someone answered.

"Get moving! Head for the highway—keep *low!*"

"Okay! Let's move out . . . *go!*"

The members of the squad leaped up, one at a time, and continued to jog toward the highway. They were moving parallel to the east fence rows, about twenty yards from the wire. The full moon was covered now by heavy clouds, and total darkness gripped the area. Before they had covered another hundred yards, rifles began to crack from somewhere inside the camp near the fences. There were still a few Japanese alive. The two Rangers ahead of the others picked up speed, turning sideways as they ran to fire at the spastic gun flashes inside the camp. In seconds, they were out of sight of their buddies.

Tech 5 Bernard Haynes, the medic assigned to the rear area squads, fired a burst from his carbine but continued to run for the highway. Tech 5 Patrick Marquis fired his M1 until the dull clank of the ejected clip told him the weapon was empty. He reloaded while following Haynes. The shots from inside the camp ceased, but bullets from the battle at Cabu bridge were still zipping around them.

"There's the creek bed!" Marquis shouted. "Head for the creek bed, Barney!"

Bernard Haynes and Patrick Marquis started to dash for the safety of the ravine through which they had traveled to reach the rear of the camp less than an hour before. Both men dove head first into the chest-high ditch.

"Dammit to hell!" Marquis muttered as he sat up and examined his M1. "My rifle barrel's full of mud!"

In a moment Tech 5 Francis "Father" Schilli dove in with them. Bullets were still snapping over their heads.

"Where's Sweezy?" Marquis asked.

"He's coming," Schilli replied as he raised his head slightly to look for his big friend. "He was right behind me."

Corporal Roy Sweezy was "lumbering along" at a steady trot, his head leaning slightly forward. Suddenly, another rifle shot was fired from inside the camp. Sweezy turned as if to fire his M1 from his hip. Then there was a short burst of automatic weapon fire from somewhere near or in the camp. Roy Sweezy's rifle flew from his hands, he jerked and fell backward into the ditch. Two bullets had struck him in the chest, passing clean through his body.

Tech 5 Bernard Haynes leaped to Sweezy's side and ripped open the wounded man's fatigue jacket. "Sucking chest wound!" Haynes instinctively yelled as he reached for a foil-covered bandage in his medical aid satchel.

Francis Schilli crawled to his friend. Corporal Sweezy, his eyes wide in a blank stare, began to gasp his final words. "God! I . . . got hit . . . by my own . . . men! My God, my own men . . . shot me!"

Tech 5 Schilli shook his head violently. "*No, Roy! . . . No . . . crossfire! The Japs.*" Francis Schilli reached for his canteen and unscrewed the cap. Slowly, he allowed a few drops of water to splatter on his friend's forehead. Then he spoke with a firm tone. "I baptize you, Corporal Roy Sweezy . . . in the name of the Father, and of the Son . . . and the Holy Ghost . . . amen!"

"Amen!" the others repeated.

Roy Sweezy had stopped gasping for breath.

"He never really bothered nobody, God!" Schilli angrily added. "He was just doing his duty!"

It was 2025 hours (8:25) when that last F Company squad reached the highway, but there were still several Rangers there waiting for them.

"Where in the hell have you guys been?" First Sergeant Bosard snapped at the last squad. "Everyone's accounted for but you guys! Most everyone is at the river by now!" The last three men were completely out of breath.

"Roy Sweezy's dead, Sarge!" Tech 5 Patrick Marquis sadly reported.

Charles Bosard stared at the three for a moment, unable to respond. The Rangers had lost one man, but that man had been a member of the sergeant's company—and a friend.

*T*ime: *2030 hours (8:30 P.M.).* Forty-five minutes after the raid began, practically all the Americans with their liberated POWs were either at the Pampanga or in the field heading for the river. They all could easily hear the sounds of the battle raging at Cabu bridge, and they began to wonder if the Filipinos could hold the Japanese until everyone was across the Pampanga. Pajota must hold a few more minutes, then Captain Prince would be ready to fire the final flare.

But an eerie silence had fallen over POW Camp Cabanatuan. The clouds had passed the moon and, once again, the area was bathed with a bright glow. Small streams of dark smoke still spiraled upward from the smoldering ruins of the camp's motor pool section. In the stockade, in the pillboxes, and under the guard towers, over 270 Japanese imperial soldiers lay dead.

Their seriously wounded would die before dawn. The contingent of imperial POW camp guards and the Kinpeidan headquarters unit had ceased to exist. One American was dead, but over 500 Allied POWs were free.

13

Luck . . . on . . . the way out!

—Captain James C. Fisher, Balangkare,
January 31, 1945

At the south bank of the Pampanga River, across from the long sandbar, Captain Bob Prince watched as the last carabao cart rolled into knee-deep water and started for Platero. It was 2040 (8:40 P.M.).

For another twenty minutes a number of Rangers waded back and forth through the river, carrying their liberated POWs, and loaded them carefully into other carts waiting on the Platero side. When everyone was finally across, Captain Prince held a short meeting with Lieutenants Tom Rounsaville, John Dove, and Bill Nellist. The Alamo Scouts were asked to establish an ambush on the north bank, adjacent to the sandbar, and prepare to hold off any pursuing Japanese. From concealed positions on that bank, they would have an excellent open field of fire over the river and into the grassland on the south side. With PFC Alfred "Opu" Alfonso under surgery in Platero, the Scouts were down to thirteen men, counting Rounsaville, Dove, and Nellist.

At 2045 hours, one hour after the raid began, Captain Prince loaded his Very pistol, held it high in the air, and fired a red flare. It was the signal indicating all Rangers and POWs were safely across the river. Captains Pajota and Joson could now withdraw.

Eight hundred yards southwest of the stockade, Captain Eduardo Joson saw the red flare and immediately ordered his few remaining men to pull out to Platero. Once in the barrio, his forces were to divide again. Half would form a second line of defense around Platero in case the Alamo Scouts waiting at the Pampanga were overrun by pursuing Japanese. The other half would form a flank guard for the Allied column moving from Platero to Balangkare. By 2050 hours (8:50 P.M.), the highway south of POW Camp Cabanatuan was completely deserted.

A mile north of the stockade, at Cabu bridge, Captain Juan Pajota also noticed the red flare signal. He could now disengage, but the battle was still raging. For a full hour, squads of Dokuho 359 Battalion had charged down the highway only to be slaughtered before reaching the remains of the bridge. The northeast banks of the Cabu, the highway, and the underbrush were littered with hundreds of dead Japanese soldiers.

Yet the Imperial Army upheld their reputation as brave fighters, even if the tactics were suicidal. The wild enthusiasm of the remaining Japanese fully indicated to Pajota that he could not disengage. If he did, not only might his enemy pursue him southeast, but some might turn northwest and accidentally stumble into the retreating Allied column.

Pajota's squadrons had still not suffered a single fatal casualty, and his ammunition supply was more than sufficient. It would be wise, he concluded, to destroy his enemy's capability to ever pursue anyone.

Edwin Rose did not know how long he had been sitting on the open box latrine inside the prison compound at POW Camp Cabanatuan. In fact, he wasn't even sure if he had drifted off to sleep. It had happened before. He had no way of knowing he had been asleep for over an hour. It was 2100 hours (9:00 P.M.). When he first left his nipa barracks for the latrine, he heard the noise of the battle. Well, a little of it anyway. Once, he saw the flashes of guns and even thought he detected voices of men rushing past the latrine area on both sides of the barbed-wire fences. But Edwin Rose was convinced it was all part of one of his fevered dreams.

Now Rose was fully awake, and he began to make his way back to the barracks. Everything seemed unusually quiet, but the world had not offered much sound to Rose in a long time. He entered his nipa quarters and found it completely empty. Had the Japanese taken everyone away for execution? He sat down on his bamboo bunk and thought for a while. Then he got up and wandered back outside to check some of the other barracks. Everyone had vanished!

Rose walked slowly to the compound gate and, finding it open, strolled out onto the camp's center road. After shuffling along for a few yards, he suddenly stumbled over something. A chill rippled through him. He was sprawled across the body of a Japanese soldier. Edwin Rose was now completely puzzled. Some strange events must have developed while he was at that latrine. All the POWs were gone. He had been left behind, and there were dead Japanese everywhere. More important, though, the gates of his hell were standing open and no one was left to stop him from leaving.

Rose returned to his hut, selected the best clothing he could find, and redressed himself. He placed his few personal belongings on a patched blanket and folded it all into a neat bundle. But no self-respecting Englishman could depart for a trip without looking his very best. With some cold water, coconut oil, and a homemade razor, he began to shave a week's growth of whiskers. After several minutes, he was ready for his journey. Out through the compound gate and down the camp's center road he shuffled. He paused only a moment at the front gate to decide which way to turn on the main highway. He decided to turn right toward Cabu bridge. By now it was almost 1:00 A.M., January 31.

With new strength and energy brought forward with the wonderful feeling of freedom, Rose traveled about 300 yards and then elected to turn on a dirt trail that led off somewhere southeast. He did not know where he was going, but common sense told him he must leave that open highway as soon as possible.

For almost an hour, he shuffled along the path, pausing now and then only to get his wind. He reached a fork in the trail and stopped for a longer period of rest to make another decision—which way was safe to travel? At that moment, there was movement in the underbrush on both sides of the trail, and a score of men carrying rifles stepped out into the moonlight. Rose was completely surrounded.

"Hello! What have we here?" Rose exclaimed with typical British composure.

No one answered, but a man, his rifle aimed at Rose's head, came forward.

"Americano?" the man with the rifle asked.

"Ah, what?"

"You . . . American?" The man lowered the rifle slightly.

"My word . . . no! I'm British!"

Edwin Rose was now in the hands of one of Captain Pajota's rear guard units.

Long before Edwin Rose prepared to leave Camp Cabanatuan, Barrio Platero had become a scene of massive commotion. It was 2100 hours (9:00 P.M.), and the villagers were already distributing water and food to more than 600 POWs, Rangers, and guerrilla soldiers. Other civilians were busy organizing the carabao carts into a single file for departure to Barrio Balangkare. Many of the POWs who could walk were given little time to recover from their confusion and shock but were raining questions upon the busy Rangers.

Other POWs were too sick or bewildered to comprehend what had happened or appreciate all the excitement.

Staff Sergeant Norton Most, waiting at his radio, would never forget the shock that gripped him when the first gaunt POWs entered the barrio in their tattered and patched clothing. He was not sure how he had expected men held captive so many months to appear. But the sight of his fellow Americans moving like limping or shuffling zombies left him appalled. When the seriously ill arrived in carabao carts and on the backs of Rangers, Norton Most and the other radio crewmen were completely overcome with emotion.

Doctor Merle Musselman had been free a little over an hour, but was already back on duty as a physician. Surgery was under way in the Platero schoolhouse on those wounded by the mortar shell blast. By the time he arrived, the "hospital" was bustling with activity. Filipino nurses were rushing in and out, bringing more fresh sheets and boiling water. The Rangers' medical corpsmen were busy aiding with the surgery.

PFC Alfred Alfonso was the first serious casualty brought to the hospital. Doctor Carlos Layug immediately went to work on the Alamo Scout's nasty groin wound, removed the shell fragment, and cleaned the damaged area. Alfonso would live, but he needed additional treatment in a better-equipped operating room as soon as possible.

A few minutes later the most serious of all the Allied casualties arrived. Doctor Layug's eyes turned saucerlike above the white surgical mask as he crossed the room to the desk where the wounded Ranger had just been placed. Captain Jimmy Fisher, the man who had worked and dreamed of the future with the Filipino surgeon earlier that day, now was prepared for surgery in the hospital he had helped create.

A plasma needle was inserted into Fisher's arm. During the rough three-mile trip from the stockade to Platero he had lost a dangerous amount of blood.

Now the skilled hands of Doctor Musselman and Doctor Layug began the surgery. Colonel James Duckworth could serve only as a frustrated consultant. He had fallen somewhere between the stockade and the Pampanga and fractured his arm. As the doctors began their work, it was immediately obvious that James Fisher's condition was extremely critical. The mortar shell fragment had done tremendous damage to his abdominal cavity.

"Perforated intestines . . . massive bleeding from the liver . . ." One doctor muttered his official statement in a calm monotone as the delicate work proceeded.

There was no antiseptic, only morphine to kill the pain, and Captain Fisher remained awake during most of the operation.

"More light! More light . . . get another lantern over here!"

Staff Sergeant John Nelson, assisting the doctors, studied the face of Jimmy Fisher with growing concern.

"Hold on, Jimmy! How's the pain?" Nelson asked.

"It's okay," Fisher replied.

"The fellows are collecting their morphine, Jimmy. We'll have more morphine in here in a few minutes."

Fisher forced a smile. "Tell them thanks . . . but save the morphine for someone who may need it more than I," he answered. "It's a long way back . . . anything can happen." He tried to turn his head to Nelson. "Did we get them all? Did we get all . . . the POWs?"

"Every swinging one of 'em," Nelson assured. "Prince is bringing up the rear. The last of them will be here soon."

Fisher drifted into unconsciousness, but in a few moments was awake again. "Did we lose any of our boys?" he asked.

"Everyone's okay . . . a few minor wounds, that's all!" Nelson replied, unaware of Corporal Sweezy's death.

"Who's got *O positive?* Who's got O positive blood!" one of the doctors called out.

Medical Corpsman Tech 5 Bernard Haynes was near the operating table and quickly responded, "I'm O positive. Let me know when you need me. I'll check outside for others."

Sergeant Haynes walked out of the schoolhouse and into the crowd of Rangers and Filipinos who were still busy organizing the column of carabao carts. The corpsman began to compile a list of men with the needed blood type. As he returned to the schoolyard, Haynes was confronted by a former POW, Father Hugh Kennedy.

"How are they doing in there?" Chaplain Kennedy inquired.

"I think everyone is going to be okay but Captain Fisher. He's in bad shape!"

"The Filipinos say the battle is still going on up at the highway bridge," Lieutenant Kennedy advised. "They suggest we pull out of here as soon as possible in case the Japanese break through."

"If they break through, Father, we have an ambush waiting at the river. Don't worry. That will slow them down."

"Are you a Catholic, son?" Father Kennedy looked Bernie Haynes in the eye.

"Well . . . I guess I'm a halfway Catholic, Father."

"Would you like me to hear your confession?"

"Now?" Haynes responded. "I . . . don't know . . . it's not a very good time, Father."

"Don't you think this may be the *best* time," Father Kennedy convincingly replied.

The two men slipped into a vacant nipa hut and remained there a minute or two while the Ranger gave his confession.

At 2140 hours (9:40 P.M.) Captain Robert Prince arrived at Platero along with twenty-five carabao carts loaded with former POWs. Now everyone, except the Alamo Scouts at their ambush point, had cleared the river area and was in the barrio.

Lieutenant Colonel Mucci had already issued orders for the column to start moving to Balangkare, beginning with some twenty Rangers and those POWs who could walk. But Captain James Fisher was still under surgery and at least another hour might be required to get the carts properly organized and under way.

Mucci and Prince both recognized that Captain Fisher must be left in the hands of the doctors. To move the wounded man now would surely mean death. But who would stay with Fisher?

Runners were bringing in word from Cabu bridge. Pajota's men were still engaged with the Japanese. The battle was going well for the guerrillas. Pajota was holding. Nonetheless, Colonel Mucci could not risk the chance that even one squad of Japanese soldiers would catch his slow-moving column.

Captain Prince returned to the Pampanga with instructions for the Alamo Scouts. As soon as the last of the column pulled out of Platero, the Scouts could withdraw from their ambush position but must serve as guards for Fisher and the medical team. Pajota and his men would set up the rear guard defense at the Pampanga as soon as he was able to disengage at Cabu bridge.

"Get to Balankgkare as soon as you can," Captain Prince said to Alamo Scout Lieutenant Bill Nellist. "See if your men and the Filipinos can clean an area for an airstrip near that barrio. We'll try to get a plane to come for Fisher!"

In a few minutes, Prince was back in Platero and now faced a task he hated to perform. Father Hugh Kennedy, Lieutenant (Dr.) Herb Ott, and Major (Dr.) Stephen C. Sitter (freed POWs), along with the Ranger medics, also volunteered to remain in Platero with Fisher until he could move with the Scouts to Balangkare. Prince entered the hospital to confront Dr. Musselman.

"How is he?" Bob Prince inquired as two officers stepped away from the operating table and into the strange shadows cast from the yellow light of oil lanterns upon the schoolhouse walls.

"Not good!" Musselman reported. "I hear you fellows are pulling out. We can't move him yet. I'm not even sure if he'll make it at all!"

"I'm sorry I must ask this," Captain Prince began, "after all you have been through in that camp . . ."

"You want me to stay back here with him?"

"You don't have to, you know," Prince quickly added. "We came here to free you men . . ."

"I'll stay," Musselman replied calmly.

The serious-natured Captain Bob Prince smiled one of his rare but sincere smiles. "Now . . . don't worry, Doctor. We're leaving some men with you. There will be thirteen Alamo Scouts and the guerrillas—"

"*Thirteen!* My God!" Musselman exclaimed.

"They are the best! Don't worry. They'll get you out. Our lines are not far away, now."

At Cabu bridge Captain Juan Pajota finally had a chance to glance at his Lord Elgin wristwatch. It was 2200 hours (10:00 P.M.). His forces had been engaged with the Japanese for over two hours. But now, a full five minutes had passed without so much as a single shot being fired by the enemy. The Japanese offensive squads had lost their momentum some fifteen minutes earlier. In their unsuccessful attempts to reach the opposite end of the bridge or cross the Cabu River, Commander Oyaebu had apparently sacrificed the bulk of his Dokuho 359 Battalion and attached units.

As incredible as it seems, Pajota's squadrons had not suffered a single serious casualty. The element of surprise, combined with excellent planning and massive and accurate firepower, had produced an impressive victory for the guerrilla commander. Most of all, the enemy had been held from reinforcing the imperial troops at POW Camp Cabanatuan. The bloody battle at Cabu bridge was over. Yet the guerrillas continued to rake the enemy area with rifle and automatic weapons fire.

Captain Pajota moved forward to his Headquarters Company and gave orders to cease fire and begin the withdrawal in leapfrog fashion across the highway. In keeping with Lieutenant Colonel Mucci's orders, all the squadrons would move first toward the southeast. Headquarters Company commander First Lieutenant Florencio Bernardo was next to Captain Pajota as they neared the highway. Suddenly, a single rifle shot from the Japanese side of the river broke the silence. Bernardo instinctively dove to the ground.

"By gum, Lieutenant," Captain Pajota said, "you fight the Japs for two hours and now, for only one shot, you fall!" He reached down to help his friend to his feet and both men began to laugh.

It would require almost three hours for Pajota's squadrons to circle southeast and swing up to the Pampanga River. Once there, they would establish the last rear guard lines to assure that no Japanese crossed the river or jeopardized Mucci's retreating column in any way.

At 2230 hours (10:30 P.M.), the first of the retreating column of Rangers and POWs reached Barrio Balangkare and began to regroup. Here, fifteen more carabao carts were added, bringing the total number to forty. But at this time, some carts were still in Platero and at least twenty were rolling along the two-and-one-half-mile dirt road between the two barrios.

Pajota's lieutenants were doing their best to keep the strange-looking convoy under control, but the mild-mannered carabao, understandably excited with the unusual fast pace, required constant attention. Keeping a close eye on those liberated POWs who were walking out of Platero and maintaining the carabao carts in orderly intervals was only part of the problem as far as First Sergeant Charles Bosard was concerned. The Filipino civilians helping the convoy movement were stopping every few hundred yards to remove their shoes, and this began to both puzzle and annoy Bosard.

"Those are American shoes," one guerrilla explained. "The submarine brought the shoes to us with all the guns. The men have saved the shoes for something special. They have never worn shoes before. Shoes fill with sand and some small pebbles. The men are only stopping to empty the shoes."

While the column rolled on the dirt road and regrouped in Balangkare, Staff Sergeant Norton Most sat with his SCR 694 radio in Platero and continued to tap out a message while Tech 5 George Disrud and Tech 5 William Lawver took turns at the generator's hand crank. They had been trying unsuccessfully for over an hour to establish contact with their Guimba base radio station. It was now 2245 hours (10:45 P.M.). The operation on Captain James Fisher was still in process. Captain Prince anxiously waited for that radio contact so he, with the last of the Rangers, POWs, and carabao carts, could pull out and catch up with Lieutenant Colonel Mucci and the first two-thirds of the column.

Near Guimba, Tech 4th Class James Irvine continued his vigil in the Rangers staff car equipped with the SCR 284 radio. It was now a few minutes before 2300 hours (11:00 P.M.). Though sleep almost conquered him several times, Irvine had succeeded in remaining awake at his radio post for fifty-seven hours since Mucci and the other Rangers departed for the raid. Around 6:00 P.M. the large group of Army brass and reporters, who had gathered about the staff car all day, broke up as a few returned to Guimba for softer quarters. The majority had stayed on, though, waiting along with the sleepy radioman for some word from Mucci.

James Irvine could feel his eyes begin to roll back into their sockets again, and he fought that powerful urge to sleep by stretching his cheek muscles and raising his eyebrows. Slowly, the flickering lids closed. His head nodded with the weight of sleep and the steel helmet. *Thud!* The helmet, with Irvine's head still inside, smashed down on the radio frame with a dull metallic sound. His head snapped back. He was groggy, but awake. The special "alarm clock" idea had worked. Irvine stretched his arms, yawned, and began to rub his sore, bloodshot eyes. At that moment a blast of static filled his radio and a message, broken with radio "skips," began to come through. Quickly he grabbed a pencil and scribbled the coded letters on his yellow message pad.

"BZ . . . GB . . . BZ . . . GB . . . Leaving Some With Friends . . ."

More static interrupted the message, and the sounds began to break up with crackling noises, then . . . silence. In a few moments, the radio was once again producing the clicking sounds of the message, "BZ . . . GB . . . Leaving Some With Friends."

Irvine knew the code letters by heart. He had repeated them to himself a million times, it seemed, during the long wait. Decoded, the message read, "Mission Accomplished . . . Starting Back . . . Leaving Some With Friends." Mucci and his Rangers had succeeded, but there must be casualties.

"They've done it!" Irvine shouted to the jubilant crowd around him. "They've done it!"

In Platero, Sergeant Norton Most was becoming increasingly concerned. It was now 2300 hours (11:00 P.M.) and he did not know if his message had been received by either Guimba's base station or even the relay post at Licab. His radio answered him only with static.

Then, the radio came alive with the acknowledgment everyone in the barrio had been waiting for. Guimba base had received his message. Most looked at his watch and began to record the time of the acknowledgment on his notepad. But in his excitement, he committed a very minor, human error. He recorded the time as 11:03. In a split second he realized his mistake and wrote the correct military time as 2303 over the common 11:03 and circled it with his initials, N.M.

The radio message acknowledgment came as a special welcome to Captain Bob Prince. The company commander had no objection, of course, to his assignment of "bringing up the rear." But Lieutenant Colonel Mucci with the bulk of the column had a long head start and no one with Prince knew exactly how far they were spread apart.

Captain Prince turned to Lieutenant Nellist. "We're pulling out now! Good luck! We'll see you fellows soon."

"Good luck!" Nellist nodded. "Tell Mucci we'll do our best to get Fisher out of this alive. Watch out for Huks! The Filipinos seem to be as concerned about *them* as they are the Japs."

In the last carabao cart in Platero, a lone POW lay on the straw and shivered with his sickness. He felt a cool sensation on his forehead and slowly opened his eyes. The eyes blinked and strained to focus on the figure standing beside the cart. The eyes blinked again. He was staring into the pretty, round face of a Filipino girl, who now wiped his cheeks with a damp cloth. His eyes, with a disbelieving gaze, fixed on her dark eyes and the raven-black hair that wrapped around her face.

A smile exploded on the face of the Filipino girl. How strange are American eyes, she thought. An interesting thing had finally been confirmed for Nurse Wilma Monsod. Now she knew the legend was true. Some Americans' eyes are truly blue.

"Hi, Joe!" she said softly and raised both eyebrows simultaneously in the characteristic Filipino expression of reassurance and agreement.

The POW's eyes flooded and his lips quivered in an effort to speak. The nurse dabbed at the tears as they began to flow down into matted hair.

"We're moving out! Let's get rolling!" a loud shout came through the darkness from somewhere near the front of the column.

As the cart jerked forward, the young girl stepped clear. The American strained to raise his head, keeping his eyes fixed on the girl. She held her arm up and with index and second finger spread, began to wave the familiar "V."

"Victory, Joe! Goodbye, Joe . . . Victory . . . Victory!" she called as the cart pulled away.

The American's mouth opened with a weak smile as if it had long forgotten such a simple exercise, and the taste of the tears met his lips. She saw his smile, dropped her arm, and faded into the darkness of contrasting shadows from the moonglow and a large banana tree.

"Keep 'em rolling up there! Let's *go!*"

Within a few minutes the last of the strange Allied column had rolled out of Platero.

Along the trail from Platero to Balangkare, Tech 4 Frank Goetzheimer, his short legs almost numb from miles of walking, welcomed a brief rest as the Allied column suddenly came to a halt. The front of the column had just reached Balangkare, and Goetzheimer sat down and placed his heavy camera equipment next to him.

"Here! Take these when you get too sleepy to walk!" A giant Ranger stood before him and was holding out his hand.

"What is it?" Frank Goetzheimer asked.

"Some kind of pep pills the medics are issuing."

"I'm sleepy now!" the cameraman replied as two little pills about a fourth the size of an aspirin tablet fell into his palm. "Damn!" he swore. The pills rolled from his hand dropped to the ground. "Where in the hell did you go . . . ?" Goetzheimer moved his equipment and began to crawl on his hands and knees, feeling in the sandy soil for the Benzedrine. He managed to find one pill, scooped it up, and washed it down with a gulp of water from his canteen. The column began to move again, and he stood up.

"What were you doing crawling about the ground, soldier? Lose your film?" a voice in the darkness teased.

"No. Lost my pills—found one, but I think I just swallowed part of Luzon with it!"

"I saw one of your Signal Corps fellows back at the last village. Good to see men from my old corps again," the voice said.

Goetzheimer turned to take a closer look at the skinny man beside him. "Who are you?" he asked.

"Major Paul Wing. Before I was assigned to Luzon, I was with the Training Film Production Lab at Fort Monmouth. The Japs made Cabanatuan my home for the last—"

"My God, sir! I'm glad to meet you," Goetzheimer interrupted. "Do you need any help? How about the carts? Don't you want to ride?"

"No . . . no, son. I'm doing okay, so far. I'll make it now."

"You should meet Goen and Lautman—our other cameramen. They are up front here somewhere. We are all disappointed. It was too dark to get any action shots when we stormed your camp. They got some good photos yesterday and we'll be active just as soon as the sun comes up. I've been carrying this equipment for two days and haven't been able to take a single foot of film. Every time I'm ready to set up—the Rangers are on the move again!"

Major Wing laughed. "Well, tell me about the Signal Corps' coverage until now. I want to hear about all our progress . . . everything!"

Shortly before 2400 hours, midnight, January 30, the Allied column of Rangers, guerrillas, their liberated POWs, and forty carabao carts began to pull out of Balangkare with Lieutenant Colonel Henry Mucci leading the way. In less than an hour the last of the column rolled out with Captain Bob Prince still in command of the convoy's rear. The trail they followed would take them three and a half miles northwest to the Morcon River, then a mile north to Barrio Mataas Na Kahoy. Most of the POWs who had managed to walk from Platero to Balangkare were now too weak to continue unassisted. They were crowded into carabao carts. Mucci then requested the Filipinos to send a runner ahead of his column to Mataas Na Kahoy. They would need ten more carts and fresh water before continuing.

At 0100 (1:00 A.M.), January 31, the small group of Alamo Scouts, medics, and former POWs who had volunteered to remain in Platero, were informed by the Filipinos that some of the Japanese soldiers had definitely survived the battle at Cabu bridge. Lieutenants Nellist and Rounsaville were also concerned that enemy troops from Cabanatuan City might decide to move north and investigate the cause of their inability to contact the stockade units. If this occurred, it would then be entirely possible that the enemy might begin to comb the countryside. The trail left by the Rangers from the Pampanga to Platero would be an easy one for the Imperial Army to follow.

First Lieutenant Saturnino Coquia, head of one of Pajota's squadrons, now advised that his "scouts" were reporting that the surviving Japanese at Cabu bridge were beginning to move about and strongly recommended the Americans move out for Balang-kare as soon as possible. He and a few guerrillas would accompany them to the next barrio. Captain Pajota was expected to arrive at the Pampanga River soon and there would establish an ambush and serve as a delaying rear guard force.

The Alamo Scout team leaders met with Doctor Musselman. The operation on Captain James Fisher was complete, but could Fisher be moved?

"I fear it will make little difference," Musselman reported. "Fisher stands only a slim chance of pulling through. But if we move him, we'll need to be extremely careful!"

The bamboo-and-cloth sack-type stretcher used by the guer-rillas for transporting wounded was considered much too awk-ward to move someone in Fisher's condition the two miles to Balangkare. Something must be employed as a stretcher that would keep his body practically motionless. The Scouts came up with the answer. A wooden door was removed from one of the finer homes in the barrio and with great care, Captain Fisher was placed upon it. Six men gently lifted the door and they were on their way. With Lieutenant Coquia leading, the last of the Americans marched out of Platero, carrying their dy-ing comrade.

It was not until 0200 (2:00 A.M.) that Lieutenant Colonel Mucci and the first of the carabao cart convoy reached Mataas Na Kahoy. There, the Filipinos were waiting with both food and water as well as eleven more carabao carts. The convoy now consisted of fifty-one carts.

Colonel Mucci wasted no time. By 0230 hours the column was once again on the move. The line of carts, carabaos, guerrillas, former POWs, and Rangers stretched a total distance of one and one half miles along the dirt road. They were heading toward the Rizal Highway and their next destination, the town of Luna. But, after traveling two miles, the column came to a halt. They now faced a new problem. The highway could still be under enemy control. For a column over a mile long to cross at any one point would take considerable time. To make matters worse, Colonel Mucci was informed by the guerrillas that it would be impossible for the carabao carts to cross the road at their direct front because the opposite bank was much too steep. They must move down the highway a mile and then cross.

First Lieutenant William O'Connell was given the roadblock assignment. A bazooka team, two squads of Rangers, and a few of Captain Joson's men were sent 400 yards northeast to halt any traffic moving from the north. A similar force established their blockade 3,000 yards southwest down the road to hold any Japanese who might be moving from the south. At 0330 hours (3:30 A.M.), Lieutenant O'Connell sent word back to Mucci. The roadblocks were ready. The column could begin the crossing.

Needless to say, the men with those two roadblocks did as much praying as watching for the enemy. If a large Japanese force proceeded along the road, every Ranger realized they could hold for a few minutes, at best. It would be almost impossible to guarantee the safety of the vulnerable column. But the bulk of the Allied force with Mucci entered the highway at 0331 hours, moved one mile southwest along the road, and finally crossed at a point just north of Luna. The entire crossing required an hour and the roadblocks were called in at 0430 hours (4:30 A.M.).

While Colonel Mucci and his column were making their way northwest cross-country, the Alamo Scouts, along with Captain Fisher, arrived in Balangkare. It was approximately 0205 hours (2:05 A.M.). The Scout team leaders organized a workforce composed of villagers and guerrillas who would assist in clearing an area to be used as an aircraft landing strip. Meanwhile, Dr. Musselman, assisted by Lieutenant Coquia and his wife, Aurolia, attended to Fisher's wounds.

By 0239 hours, a flat parcel of land was selected on the northwest edge of the barrio and work began on the airstrip. It would take them till dawn to complete their task.

It was almost daybreak when Edwin Rose and the squad of Pajota's guerrillas entered a small barrio. Naturally, the bamboo telegraph had notified the villagers of their impending arrival, and fresh fruit, water, rice, and broiled chicken were ready for the guests. While Rose enjoyed his feast a young, attractive girl, perhaps sixteen or seventeen years old, knelt in front of him.

"Where am I?" Rose asked.

"Barrio Macatbong," the girl replied with a big grin. "From what place are you, sir?"

"Why . . . from the prison camp!" Rose answered between heaping mouthfuls of chicken.

"Did the Americans leave you there?"

"Americans?" Rose looked puzzled. "What Americans?"

The young girl turned to reply to a barrage of Tagalog, as everyone nearby seemed to jabber at once. Then she faced Rose again. "The Americans who came to kill the Japanese last night!" she told him.

"Really? My word . . . so that's it, eh!"

"Yes, sir. My husband will be here tomorrow," she added with a reassuring smile. "His men will accompany you to the Americans after they take Cabanatuan City from the Japs."

"Who is your husband?" Rose finally asked.

"Captain Pajota, sir."

In two more days the war would be over for Edwin Rose, the POW the Rangers accidentally left behind.

The first rays of warm sunlight cracked over the emerald island of Luzon. The Black Widows of the 547th Night Fighter Squadron were returning to their nest near Lingayen Gulf.

During the long night of January 30 and through the early hours of the thirty-first, the P61s accomplished their mission, keeping Nueva Ecija's roads clear of enemy traffic. The venom of the deadly Widows had destroyed a total of twelve Japanese trucks, one tank, and hundreds of troops trapped in those vehicles or around campfires near the road. The only damage to the Widows was a few small holes in one aircraft from ground fire.

As the P61 crews settled down for a well-earned rest, their ground personnel began their service, all proud of the fact that the 547th had never lost a single airplane due to mechanical failure. And, while the night killers rested, a squadron of sleek North American P51 fighters not far away warmed their powerful Allison and Packard engines. Within an hour the silver planes scrambled into the sky and roared off toward the rising sun at 380 miles per hour to seek new prey.

At the Cabu River, Battalion Commander Tomeo Oyabu sat on his haunches and sucked air between his teeth as he listened to the casualty report from a bloodied noncommissioned officer. it was almost 0600 hours (6:00 A.M.) January 31.

All his junior officers were dead. His truck with its machine gun was completely destroyed, his four tanks disabled beyond repair. Except for part of his First Horino Company and Fourth Iwashiro Company, everyone else in Dokuho 359 Battalion and its attached units was dead. The bodies of over 1,000 of his men, some of the best imperial soldiers on Luzon, lay scattered along the Cabu River bank, throughout the underbrush and bamboo thickets, and piled and tangled on the highway near the burned-out truck at the bridge. Most had been blasted beyond recognition by the continual barrages from the enthusiastic Filipinos that night.

Commander Oyabu mustered Horino and Iwashiro companies together to take a head count. The survivors of the battle totaled 255. Only two were without serious wounds. And no one was in condition to proceed immediately to Cabanatuan City.

Oyabu was not even certain what army had hit his battalion. His enemy obviously lacked tanks and artillery. Based on the firing he had heard in the south during his long night's battle, he could only assume that the prison stockade was also hit. The unit that attacked him had withdrawn—disappeared in the night as quickly as it had appeared. He knew that only guerrillas fought with such tactics, and concluded that it would be safe to continue to Cabanatuan City, but not for a while. Oyabu withdrew the remainder of his unit a few hundred yards northwest to the banks of the Pampanga River where his men could doctor their wounds and rest.

Shortly before reaching the Casili River, Colonel Mucci halted at a small barrio for a brief rest and to give his column a chance to close up. It was 0530 (5:30 A.M.), and Captain Prince, with about 25 percent of the Rangers, POWs, and carabao carts, was at least two miles behind.

While the column rested, Sergeant Norton Most set up his radio and attempted to establish contact with James Irvine at the Guimba base. First, Sergeant Most's radio produced only static, and then it ceased to function. Immediately, the radiomen went to work on the equipment and discovered that there was really nothing wrong with the radio. Their signal was simply not getting through. But Mucci did not wish to wait any longer and the column rolled on for another half mile.

As they approached the next small barrio, Lieutenant Toribio Paulino, one of Pajota's officers assigned to assist the Rangers, received a message from a runner. Paulino was told the disturbing news that the Huks had control of the next village.

"It is not safe to go through that place," Paulino warned Colonel Mucci. "The Huks have over 100 armed men. They are waiting for us. It could be trouble."

Colonel Mucci had no desire, of course, to mingle in Filipino political squabbles, but he also had a mission to complete.

"Is there another road around the barrio?" he asked Lieutenant Paulino.

"None, sir!"

"Then send someone up there and tell the Huks we are coming through!" Mucci snapped.

"I will go myself, sir," Paulino replied. "The Huks caused the death of my brother, Captain Simplicio Paulino, at Talabutab Sur exactly a month ago!"

Colonel Mucci and the column waited, and in a few minutes, Lieutenant Paulino returned.

"The Huks will permit only Americans to pass, sir," he reported.

"They will not allow any USAFFE soldiers or Filipino civilians to go through that place!"

Now the Ranger commander was in another serious situation. With Captain Prince some two miles away and the Ranger column strung out over that entire distance, it would be difficult to assemble his troops to storm the town. Of primary concern was the safety of the POWs. Lieutenant Colonel Henry Mucci employed quick thinking, combined with his usual flair for activating spontaneous ideas.

"Lieutenant, go back and tell those Huks that we *all* are coming through. If they offer any resistance whatsoever—if even a dog snaps at one of my men, I'll call in artillery and *level* the village!"

Paulino had a deep, worried look. "The radio, sir . . . the men say it does not work!"

Mucci grinned. "The Huks don't know that!"

Once again, the column rolled forward and began to pass through the village between rows of armed Huk soldiers. Curious villagers stared at the strange sight, while the opposing Filipino groups exchanged evil looks. But none said a word. Colonel Mucci's bluff had worked.

For two more miles the column rolled west until they came to the small town of Sibul. It was 0800 (8:00 A.M.). At Sibul, the Filipinos were waiting with fresh water, food, and twenty additional carabao carts. Mucci's column now included a total of seventy-one of the two-wheeled vehicles. Another rest was called, and Sergeant Norton Most set up his radio again to try to contact the Guimba base. This time he succeeded. The large town of Talavera, less than twelve miles away, had fallen to the Allied forces. While the Rangers were on their mission, General Krueger's army had advanced half the distance from Guimba to Cabanatuan City.

At Guimba, Tech 4th Class James M. Irvine tried to concentrate on his radio signals as scores of high-ranking Army officers and newsmen crowded around the staff car. Irvine had now been awake at his radio post for over sixty-seven hours.

The important message from Colonel Mucci began to come in on the radio. Irvine printed it, with a soft lead pencil, on his standard Army message pad.

"Will be at highway! BZ-VJ/ about / DHE / or QXM. Have P1 / need trucks to transport / JE / Also ambulances for approximately / HE / 310900/."

Decoded, the message informed Sixth Army headquarters at Guimba that Mucci's Rangers would be at the National Highway in about two hours. He needed trucks to transport 412 men and ambulances to move 100 litter cases. The date and time were expressed as January 31, "0900" (9:00 A.M.). Due to the excitement at the staff car, it would be another fifteen minutes before James Irvine could notarize the message with his initials. Mucci's column was now moving for the National Highway.

On the edge of Barrio Balangkare, the Alamo Scouts continued to wait for the plane to come and pick up Captain James Fisher. It was 1100 hours (11:00 A.M.) and still no sign of a plane of any type.

In a large wood-and-bamboo home in the barrio, Staff Sergeant John Nelson sat at the side of his dying friend. Captain Fisher had drifted in and out of consciousness since dawn. Once more, his eyes opened and stared into the tired face of Nelson.

"How you doing, pal?" Nelson asked. "Can you hear me, Jimmy?"

Captain Fisher managed a weak smile and his lips moved slowly as he tried to answer. "Luck . . . on . . . the way out!" He said. Then his eyes closed for the last time.

Sergeant Nelson, his voice choked with emotion, replied softly, "Luck, on the way out . . . Jimmy!"

At noon, Major Stephen Sitter, M.D., First Lieutenant Herb Ott, D.V.S., Second Lieutenant Claude Daniel, D.D.S., First Lieutenant Merle Musselman, M.D., First Lieutenant Hugh Kennedy, Chaplain, the Ranger medics, and Alamo Scouts gathered in a grove of trees about 200 yards from the edge of the Balangkare. Around them, almost 300 Filipinos—guerrillas and civilians— stood silent while the Americans said farewell to one of their own.

Lieutenant William Nellist spoke first, as Captain Fisher's body, wrapped in canvas, was lowered into the grave.

"O God! We commend to you the soul of a very brave man . . ." he began.

Afterward, Father Hugh Kennedy conducted the formal burial service.

The Americans waited for another two hours. Still, no plane arrived. They could wait no longer. The Filipinos, thanks to the bamboo telegraph, informed them—Talavera was in American hands. The Alamo Scouts decided it would be best to try to reach their lines before dark. As the group of Americans passed the grove of trees where they had buried the 6th Rangers' battalion surgeon, they noticed a number of Filipinos on their knees, praying before a small cross. Next to the cross, on one of the trees, the citizens of Balangkare had nailed a sign that read, "Doctor-Captain James C. Fisher Memorial Park"!

At 1100 hours (11:00 A.M.), the rear of the Rangers' carabao column was still a mile from the National Highway, and Captain Prince could only conclude that Lieutenant Colonel Mucci, at the front, had already reached or crossed the road.

Suddenly, at the rear of the column, the roaring hum of approaching fighter planes cut the still morning air. Everyone's eyes searched the sky.

"Oh, my God!" one Ranger shouted. "It's the Japs! Out of the carts!"

"*Take cover!* Get in the grass! Take cover!" came a command.

There was no time to move the slow carabaos from the road.

"No . . . oh, no!" a POW exclaimed as a Ranger helped him from the cart. "Not after all this . . . not *now!*" He landed on shaky legs and headed for the tall grass.

Seconds drifted by and the first plane came into the rifle sights of the Rangers.

"Suppose they are our guys?" PFC Bill Proudfit whispered to the man next to him.

"Damn! They may still strike us!" came the reply. "They wouldn't know who we are!"

The first fighter was almost in rifle range now, dropping slowly, nose pointed at the column of carabao carts, fuselage almost level with the ground. It was in a perfect approach for a strafing run.

"He's at about 500 feet! *Ready!*"

Fingers began their slow squeeze on triggers of a variety of weapons. But before anyone could fire, the silver fighter lifted its nose and soared toward the heavens, revealing its wing markings.

"They're ours!" came the shouts along the column.

Up and up the fighter climbed until she was only a shiny speck near 10,000 feet. Then she flipped over and began an eighty-degree dive toward the column. The scream from her powerful engine reached ear-splitting proportions as she streaked earthward. At 1,000 feet, the pilot pulled out of his dive and roared over the column, tilting the wing first to the left, then to the right, then, back again. As the men on the ground watched, three more fighters buzzed over, each waving its wings. Cheers and shouting engulfed the column. The planes banked north and joined in a tight formation.

"Go get 'em, boys!" a Ranger yelled.

"What kind of plane is that thing?" a POW asked PFC Proudfit.

"They're P51s, soldier!"

Far up "on the point," several hundred yards ahead of Colonel Mucci's column, Tech 5 Patrick Marquis slung his M1 rifle over one shoulder and began to sing.

> Home, home on the range,
> Where the deer and the antelope play,
> Where seldom is heard,
> A discouraging word, and—

"Halt!" a voice from the bushes ahead of Marquis shouted.

"Advance, and be recognized!"

"Are you kidding!?" Marquis replied.

"Who are you?"

"Ranger!" Marquis shouted back, a little "high" on Benzedrine, "what do you think I am?"

Patrick Marquis had just run into a reconnaissance patrol of the United States Sixth Army's front lines. In less than an hour, the liberated POWs and Mucci's tired Rangers were loaded up in trucks and ambulances for a jubilant ride into Guimba. There, the POWs from Cabanatuan began immediate medical treatment at the 92nd Evacuation Hospital. For them, the war was over.

As the happy welcome got under way in Guimba, the Alamo Scouts, medics, Dr. Musselman, and Father Kennedy were making fairly good time on their foot journey northwest. About 1500 hours (3:00 P.M.), as they approached a small barrio when they planned to take a break, they were confronted by about twelve armed Filipinos.

"Careful, sir. They are Huks!" a guerrilla spoke quietly to Lieutenant Bill Nellist.

"They look like a bunch of bandits to me!" Nellist stated to Lieutenant Rounsaville.

"Yeah, but they could do a lot of damage," Rounsaville replied.

The Alamo Scouts began to spread out but continued to move forward toward the waiting Huks, who were now arguing with the guerrillas. A Huk shoved one guerrilla backward and shouted something in Tagalog.

Sergeant Galen Kittleson calmly released the safety on his Thompson submachine gun. "If they stay bunched up like that, I can take 'em with one burst," he whispered to Lieutenant Nellist.

Nellist was now directly in front of one Huk, who obviously had no intention of stepping aside. The huge Alamo Scout lieutenant looked down on the little man blocking his way.

"You shall not pass!" the Huk shouted.

"Why don't you go to hell!" Nellist barked.

The startled Huk moved from the trail and the Americans continued without uttering another word.

By evening the group had safely reached the Allied lines.

Battalion Commander Tomeo Oyabu, at the Cabu River, had his orders. Dokuho 359 must assist with the defense of Cabanatuan City and delay the Americans as long as possible. Oyabu would obey those orders even if he was a day late and no longer commanded a full fighting battalion. Three of his wounded soldiers had died during the night of January 31 and were left on the banks of the Pampanga River.

Now, Oyabu and 252 imperial soldiers staggered back to the highway, crossed over, and continued east for three-quarters of a mile to avoid the bridge area. They tramped through the muddy Cabu River bed and cut back to the highway just north of Pangatian. Down the highway, past the deserted POW camp they marched, paying little attention to the blackbirds that circled above the stockade and dropped inside the compound to feed on the dead.

Dokuho 359 could easily hear the battle at Cabanatuan City as they marched. And when they reached the suburbs, they ran head-on into a small unit of the United States 1st Cavalry. The Americans had smashed into the city from both the west and the north.

The determined Oyabu knew his men were unable to conduct a charge. He elected, instead, to issue orders for them to take a position along the highway. They held that position through the night of February 1. By midmorning of the second, Oyabu could take no more and withdrew from the battle, leaving 180 dead members of the battalion behind.

Like wounded wolves pursued by a stronger pack, Oyabu and his remaining seventy-two men soon became easy prey for the Filipino guerrillas. Within fourteen hours, the Oyabu Dokuho 359 Battalion had ceased to exist.

EPILOGUE

Time is the villain! it changes all; annihilates the bitterness and everything—including purpose, including love.
—General Carlos P. Romulo, 1943

With the help of the Filipino guerrillas and civilians, the United States 6th Rangers and Alamo Scouts successfully liberated 516 Allied prisoners of war from Camp Cabanatuan at Barrio Pangatian in Nueva Ecija province, Luzon, that night of January 30, 1945. In the action, the American Rangers lost two soldiers killed—Captain James C. Fisher, M.D., and Corporal Roy Sweezy. Seven Americans were wounded seriously. The Filipinos, under the command of Captains Juan Pajota and Eduardo Joson, suffered even fewer casualties—twelve received superficial wounds, none were killed. All of the Allied wounded recovered.

During those same hours of combat, slightly more than 1,275 Imperial Japanese Army soldiers were killed and approximately 260 were wounded. These figures, of course, include Japanese casualties from both the POW camp assault and the battle at Cabu bridge. The surviving Japanese soldiers from this engagement were apparently all killed during the Allied liberation of Cabanatuan City.

On January 31, some of Captain Juan Pajota's men located the body of Corporal Roy Sweezy in the creek bed on the east side of the stockade and carried him to Barrio Balangkare. They buried Roy Sweezy next to Captain James Fisher in the "Memorial Park."

The official document listing the names of the rescued POWs was originally classified "secret" and is known as the "Cabanatuan List." Within a few days after the raid, the families of those liberated were notified by the U.S. military, but the *complete* list was never released for publication.

One POW had died at the gates of the stockade of an apparent heart attack only moments before being carried to freedom. Englishman Edwin Rose was not processed with the bulk of POWs at Guimba on January 31 and February 1. The "Cabanatuan List" contains 515 names—424 U.S. Army personnel, one Filipino civilian (the records do not indicate why this individual was in the camp), twenty-eight U.S. civilians, two Norwegian civilians, three Dutch Army, twenty British Army, two U.S. Marines, thirty-eight U.S. Navy personnel, two British Navy, and one British civilian. Rose's name would bring the total number of POWs rescued to 516.

By the end of February 2 Cabanatuan City and the Naotake Command had fallen and the city was liberated by Allied forces. Soon after, world newsmen, correspondents, and photographers received a briefing on the most successful mission of its type in U.S. military history—the "Cabanatuan POW Camp Story." Even then, the details released were distorted and not complete.

The official press release issued by General Douglas MacArthur immediately following the raid stated, in part, "I have awarded the Commanding Officer of the rescue mission the Distinguished Service Cross, all other officers the Silver Star and all enlisted men the Bronze star for this heroic enterprise. No incident of the campaign has given me such personal satisfaction."

General Walter Krueger personally presented the awards on March 3, 1945. Actually both Colonel Henry Mucci and Captain Robert Prince received the Distinguished Service Cross. The other American officers received the Silver Star and enlisted men, the Bronze Star. In addition, all members of both C Company and the 2nd Platoon of F Company received the special "Unit Citation." Although officers in the Army, for some reason Captain Juan Pajota and Captain Eduardo Joson did not receive the Silver Star. They had to settle for the Bronze Star.

The news of the raid, the tragic Bataan Death March, and the "death camps" flashed about the world. "Cabanatuan" was a front-page story for a few days, but the rapid developments in a world at war soon superseded it. In less than three weeks, a place where more than 1,000 Americans were dying for every mile gained became a common name—Iwo Jima.

Luzon was not declared "secure" until July 4, and General Tomoyuki Yamashita, with the remnants of his defending force in northern Luzon, did not surrender until September 2. His Fourteenth Area Army of 450,000 troops (counting eleventh-hour reinforcements) was down to about 100,000 sick and wounded men. Less than 50,000 were still with Yamashita at his surrender. As late as 1974, individual Japanese imperial soldiers were still surrendering in remote areas of the Philippines. It is reported that a few are still holding out. In total, the liberation of the Philippines had cost the Americans over 15,000 killed and 50,000 wounded.

But what was the major significance of the raid on Cabanatuan? From a military point of view, the assault was a perfectly coordinated effort, well planned and executed. It was the first and, to this date, the most successful mission of its type carried out by the United States Army. Yet the basic planning involved nothing particularly revolutionary in tactics. Only the performance of each soldier involved was extraordinary. From a practical standpoint, the raid reminded a troubled world that the United States may go to great extremes to rescue a few of her citizens. But the psychological effect was most overwhelming. The suicidal tactics of the Japanese military (the kamikaze being only one) indicated that Japan would not surrender her mainland without a fight to the last man. The rescued POWs from Cabanatuan were living proof of the atrocities that had been committed during the Bataan Death March and in the death camps. With this knowledge, the Allied world became even more outraged. In the minds of Americans at home and on the war front, *anything* that might save lives in the long run must be employed. Any method, any weapon, could be justified if it shortened the war. A brutal military power that obviously had no regard for human life must be destroyed. The indirect result was Hiroshima and Nagasaki.

On August 10, 1945, the Japanese agreed to surrender, and at

9:00 A.M., Sunday, September 2, the formal surrender documents were signed aboard the U.S.S. *Missouri,* anchored in Tokyo Bay. On the morning of July 4, 1946, during an official ceremony in Manila's Luneta Park, the American flag was hauled down. The flag of the new Republic of the Philippines went up. For the first time in over 400 years, the Philippines was a free and independent country.

What became of the individuals mentioned in this book? Imperial Army General Masaharu Homma and General Tomoyuki Yamashita, along with many other Imperial Army officers, stood trial for war crimes. Homma was executed for having command responsibility during the Bataan Death March and ignoring early atrocities committed by his forces on the islands. Yamashita was executed for having command responsibility while Japanese atrocities continued unchecked during the liberation. Captain Yoshio Tsuneyoshi, the first commandant of the Death Camp O'Donnell, was found guilty of mistreatment of prisoners of war. On November 21, 1947, he was sentenced to be confined at hard labor for life. Lieutenant Colonel Shigeji Mori, commandant of the Death Camp Cabanatuan, was found guilty of mistreatment of prisoners of war. On November 7, 1947, he was sentenced to be confined at hard labor for life. Colonel Mori was not the commandant at Cabanatuan at the time of the raid.

USAFFE Generals Jonathan M. Wainwright, Edward P. King, Jr., George M. Parker, and Albert M. Jones, and many other high-ranking U.S. POWs were shifted from one death camp to another until the end of the war. They were liberated from their last camp in Manchuria by Russian troops. General Wainwright stood with General MacArthur on the U.S.S. *Missouri* to witness the signing of the Japanese surrender. Within a few years, all retired from the military except MacArthur, whose colorful career came to an abrupt halt, of course, during the Korean War.

Nurse Josefa F. Hilado was awarded the Silver Medal (the highest award of the American Red Cross) and the Philippine Legion of Honor and became a candidate for the U.S. Medal of Freedom and the Florence Nightingale Medal for her heroic service during the Death March and those horrible months at Camps O'Donnell and Cabanatuan. She later married, and Josefa Hilado Torre emigrated to the United States. Today, still working as a nurse, she is with a large midwestern Veterans' Hospital. Private Adriano Olivar, Jr., with one leg blown away in Bataan, survived the Death March and O'Donnell. This extraordinary and determined man finished school and fulfilled his dreams by becoming a doctor. Later, he emigrated to the United States and has a successful medical practice near Chicago.

Of the former American POWs, Corporals Albert Charmelo, Leonard Hicks, and Louis Latchman and PFCs Frank Fontana, George Dravo, and Forrest Dreger all were shipped from Luzon in late 1944 to POW camps in or near Japan. They were among the few who survived to see the end of the war, and returned to civilian life in late 1945 and early 1946.

From POW Camp Cabanatuan, medic PFC Eugene Evers returned to civilian life and lives in Iowa. First Lieutenant Merle McNeal Musselman, M.D., who volunteered to stay behind the night of the raid to attend to Captain Fisher's wounds, returned to his native Midwest and is still serving his country, as a civilian physician. Colonel James Duckworth, M.D., returned to the United States and served as a civilian physician until his death several years ago. Sergeant Abie Abraham lived to testify against the Japanese during the postwar trials, but his service in the military was not over. Within a short time after his liberation from Cabanatuan, General MacArthur personally assigned the tough little NCO a task that was unfair, considering all that Abraham had been through. He could have declined MacArthur's "requested assignment," but did not. Abie Abraham was allowed to spend a few days with his family (who had survived civilian prisons in Manila) and then returned to Bataan to carry out his duty. Abraham, with a team of Filipinos, sought the American graves along the Death March route and exhumed thousands for reburial in national cemeteries. For more than two years after the war, Master Sergeant Abraham continued to search for the remains of his comrades until ill health finally forced him back to the United States. He later wrote his own book, describing in detail his nine years of service in the Philippines.

Of the American guerrillas, Major Robert Lapham returned to the United States and recently retired as a vice-president of Burroughs Corporation. Today he resides in Arizona. Colonel R. W. Volckmann returned to the United States and entered private business, later to write his own book about his guerrilla campaign in northern Luzon. Captain Harry M. McKenzie, a civilian living in the Philippines before the war, returned to private business. The moment Manila fell to the Allies, Colonel Bernard Anderson rushed to Santo Tomas civilian prison to seek his fiancée. He received the heartbreaking news that she had died of a ruptured appendix a few days before freedom. The Japanese had refused to operate and claimed they had no medicines for civilian prisoners. Anderson returned to the hills and continued his fight with the enemy until Japan's surrender. He remained in the Philippines as a civilian executive for many years. Now, he resides in a peaceful town in Florida.

At the peak of the Vietnam War, in November 1970, a team of United States Special Forces (Green Berets) were carried by helicopter behind enemy lines on a special mission. They launched an assault on the North Vietnamese POW camp known as Son Tay, near Hanoi. There are some interesting relations (with regard to participants) between the raid on Cabanatuan and the raid on Son Tay, although the raids occurred in different countries and different wars, almost twenty-six years apart. As a guerrilla in northern Luzon in 1945, Donald B. Blackburn was well posted on the situation at Cabanatuan. Twenty-six years later, Brigadier General Donald Blackburn helped organize the raid on Son Tay. Captain Arthur D. Simons, as B Company commander of the 6th Rangers in 1945, missed out on the Cabanatuan assignment due to his earlier orders to Santiago Island. In 1970, Colonel Arthur "Bull" Simons trained his Green Beret team and led the raid on Son Tay. One of those Green Berets on that raid, manning a helicopter machine gun, was none other than Master Sergeant Galen Kittleson. This former Tommygunner with the Alamo Scouts holds the distinction of being the only American soldier to have participated in three major assaults on enemy POW stockades. The first two were in World War II (the raid in New Guinea to free Dutch POWs and Cabanatuan). The third was Son Tay. Colonel Simons has retired from the military.

Of the other Alamo Scouts, Lieutenant Tom Rounsaville stayed with the Army and recently retired as a colonel. Lieutenant Bill Nellist returned to civilian life in the United States, as did most of the Scouts. At the end of the war, Nellist and Rounsaville asked Filipino-American Rufo Vaquilar what his plans were. "I think I'll just keep going down this dusty road. I'll see you guys some day," Vaquilar replied. They never saw him again. But Vaquilar had not completely disappeared. In 1976, I found him living peacefully in California surrounded by a number of grandchildren.

Huk leader Luis Taruc had a long bitter war ahead, after the liberation. Soon the Huks began a vigorous military campaign against the government. Taruc, his first wife dead from disease and his second killed in a battle with federal troops, finally surrendered in the mid-1950s. By 1975, he had become leader of Faith Incorporated in the Philippines, working as a liaison with the Marcos government. At long last, Taruc had found a peaceful way to help his farmers and underprivileged.

General Walter Krueger retired just after the war and died a few years later. Mario S. Garcia, the Cabantuan City Constabulary officer and Death March survivor who worked with the guerrillas, later was elected mayor of Cabanatuan and then retired to ranching. Captain Eduardo Joson later became governor of Nueva Ecija. Lieutenant Colonel William C. Odell, the 547th Night Fighter Squadron commander, is now a writer, having more than sixteen published works to his credit. Kenneth R. Schrieber, the pilot of the P61 "Hard to Get," stayed in the service until 1947. In 1951, he was recalled to flight status for the Korean War and retired as a lieutenant colonel in 1966. Today he still works for the government in a civilian capacity.

Directly or indirectly, Colonel Mucci kept his promotion promise to Robert W. Prince. The Ranger C Company commander finished the war as a major then returned to his favorite Northwest coast area to enter the apple business. Today, Bob Prince travels the world representing the Apple Growers Association in an executive capacity.

Henry A. Mucci was transfered from the 6th Rangers he had developed into such an effective fighting force to the 6th Division to command the 1st Infantry Regiment in February 1945 and was promoted to full colonel. He was wounded by a mortar burst, which ultimately led to a 1946 medical discharge. After an unsuccessful try at politics in his native New England, Mucci joined the petroleum industry and functioned as an executive. In this capacity, he worked in Asia for fifteen years and in 1977 he announced he would retire to Florida.

The other Rangers involved in the raid eventually returned to civilian life, pursuing a wide variety of careers. Tech 5 Francis "Father" Schilli, for example, returned to farm implement and violin repair. PFC Bill Proudfit returned to Iowa and is a bricklayer. In October 1976, Bill Proudfit traveled to Leyte to attend an anniversary celebration of MacArthur's return to the Philippines. There, Bill was presented an old American flag that the Filipinos had been saving for the first Ranger to return to that area. It was the same flag the 6th Rangers raised on Dinagat, October 18, 1945, two days before the major Allied invasion.

For Juan Pajota and his squadrons, the war continued into northern Luzon until the Japanese surrender. By that time, Pajota had been promoted to the rank of major. After the war, he was appointed temporary military governor of Nueva Ecija. Then came the bitter irony. Although Pajota and many of his men were "recognized" as official members of the U.S. Armed Forces, none of Squadron 202 and most of Squadron 200 who fought at Cabu bridge (and many battles later) were not recognized.

The argument over "recognition" continues today. Of the more than 100,000 Filipinos still unrecognized (mostly of USAFFE and guerrilla squadrons), the majority have long since lost hope for U.S. veteran benefits. The U.S. military stands firm with its claims that a fair system was employed for recognition after the war. The system may have been fair but its employment left much to be desired. In 1946, most former guerrillas had returned to the farms and barrios and could not be located. Corruption on the part of some Filipinos and Americans involved in the recognition process is a matter still debated. Juan Pajota came to America in December 1976 to file for U.S. citizenship. But the citizenship for all World War II Filipino veterans had been blocked in federal court. A year later the case was resolved in favor of the veterans, but Major Pajota died of a heart attack a few days before he could see his lifelong dream to become an

American fulfilled. It was an honor to have Pajota as my house guest for that year before his death.

The war also did not end quickly for Unit F (Photo) of the 832nd Signal Service Battalion. Little five-foot-five-inch Tech 4 Frank J. Goetzheimer, proving once again that bravery is something more than size, volunteered for the 503rd Parachute Regimental Combat Team's airborne assault on Corregidor. On February 17, 1945, he landed with the first wave of paratroopers and was later awarded the Oak Leaf Cluster for his Cabanatuan Bronze Star. Behind him, in the second wave, came Corporal Robert C. Lautman and 1st Lieutenant John W. Lueddeke making their very first parachute jump—on a small rocky island.

But while on Luzon, luck ran out for the 832nd. PFC Wilber B. Goen also jumped onto Corregidor with Goetzheimer in that first wave. The unit was later assigned a mission in northern Luzon with the 37th Division. Following closely behind a tank and snapping photos with his four-by-six Speed Graphic, PFC Goen was struck by shell fragments and died in a field hospital four hours later.

The parents of Captain James C. Fisher moved with two basic courses of action upon learning of the death of their son. First, they made arrangements for Doctor Carlos Layug and his wife, Julita, to journey to the United States for medical postgraduate studies. It was a generous move to reward one of the Filipinos who had assisted in attempting to save Jimmy Fisher. Today, in Cabanatuan City, Doctor Layug has retired from practice, but outside his medical clinic there is still a sign which reads *"James C. Fisher Memorial Clinic."*

The second step for the Fishers was to find a method whereby the Filipinos would know of the appreciation for their brave assistance to the Rangers. The Fishers decided to have a memorial tablet placed on the tree marking the spot where Captain Fisher was buried. They pleaded with the Army to leave his grave at Balangkare, but the Graves Registration Service had acted swiftly. Captain Fisher had already been reburied in a military cemetery. During wartime there was little bronze available, so the plaque had to wait. Some eight years later, through the help of General Carlos Romulo and many others, a monument was erected. Standing in Barrio Balangkare, Nueva Ecija, is a large circular concrete apron with a stone fence and benches on its perimeter. In the center, one can walk up four steps and confront two bronze plaques set in concrete cubes some eight feet in height. The words on one plaque are in English, those on the other, Tagalog. They read:

"This tablet is erected to honor the humane kindness of the people of Balangkare Sur, to an American Officer, who died here and was buried under this tree January 31, 1945. Captain James Canfield Fisher, Medical Officer of the 6th United States Rangers, had gone with them on their expedition to free 516 prisoners held by the Japanese at Cabanatuan. Wounded there, he was brought back here. At the risk of their lives, the men and women of this barrio gave him shelter and protection during the last hours of his life. This act of courageous Filipino friendliness will never be forgotten by Dr. Fisher's family and by his comrades in the American Army. May the memory of dangers shared and blood they shed together, unite our peoples forever. Men die . . . the spirit lives."

AUTHOR'S NOTES

Most of the information for this story comes from those who participated. There is little printed data available on the raid, although a fair amount of published material is obtainable on the Bataan Death March and the war in the Philippines. I have listed related works in the bibliography.

My sincere thanks must surely go to those who gave freely of their time so that this story could finally be told in its entirety. Over six years of research were required to complete it—procuring the appropriate documents, maps, and photographs and locating the key individuals who were involved. A skeleton of the story was not complicated to form, as it could be outlined and assembled from "after action" reports, unit history reports, and related documents. But its structure was like a simple picture, leaving the scene full of empty spaces similar to a half-finished jigsaw puzzle on a table. The declassification of heretofore "secret" government information on World War II in Luzon helped fill a few of the spaces. As strange as it may seem, many of these thirty- to thirty-five-year-old documents were only recently declassified.

Those individuals who participated were able to complete the puzzle. Each remembered his particular assignment in often re-markable detail. Between 1945 and the time I began my research, about 20 percent of those who were involved had passed away. Another 8 percent died during the research phase. Those remain-ing were literally scattered about the world—all over the United States, the Philippines, and elsewhere. Colonel Henry Mucci, for example, was finally located in Thailand. P61 "Black Widow" pilot Kenneth Schrieber of the "Hard to Get" was working in Panama.

Yet I was fortunate to find, and privileged to talk with, over 50 percent of those who did participate. More than 500 people were interviewed during those six years. Often, months after an inter-view, I uncovered another bit of information that had to be reveri-fied. I always preferred to have at least two witnesses to each event.

The total accumulation of data filled three file cabinets and contained everything from information on the amount of am-munition used by the P61s on January 30, 1945, to the type of wristwatch that Captain Pajota was wearing. Those who helped not only gave freely of their time but turned over for my viewing their treasured scrapbooks, snapshots, maps, personal diaries, and memorabilia. Unfortunately, there simply is not enough space to list and thank each one, but they do have my deep appreciation.

Conversation in this book was reconstructed through the as-sistance of those engaged in the dialogue or, in some cases, by the memory of two other people who were present during a meeting or event. Where possible, both parties were asked to verify to the best of their ability what was said and how it was said. Descrip-tion of emotions was organized in the same manner, occasionally punctuated by my own observations of the individual during in-terviews.

In some cases, especially with former POWs or Bataan Death March survivors, reminiscences were painful. Often, a delicate ap-proach to certain subjects was necessary. The human brain can play many games with us all, in particular those who suffered much. For example, when I questioned Doctor Merle Musselman about the POWs' homemade radio assembled and used at Ca-banatuan, he remarked, "Oh, my God! Do you know I still have nightmares about that radio! I did not want to know where it was. If the Japs knew about it, we would have been tortured and beaten until we revealed its location. To know its location could mean death. Sometimes . . . I dream I know the radio's location and I wake up, heart pounding . . . until I realize that was over thirty years ago."

Before this story could be written I felt it necessary for me to study the actual terrain on which the battles were fought. I journeyed to Luzon to see Bataan and Nueva Ecija. Weeks of hiking and bouncing jeep rides produced the results I needed—firsthand knowledge of the trails, rivers, and mountains where it all occurred.

Interviews with Filipino witnesses (both civilian and military) to the Bataan Death March and the raid yielded a colorful conclusion to my trip. Luzon, of course, is an island. The lifestyle and customs of its inhabitants, influenced by the tradition, had permitted the majority to maintain close contact with one another since the war. It is a fact that in various provinces on Luzon life has changed little since 1945.

I am grateful to the Philippine government for their gracious hospitality and assistance. My thanks go to Mr. Mario S. Garcia, former mayor of Cabanatuan City, for his kindness and help, and likewise to the hundreds of Filipinos who made my stay in their country most fruitful and pleasant.

Special thanks to Consular Jose R. Nuguid, former congressman of Bataan, whose "contacts" proved very valuable. Thanks also to Robert Prince and Juan Pajota, whose great memory for detail provided many missing pieces to the puzzle.

It is seldom that one has the opportunity to meet men of such high caliber and dignity.

My thanks to Mr. Sam Kajita, who assisted with the difficult Japanese-to-English translations of special Imperial Army Records, and to Ms. Sharon Wenda, whose artistic talents produced such useful maps for this book.

My deep appreciation to my friend, Lieutenant Colonel Chan Wysor, Special Forces, USAR, for his enthusiastic encouragement, and to those I love for their understanding when so many trails seemed to lead in circles or to dead ends.

While on Luzon in January 1976, I stood on a dirt road in the center of a large rice field near Barrio Pangatian—the same road that once ran through the center of POW Camp Cabanatuan. To the south I could see the small chapel that the Filipinos erected just before World War II. It is the only thing left of what was once the POW camp.

Around me was nothing but fresh green rice. There were no markers, no monument, and no flags. Not even a strand of barbed wire remains to remind one of what once was there. In late 1945, Graves Registration of the U.S. Army exhumed those buried at the camp cemetery for reburial in other places.

Mayor Garcia and his staff, in nearby Cabanatuan City, had a program under way to convert the former POW camp area into a memorial park. In 1975 the U.S. Embassy in Manila was approached with a request for a small contribution to be applied toward the cost of erecting a marker. The Filipinos would pay the balance and furnish the land. Mayor Garcia was advised that the United States had "no funds available for such a program."

At that time the United States officially rejected the opportunity to help mark the site where over 3,000 of her young men died a slow horrible death, where over a hundred American volunteers risked their lives to snatch 517 comrades from death's grasp during the raid on Cabanatuan.

A few years ago a monument was erected at the same site. The Filipinos donated the land and furnished the labor, but the irony of the Cabanatuan story continued. The funds for the memorial were raised by former American POWs and veterans as a tribute to their comrades who suffered and died before the raid on Cabanatuan.

ROSTERS

The following officers and enlisted men of the U.S. 6th Rangers are officially credited by government archives for being on the raid on Cabanatuan. Ranks are as of early 1945.

LIEUTENANT COLONEL
Henry A. Mucci

CAPTAINS
James C. Fisher
Robert W. Prince

FIRST LIEUTENANTS
John F. Murphy
William J. O'Connell
Melville R. Schmidt
Clifford K. Smith

FIRST SERGEANTS
Robert G. Anderson
Charles H. Bosard
Ned H. Hedrick

TECHNICAL SERGEANTS
   Melvin H. Gilbert
   Daniel H. Watson
   Ralph C. Franks

STAFF SERGEANTS
   John W. Nelson
   Charles W. Brown
   David M. Hey
   James V. Millican
   Richard A. Moore
   Cleatus G. Norton
   James O. White
   Norton S. Most
   Floyd S. Anderson
   Lyle C. Bishop
   William R. Butler
   Thomas H. Frick
   Clifford B. Gudmunsen
   Clifton R. Harris
   Preston N. Jensen
   Mike Koren
   Lester L. Malone
   Theodore R. Richardson
   August T. Stern, Jr.
   Manton P. Stewart

SERGEANTS
   Claude R. Howell
   Albert F. Outwater, Jr.
   Vance R. Shears
   James M. Tucker
   Leo M. Wentland
   Milo C. Mortensen
   Arthur T. Williams
   Harry G. Killough
   Joseph O. Youngblood

TECH 4S
    Homer E. Britzius
    Robert L. Camp

CORPORALS
    Martin T. Estesen
    Waymon E. Finley
    James B. Herrick
    Marvin W. Kinder
    John G. Palomares
    Roy W. Sweezy
    Robert L. Ramsey

TECH 5S
    Bernard L. Haynes
    Edward L. Biggs
    Patrick F. Marquis
    Francis R. Schilli
    William A. Lawver
    Robert W. White
    Dalton H. Garrett
    Alymer C. Jinkins

PRIVATES FIRST CLASS
    Robert C. Strube
    Warren M. Bell
    James W. Conley
    Donald A. Adams
    Carlton O. Dietzel
    Eugene H. Dykes
    Howard R. Fortenberry
    Thomas A. Grace, Jr.
    Dale F. Harris
    Norman F. Higgins
    Frank C. Hudoba
    F. J. Hughes
    Edward N. Knowles
    John V. Pearson

Joseph M. Pospishil
William H. Proudfit
George H. Randall
Buford K. Spicer
Frank R. St. John
Gerhard J. Tiede
Vernon Ablott
John D. Blannett
William F. Crumpton
Virgil S. Dixon
Waverly R. Duke
Edwin G. Enstrom
Mariano Garde
William H. Garrison
Paul J. Grimm
Howard J. Guillory
Clarence W. Heezen
Andrew J. Herman
Eugene J. Kocsis
Edward Littleton
Joseph Lombardo
Alfred A. Martin
Billy McElroy
Alfred J. McGinnis
Ralph C. Melendez
Leroy B. Myerhoff
Edward Paluck
Jack A. Peters
Roy B. Peters
Alva A. Polzine
Leland A. Provencher
Merrie K. Purtell
James M. Reynolds
John B. Richardson
Alvie E. Robbins
Edgar L. Ruble
Roy D. Sebeck
Melvin P. Shearer

Charles Q. Snyder
Conrad J. Solf
Peter P. Superak
Charles S. Swain
Russell J. Swank
Ronald R. Thomas
Alexander E. Truskowski
Jasper T. Westmoreland
Ray E. Williams

The following men of Combat Photo Unit F, 832nd Signal Service Battalion, are credited for accompanying the 6th Rangers on the raid. Ranks are of early 1945.

FIRST LIEUTENANT
John W. Lueddeke

TECH 4
Frank J. Goetzheimer

PRIVATES FIRST CLASS
Wilber B. Goen
Robert C. Lautman

The following men of the Alamo Scouts, Sixth U.S. Army, are credited for their involvement in the raid. Ranks are as of early 1945.

FIRST LIEUTENANTS
Thomas Rounsaville
William Nellist
John E. Dove

SERGEANTS
Harold Hard
Galen Kittleson

PRIVATES FIRST CLASS
Rufo Vaquilar
Franklin Fox
Gilbert Cox
Wilbur Wismer

Francis Laquier
Alfred Alfonso
Andy Smith
Sabas Asis
Thomas Siason

The following roster of Allied prisoners of war who were liberated the night of January 30, 1945, during the raid was known officially as the "Cabanatuan List." It was originally classified "secret" and remained so for years after World War II. The list has been copied from the original, which was compiled by the United States Sixth Army headquarters at Guimba within forty-eight hours of the raid. Names were misspelled and many ranks were incorrect. Apparently, several clerks attempted to procure necessary information from over 500 POWs who were confused, sick, or still in a state of shock. Several POWs gave the Philippines as their home address. Most of these men lived in the islands before the war. A few had families who were unable to evacuate during the Japanese invasion.

NAMES	HOME ADDRESS GIVEN
COLONELS	
Alfred Olivar (Chaplain)	Washington, D.C.
James Duckworth, M.D.	San Francisco, California
COMMANDER	
Lea Sartin	Houma, Louisiana
LIEUTENANT COMMANDERS	
Jerry Steward	Los Banos, Luzon
Robert Strong, Jr.	Arlington, Massachusetts
Hjalalmar Erickson	Los Angeles, California
LIEUTENANT COLONELS	
Albert Fields (or Fralds)	Coffeyville, Kansas
William Galos	none listed
Robert Johnston	Columbus, Georgia
Edward Kallus	Caldwell, Texas
Donald Sawtelle	Corpus Christi, Texas

Thomas Willson   Little Rock, Arkansas

James Green   Mt. Bontoc, Luzon

MAJORS

William Knoblock   Camarenes Sur, Luzon

Stephen Sitter   Milwaukee, Wisconsin

Robert Hill   Manila, Luzon

Paul Wing   Lexington, Kentucky

Ralph Hubbard   Oklahoma City, Oklahoma

John Borneman   Niagara Falls, New York

Emil Reed   Dallas, Texas

CAPTAINS

Robert Roseveare   Manila, Luzon

Wilson McNeil   Lawton, Oklahoma

Bertram Bank   Tuscaloosa, Alabama

Matt Dobrinic   Taylor Springs, Illinois

Robert Lewis   Cape Elizabeth, Maine

Robert Whiteley   Palo Alto, California

Jules Yates   Scranton, Pennsylvania

Frederick Amos   Humboldt, Kansas

Curtis Burson   Denver, Colorado

John Dugan   Melton, Massachusetts

Robert Duncan   San Francisco, California

Lloyd Floyd   Enterprise, Oregon

Jules Gates   Scranton, Pennsylvania

Ralph Hibbs   Oskaloosa, Iowa

Charles Katz   Oak Park, Illinois

Ben King   Austin, Texas

Raymond Knapp   San Antonio, Texas

Charles Leasum   Stergon Bay, Wisconsin

Robert Sly   Eugene, Oregon

James Trippe   Los Angeles, California

Dallas Vinette   Tarts, New Mexico

John Lucas   Washington, D.C.

Caryl Piccotte   Oakland, California

Denton Rees   Milwaukee, Wisconsin

Donald Robins   Detroit, Michigan

Homer Colman   Grand Junction, Colorado

FIRST LIEUTENANTS

Seaton Foley	San Rafeal, California
Francis Lunnie	Concord, Vermont
Walter Stone	Chicago, Illinois
George Kane	Atlanta, Georgia
Hugh Kennedy (Chaplain)	Scarsdale, New York
Merle Musselman, M.D.	Nebraska City, Nebraska
Herbert Ott	Wheaton, Illinois
Earl Baumgardner	Yonkers, New York
Knut Engerset	San Pedro, California
George Green	Auburn, Alabama
Issac Lavictaire	Pigean, Michigan
Alma Salm	Oakland, California
Emmet Manson	Worthington, Minnesota
Eugene Okeefe	South Orange, New Jersey

SECOND LIEUTENANTS

Frank Burgess	San Diego, California
Donald Miller	South Gate, California
Daniel Limpert	Albuquerque, New Mexico
Charles Fox, Sr.	Oakland, California
Ambrose Wangler	Graveport, Ohio
Jerome Triolo	El Paso, Texas
Edward Thomas	Grand Rapids, Michigan
John Temple	Pittsfield, Massachusetts
Willard Smith	Altadena, California
Melvin Johnston	Long Beach, California
Richard Hedreck	Manila, Luzon
William Haines	Waynesburg, Pennsylvania
Buerly Gibbon	Marshall, Michigan
William Gentry	Harrodsburg, Kentucky
William Duncan	Pelahatchia, Mississippi
Calude Daniel	Bogalusa, Louisiana
Clifton Chamberlain	Marlin, Texas
Robert Burke	Quebec, Canada
Jarry Brown	Brownsburg, Indiana
Raymond Bliss	none listed
William Romme	Terre Haute, Indiana

John Zimmerman	Lynchburg, Virginia
Jack Jennings	Sausalito, California
Tony Wheeler	Seagraves, Texas

WARRANT OFFICERS

Grover Gilbert	Ludlow, Illinois
James Pfeiffer	Buffalo, New York
Ralph Ellis	San Antonio, Texas
Eric Lundblad	San Francisco, California
James Shimel	Philadelphia, Pennsylvania

SERGEANTS

Stanley Bronk	Seattle, Washington
Dale Lawton	Mineral Point, Wisconsin
Marvin Laycock	Libertyville, Illinois
Orville Drummond	Clovis, New Mexico
George Clow	Omaha, Illinois
Damon Howard	Norway, Minnesota
John Batcheler	Ashland, Oregon
Harold Beasley	Timpson, Texas
Donald Bridges	Emervylle, California
David Chavez	Albuquerque, New Mexico
Nathan Cleaves	Portland, Maine
Earnest Clements	Wrens, Georgia
Richard Craycroft	Vine Grove, Kentucky
Frederick Crocker	Spartanburg, South Carolina
George Darling	Deming, New Mexico
Wilber Disosway	Hampton, Virginia
John Kelly (Sergeant Major)	San Diego, California
Archibeque Esperidion	Albuquerque, New Mexico
Julius Farrell	San Diego, California
Jack Fogerson	Clovis, New Mexico
Virgil Ford	Memphis, Texas
Walter French	Hardy, Arkansas
Fred Gaston	San Francisco, California
Samuel Goldy	Gloucester City, New Jersey
Cecil Heflin	Lake, Mississippi
Elmer Howell	not given
Everett Keyes	Concord, New Hampshire

Joseph Knapp	Fairport Harbor, Ohio
William Lambert	Fort Meyers, Florida
Sylvester Lane	New Port, Kentucky
Burney Machovic	Ridgefield Park, New Jersey
Lewis Taylor	Phoenix, Arizona
Roy Smith	Pelly, Texas
Austin Rogers	Florence, South Carolina
Hassel Short	Whitesboro, Texas
Alma Owen	Salt Lake City, Utah
Charles Novak	Philadelphia, Pennsylvania
Richard Neault	Adams, Massachusetts
Charles Mortimer	Crowe, Virginia
Leon Tice, Jr.	Odgenburg, Pennsylvania
Harry Pinto	Mount View, California
Clifton Copeland	Indianola, Mississippi
Kenneth Mize	Beattie, Kansas
Milo Folson	none listed
Edward Witmer, Jr.	Stansburg, Pennsylvania
Gerald Wagner	Rapid City, South Dakota
Charles Walker	Springfield, Illinois
Leon Swindell	Tifton, Georgia
William Thamos	Bloomsburg, Pennsylvania
Robert Doyle	none listed
George Dunn	Riverside, California
Abie Abraham	Manila
Ermon Addington	Harrison, Idaho
Louis Albin	San Antonio, Texas
Robert Baker	Valdosta, Georgia
Floyd Barnhardt	Chicago, Illinois
Chester Brown	Trenton, Missouri
Julian Brown	Madison, Florida
Edward Burns	Bowman, North Dakota
Roger Campbell	Marble, New Mexico
William Claxton	Los Angeles, California
Floyd Cooney	New Castle, Indiana
John Culp	State Line, Mississippi
Jacob Dusich	Queson, Philippines
Roy Gatewood	Elijah, Missouri

Leonard Gibbs	Willis, Texas
Harold Glass	Long Beach, California
Clinton Goodbla	West Wind, Iowa
Robert Guice	Heflin, Louisiana
Frederick Guth	Whitmore, California
George Gwin	Dubuque, Iowa
Almer Hannah	Liberty, Missouri
Arthur Harrison	Fresno, California
Roy Hoblet	Fayetteville, Arkansas
Oliver Hoover	Huntington Park, California
Robert Howe, Jr.	Batavia, New York
Melvin Johnson	Biggs, California
Gust Katrones	Manila
Marcos Keithley	Oakford, Illinois
Walter Ruig	San Roque, Luzon
John Ryan	Baltimore, Maryland
Lavergne Ritchie	Trenton, Illinois
Calvin Rhoades	Wolfe City, Texas
Everett Reyes	Concord, New Hampshire
D. C. Raines	Bonifay, Florida
Frederick Rabin	Long Beach, California
Arnold King	Hutchinson, Kansas
Togan Kinnison	Lincoln, Nebraska
William Kippen	Cleveland, Ohio
Charles Kyllo	Salt Lake City, Utah
Stanislaus Malor	Salem, Massachusetts
Charles Mokewen	Ithaca, New York
Paul McKinley	Portland, Oregon
Eldred McPherson	Fortuna, California
Edward Miller	Hagerstown, Maryland
Walter Miller	Los Angeles, California
Darvin Patrick	Hummelstown, Pennsylvania
Alfred Pharr	Jasper, Texas
Charles Quinn	Dayton, Ohio
Donald Smith	Boulder, Colorado
Henry Staples	Binghamton, New York
Blake Vanlandingham	Crosses, Arkansas
Ari Vico	Crockett, California

Stanley Wallace	Sikestown, Missouri
Frederick Walther	Provo, Utah
Finas Williams	Washington, D.C.
William Smith	San Diego, California
Milton Englin	Seattle, Washington
Eugene Commander	San Diego, California
Harry Arnold	Liberty, Missouri

CORPORALS

Millard Basinger	Pomona, California
Lloyd Blanchard	Port Arthur, Texas
William Davis	Medford, Oregon
Hugh Branch	Cut Bank, Montana
Cecil Hay	Marlin, Texas
Alfred Taube	Omaha, Nebraska
Patrick Bryne	Chicago, Illinois
Paul Nateswa	Seama, New Mexico
William Peterson	Lake Park, Iowa
Richard Scott	Helena, Montana
Gareth Reed	Walla Walla, Washington
Ray Wilson	Long Beach, California
Deno Zucca	Pocahontas, Illinois
Neil Piovino	Chicago, Illinois
Edward Berry	Topango, California
Dennis Rainwater	Paris, Arkansas
Max Greenburg	none listed
Meil Jovina	none listed
Glen Hagstrom	Spokane, Washington
Richard Chapman	Guilford, Connecticut
Quentine Devore	Wray, Colorado
Ted Easton	Venice, California
Paul Gernandt	Davenport, Iowa
John Reiff	Glen Ullin, North Dakota
Frank Potyraj	Grand Rapids, Michigan
Fred Schumm	Staten Island, New York
Edward Seaman	Middleport, New York
Carl Stuard	Walthill, Nebraska
Roy Terry	Bakersfield, California

Karl Tobey	Fallon, Nevada
Rufus Turnbow	Konawa, Oklahoma
Albert Parker	Deming, New Mexico

PRIVATES FIRST CLASS

Lloyd Anderson	Everett, Washington
Richard Barnes	San Antonio, Texas
Louis Barry	Louisville, Kentucky
Eugene Clark	Lincoln, Nebraska
David Coull	Atlantic City, New Jersey
James Cowan	Fullerton, California
Howard Hall	Haleyville, Alabama
Allen Gutridge	Baker, Oregon
Spiriano Greigo	Albuquerque, New Mexico
John Gordon	Chicago, Illinois
Frank Franchini	Albuquerque, New Mexico
John Dugan	Springfield, Ohio
Lawrence Hall	Jellico, Tennessee
Joseph Henry	Kelso, Washington
Raymond Holland	Deland, Florida
Louis Macholl	Marcellus, New York
Robert Paco	Greenville, South Carolina
George Parrott	Bryan, Ohio
Don Robertson	Ardmore, Oklahoma
Roy Jones, Sr.	Visalia, California
Samuel Korrocks	Oakland, California
J. B. Miller	Brownwood, Texas
Pat Parker	Caliun, Oklahoma
Carroll Sherman	Baton Rouge, Louisiana
Field Reed, Sr.	Harrodsburg, Kentucky
Ralph Rodriques	Bernalilla, New Mexico
William Shults	Corsicana, Texas
Ted Thomas	Mangum, Oklahoma
Robert Unger	Berkley Springs, West Virginia
John West	Roswell, New Mexico
Louis Zeliz	Chicago, Illinois
Dale Forrest	Richmond, California
Jack Ostrom	Miles City, Montana

Samuel Horrocks	Oakland, California
Sjpriano Srugo	none listed
Robert Strasters	Salt Lake City, Utah
Lester Vitek	Chelsea, Iowa
Peter Soppoknerky	none listed
Lorne Cox	Medford, Oregon
Harold Amos	Afton, Iowa
Richard Beck	Atlanta, Georgia
Clarence Bower	Mount Sterling, Ohio
Paul Browning	Princeton, New Jersey
Preston Bryant	Blue Springs, Nebraska
Benjamin Cabreiro	Hilo, Hawaii
Carl Carlson	Bronx, New York
Julius Cobb	Colorado Springs, Colorado
Sidney Coy	Louisville, Kentucky
Robert Decker	Omaha, Nebraska
Cecil Easiley	Houston, Texas
Claude Gibbons	Tracy, California
Herbert Herzog	Akron, Ohio
Charles Jensen	Chicago, Illinois
Vernice Kauffman	Fayetteville, Pennsylvania
Norman Lev	Chicago, Illinois
Sanford Locke	Suffolk, Virginia
George McHale	East Saint Louis, Illinois
John Moores	Woodbine, Iowa
Winthrop Pinkham	Dover, New Hampshire
William Rieck	Utica, Michigan
William Seckinger	Lilly, Pennsylvania
Ernesto Serrani	Coyote, New Mexico
Jeff Smith	McCrory, Arkansas
Donald Snyder	Pittsburg, Pennsylvania
Marshall Stoutenburgh	Kelly Corners, New York
Ira Taylor	Lexington, Texas
Joseph Thibeault	Lawrence, Massachusetts
Foch Tixtier	Albuquerque, New Mexico
Charles Tupy	Waucoma, Iowa
Dale Vonlinger	Mansfield, Illinois
Grandison Vroman	Ithaca, New York

Eugene Watson	Tucson, Arizona
Ben Williams	Espanola, New Mexico
Benjamin Williams	Crandall, Mississippi
Chester Easton	Englewood, California
Fred Vinton	Jackson, Michigan
Herman Silk	Isable, South Dakota
Lawdell Yates	Coolidge, Arizona
Thomas Wood	Detroit, Michigan
Frank Wilson	Salinas, California

PRIVATES

Herman Ancelet	Basco, Illinois
John Bailey	Chicago, Illinois
Lellon Barnes	Carrizoao, New Mexico
Archie Bellair, Jr.	Port Neches, Texas
Merwyn Chenoweth	Grass Valley, California
Lawrence Courtney	Monroe, Wisconsin
Carno Elkins	Tuskaloosa, Oklahoma
Eugene Evers	Dyersville, Iowa
Travis Flowers	Scranton, North Carolina
Thomas Gorman, Jr.	Elsayundo, California
William Harrison	Bozeman, Montana
Dean Henderson	Gooding, Idaho
Charles Hickey	Portland, Oregon
James Hildebrand	Chicago, Illinois
Arthur Hilshorst	Mt. Washington, Ohio
John McCarthy	Henly, Ohio
Vernon Jones	Alameda, California
Willie Jornogln	Peoria, Illinois
William Kirkpatrick	Eugene, Oregon
Walter Lawrence	Sioux City, Iowa
Clarence Mitchell	Huntsville, Texas
Lee Moore	St. Joseph, Missouri
James Ogg	Los Angeles, California
Jack Peak	Leonard, Texas
Felix Petcrck	Yuma, Arizona
Edgar Peters	Lake Park, Iowa
Robert Ross	Coffeyville, Kansas

Jesus Santos	Hebberville, Texas
Edward Searkey	Lynn, Massachusetts
George Sharpshire	Scottsville, Kentucky
Carl Smith	Oakland City, Indiana
Ralph Spinelli	Sewickley, Pennsylvania
Joseph Stanford	Pittsburgh, Pennsylvania
George Steiner	Loomis, California
Melvin Baxter	Mangum, Oklahoma
Joe Chavez	Belen, New Mexico
Bruce Choate	Little Rock, Arkansas
William Duncan	Troutsville, Virginia
Elbert Easterwood	Weatherford, Texas
John Elms	Shafter, California
Alfred Farrell	East Rockaway, New York
Burnise Fay	Albuquerque, New Mexico
Nelson Fonseca	San Jose, California
Gordon Fultz	Cresson, Pennsylvania
Dale Gilbert	Ashton, Illinois
Virgil Greenaway	Old Hickory, Tennessee
Lloyd Jackson	Holcomb, Missouri
Troy Holt	Fayetteville, Arkansas
Farley Hall	Huntington, West Virginia
Edward Johnson	Chicago, Illinois
Herman Kelier	Pineola, North Carolina
Richard Kellog	Salinas, California
William Lash	Willoughly, Ohio
Gerome Leek	Marshall, California
Vincent Lemely	Livingston, Montana
J. M. Lillard	Caddo, Oklahoma
Joseph Limbauch	Orosso, Michigan
Chester McGlosson	Latonia, Kentucky
Peter Connacher	Portland, Oregon
Sam Sina	Roseada, New Mexico
James Turner	Varnado, Louisiana
Macario Villaloboz	Rapid City, South Dakota
William Warren	Wichita, Kansas
Buster Wilkerson	Deming, New Mexico

Lawrence Williams	Glendive, Montana
James York	Syracuse, New York
Edward Gordon	Jackson, Mississippi
James Newman	Fort Worth, Texas
Don Adams	Artesia, New Mexico
William Alhschwede	Thayer, Nebraska
John Alford	Pensacola, Florida
Uriah Ash	Fairmount, West Virginia
William Baker	Oakland, California
Lee Bennett	Mound City, Missouri
Russel Boatwright	Colorado Springs, Colorado
Robert Body	Detroit, Michigan
James Boyle	Joshua, Texas
John Braunberger	Portland, Oregon
Charles Buchanan	Vicksburg, Mississippi
Joe Burks	Dumas, Texas
Ben Chavez	Soboyeto, New Mexico
Harold Memmler	Chicago, Illinois
Norman Moen	none listed
Roy Morris	Covington, Kentucky
Henry Peontck	Springfield, Illinois
Breed Phillips	Tangipahoa, Louisiana
Loren Pierce	Princeton, Minnesota
Peter Prinat	Cleveland, Ohio
Ira Pitts	Shawnee, Kansas
Earl Quay	Springfield, Missouri
Frank Rawlinson	Philadelphia, Pennsylvania
Lawrence Robinson	Wayland, Kentucky
Marvel Ross	Syracuse, New York
Alfredo Sanchez	Clayton, New Mexico
Joe Schneider	Los Angeles, California
Lamar Wilkinson	Provo, Utah
Clarence Warton	Laredo, Texas
Oliver Wetzel	Spencer, Iowa
Joseph Wengronowitz	Chicago, Illinois
James Teel	Texarkana, Texas
William King, Sr.	Red Bay, Alabama

Willis Vincent   Klamath Falls, Oregon
Philip Rohde   Hamden, Connecticut

   U.S. NAVY ENLISTED MEN
P/C John Walker   Vandergrift, Pennsylvania
LM 1/C William Thompson   Garott, Kansas
CBM Walter Kain   Baltimore, Maryland
C/R Ralph Ham   Zambales, Philippines
CTM Everett Dillard   Cavite, Philippines
F 1/C Ralph Taylor   LaFollette, Tennessee
GM 3/C George Tarkanish   Youngstown, Ohio
M/M 1/C Delbert Sparks   Louisville, Kentucky
C/QM Martin Seliga   Fitchburg, Massachusetts
F 2/C Melvin Moritz   Sedro-Wooley, Washington
CMM Robert Monrow   Monterey, California
CY Max McCoy   San Luis Obispo, California
WT 2/C Orvin Kringler   Westend, Iowa
Bernard Holen   none listed
CMM Fern Boaz   Glencoe, Kentucky
S 1/C Lynn Brotherson   none listed
F 2/C Joseph Burke   San Francisco, California
QM 1/C Clovis McAlpin   Gilmer, Texas
Charles Kelly   Camarines Sur, Philippines
Joseph Herron   Preston, Iowa
CMM Robert Pitchford   Long Beach, California
SK 1/C John Burtz   Farrell, Pennsylvania
F 2/C William Girard   Ashland Den, Kentucky
CM 1/C Clarence Hall   Grand Crossing, Florida
Pay Clerk Paul Jackson   Long Beach, California
B 2/C Paul Kelsey   Suffern, New York
CBM Thomas Kreiger   Spring City, Pennsylvania
CY James McCarthy   New York City
1/C PO J.E.A. Morin   Danvers, Massachusetts
CMM Ernest Rickett   Shanghai, China
CBM Harry Stefl   Pasay, Philippines
EM 2/C Virgil Wemmer   Salinas, California
CGM Harry Willis   Hamilton, Ohio

AC MM Carl Silverman   Wareham, Massachusetts
GM 1/C Thomas Slater   Philadelphia, Pennsylvania

U.S. MILITARY—RANK OR BRANCH NOT LISTED

Thomas Mason, Jr.   Elkland, Pennsylvania
Otis Bills   Phoenix, Arizona
John Cook, Jr.   San Marco, Texas
George Distel   Washington, D.C.
Kenneth Gorden   Merrifield, Minnesota
Albert Hayes   Lawrenceburg, New Mexico
Olin Johnson   Clovis, New Mexico
Alfred Jolley   Safian, California
Ira Jeffries   Marlington, West Virginia
Jearuld Drown   San Diego, California

U.S. CIVILIANS

Edward Normandy, Jr.   Manila
Osborne Jones   none listed
Hugh Keays   Cleveland Heights, Ohio
George Weedon   Elberton, Washington
Max Wait   North Little Rock, Arkansas
Theodore Rosenberg   Easton, Pennsylvania
Raymond Osborne   Dayton, Texas
Leonard Menges   Manila
Frank Ellsworth   Long Beach, California
William Fossoth   Pampanga, Philippines
Ray Fouts (or Fouth)   Manila
Hale Hutchins   Salt Lake City, Utah
Clyde Jenkins   Bellflower, California
Jesse Light   Manila
Worden Clark   Wisconsin
Vernon Booth   Manila
Mason Blair   Onawa, Iowa
Robert Bary   Orlando, Florida
Dean Albee   Eureka, Montana
Joseph Embree   Silver Springs, Missouri
J. W. Georgenton   Los Angeles, California
John Huntley   Manila (Hope, Arkansas)

Elmer McNeilly	West Orange, New Jersey
John Spradlin	Pasay, Rizal, Philippines
Christopher Sullivan	Manila
John Thompson	Long Beach, California
Dick Verkey	San Francisco, California
Carl Stoops	Manila

BRITISH MILITARY

Sgt. Robert Bell	Lancashire, England
Gnr. Stanley Dellar	Hitchchin Herts, England
Pvt. George Heeley	Birmingham, England
Cpl. Sidney Stevens	Lincolnshire, England
Gnr. Reginald Wyatt	Kent, England
Cpl. George Laytol	Cambridgeshire, England
Sglman. Thomas Potter	Lavenshire, England
Sglman. Walter Riley	none listed
PFC Dennis Keating	Essex, England
John Allan	London, England
Sgt. Lesley Palmer	Suffolk, England
L/Sgt. Herbert Markham	Nottingham, England
Driver George Barber	Nottingham, England
Pvt. John Cuncliffe	Manchester, Lanco, England
AC-1 David Hallan	Chesterfield, Derby, England
Gilbert Maker	Morden, Surrey, England
L/Cpl. J. C. Slaughter	Norfolk, England
Pvt. George Martin	Lancastershire
Sglman. Thomas Potter	Lancastershire
Sgt. George Shardlow	North Leicester, England

BRITISH CIVILIANS

Leslie McWilliams	Cheltenham, England

DUTCH MILITARY

Sgt. Dutch Klein	Buitenzorg, Java
Pvt. Gerard Van Diggelen	Malay, Java
Sgt. Casper Muelman	Utrecht, Holland

NORWEGIAN CIVILIANS

Bgorne Leira	Aalesund, Norway
Aksel Svendsen	Frederecksted, Norway

The following Filipino officers and men were awarded the Bronze Star "for heroic achievement on 30 January 1945" (USAFFE General Order 42 dated February 27, 1945, and General Orders 8 and 14 dated January 8, 1947).

CAPTAINS
Juan Pajota
Ruperto Villamin
Luis De La Cruz
Carlos Layug
Eduardo Joson

FIRST LIEUTENANTS
Francisco Manahan
Benedicto Trinidad
Carlos Tombo
Estanislao Abaga
Ceferino Sarmenta
Alejandro Medina
Amado Santiago
Marceliano Hidelgo
Florencio Bernardo, Jr.
Hermando Bernabe
Jose Hipolito
Cirilo Duatin
Artemio Espidol
Saturnino Coquia
Alfonso Manahan
Marcos Abad
Conrado Paulino
Arturo Fernando

FIRST SERGEANTS
Thomas Morales
Patero Viloria
Porfirio Calivoso
Federico Gamotea
Igmedio Albes
Carlos de Villa-Abrille

MASTER SERGEANTS
    Felino Paulino
    Crispulo San Jose
    Napoleon Villanueva

STAFF SERGEANTS
    Lif Rea
    Claro Mipalar

SECOND LIEUTENANTS
    Procopio Esquerra
    Candido Cruz
    Leonardo Juan
    Andres Frijinal
    Olympio Isidro
    Nicetas Arcinas
    Benigno Graneta
    Arsenio Padama
    Bernandico Tabifranca
    Benito Valdez
    Fidel Mendoza
    Sessinio Cabilin
    Anselmo San Pedro
    Katuiran Villaromas
    Julianto de Guzman
    Pedro Aisperna
    Bienvendo Erive
    Arturo Tolentino
    Manuel Bringas
    Clodualdo Bringas
    Toribio Paulino
    Florentino Eugenio
    Laureano Gadlamo

SERGEANTS
    Cenon Paconla
    Salvador Abello
    Simeon Cruz
    Pedro Delfin

Manuel Diola
Pedro Iglesia
Pedro Ignacio
Leandro Ignacio
Vicente Pascual
Benjamin Reyes
Jose Santiago
Anacleto Sawit
Lenocio Gutierrez
Eugenio Jengo, Jr.
Juan Calses
Casiano Eugenio
Leopoldo Melchor
Jose Torres
Felix Gamotea
Lorenzo Hipolito
Ciriaco Matias
Perigrino Capaycapay
Norberto Reyno
Mario Ordonez
Pedro Flores
Felix Quijada
Graciano Hipolito
Antonio Salamat
Julian Nicholas
Castro Villa
Pastor Guzalan
Simplicio Madrid
Fausto Palante
Alfredo Sagisag
Basilio Payawal
Cipriano Valeriano
Eliseo Bringas
Felipe Mingala
Florencio Laureano
Ramon Cruz
Teodore Guisico
Severino Sarmenta

Emelino Rimando
Ildefonso Andasan
Saturnino Sagun

TECHNICAL SERGEANTS
Asisclo Bonita
Salomon Cabrera

CORPORALS
Deogracias Palapal
Daniel Bautista
Benjamin Serizo
Romulo Antonio
Ceasar de la Cruz
Justo Dumdao
Guadencio Farin
Felemon Guiang
Ricardo de Leon
Salvador Malubag
Pedro Ocay
Pontaleon Rafael
Leonicio Rivera
Silverio Ruz

PRIVATES FIRST CLASS
Benito Galaranan
Glicerio Villanueva
Eusebio Andasan
Circilo Hulandan
Villal Feliciano
Agapito Gaverto
Mario Padilla
Juan Sana
Silvino Tapalis
Eugeniano Tolentino
Antonio Aldas
Samson Alvarado
Francisco Bello

Mauro Duatin
Francisco Dizon
Victorino Emeterio
Teofilo Sibayan
Hermos Marcos
Eustaquio Pineda
Bernardo Fabe
Pedro Castro
Gabriel Dans
Eugenio Omania
Pantaleon Sanhi
Julio Balangiut
Cipriano Bayro
Joaquin Viray
Andres Castillo
Cornelio Piad
Guillermo Rivera
Leonilo Aguirro
Modesto Obispo
Enrique Briones
Agapito San Pedro
Pedro Castro

PRIVATES

Gregorio Sarmiento
Pedro Buenaventura
Cesario Asuncion
Manuel Briones
Mamerto Carrillo
Albert Concepcion
Ambrosio Dizon
Dalmacio Duan
Enrique Gabriel
Teodore Grospe
Marcos Ignacio
Artemio de la Jose
Bernardo Masconiana
Martin de los Santos

Santiago Estaya
Jimmy Aniez
Eusabio Valdez
Vicente Arenas
Miguel Ramos
Victorino Galindo
Moises Corpuz
Remegio Estafanio
Marcelino Gatoc
Fernando Manalastas
Jacinto Principe
Marcelo Ramos
Bienvenido Rupac
Wenceslao Ramos
Marcelino Catipon
Simeon Domingo
Leo Robles
Ernesto Maderano
Dominador Barangan
Fortunate Dumayas
Andres Liwag
Domingo Valdez
Alejandrino Mendoza, Jr.
Jose Mendoza
Isidre Jose
Vicente Leogando
Magno Mactal
Delfin Pascual
Rafael Pablo
Jose Alejo
Gerardo Garcia
Tranquilino Corpuz
Domingo Esmundo
Tomas Bautista
Damian Domingo
Anacleto Mendoza
Rodolfo Quilit

Alfredo Quimuyog
Silverio Abad
Ignacio Abraham
Aurelio Agustin
Eugenio Almuete
Ceferino Aguilar
Moises Alenjandro
Simeon Ambos
Leonardo Angeles
Eufronio Aquino
Avelino Arrocena
Arcadio Asuncion
Andres Asuncion
Bienvenide Bautista
Tomas Barlis
Avelino Bondoc
Jose Bonilla
Lauro Bumanlag
Eusebio Cinio
Juanito de la Cruz
T. Constantino
Pamfilo Duque
Teodulo Corpuz
Deogracias Domingo
Mauro Domingo
Isidro Dorono
Florentino Dumaya
Pedro Elvinia
Bomifacio Eugenio
Napoleon Fausto
Fructuoso Federico
Gaudencio Fermin
Sixto Fernandez
Silvestre Galagar
Leonardo Galleta
Arcadio Garcia
Jesus Garcia

PRIVATES

Isidro Garcia
Moises Garcia
Victoriano Garcia
Alfonso Gabriel
Clemente Gregorio
Deferino Grospe
Felix Hizon
Juan Imperial
Lorenzo Ignacio
Diego Janitiano
Migel Jinitiano
Ricardo da Jose
Juan Lagasca
Luciano Lagasca
Eustaquio de Leon
Antonio Lina
Rufino Lina
Emeterio Labaupa
Marcos Lazatin
Fromencio Jomoc
Severino Magdangal
Delfin Macapagal
Benito Magno
Eulogio Manuel
Primitino Mauricio
Anastacio Mendoza
Jacinto Melegrito
Flaviano Mercado
Teodoro Molina
Jose Nepocina
Carlos Ninial
Camelo Olpindo
Antonio Pascual
Pablo Pastor
Dionisio Padaca
Serafin Pangalinan
Bartolome Quebuyen

Martin Quilon
Sotero Ramos
Norberto Realino
Arturo Sta. Reyes
Fabian Salazar
Monico Salmo
Aurelio Sarmiento
Eudon Seril
Heminiano Simplina
Jose Sumang
Anselmo Salvador
Pedro Palma
Segundo Fernando
Arcadio Dizon
Quirino Fernando
Jose Bautista
Francisco Fabres
Ricardo Florea
Sgnacio Taguding
Maximiano Reyes
Jose Cudal
Nestor Baysa
Silvino Galindo
Domingo Mariano
Catalino Arcangel
Jose Gamido
Celestino Espino
Daniel Costillo
Gabriel Disto
Benjamin Reyno
Emiliano Malilay
Venancio Malilay
Dominador Matadling
Leon Montemayor
Mariano Marcelo
Alberto Dandan
Feliciano Uminga
Faustino Alog

Remigio Salgado
Eduardo Salgado
Ireneo Latchica
Bonifacio Moreno
Riccardo Laperador
Bernardo Gabi
Jose Fajardo
Ireneo Ramos
Alejandro Ponce
Gregorio Ignacio
Mariano Lazo
Jose Balmonte
Ambrocio Rullian
Alejandro Gamboa
Guillermo Fajardo
Apolinario Perez
Martin Perez
Alberto Taroc
Paulinon Roxas
Maximino de Umania
Lorenzo Samson
Alfredo Santos
Bienvenido Tora
Apolinareo Trinidad
Benito Tumpalan
Aquiliano Vallarta
Ponciano Vilante
Rufino Viloria
Lauro Vigega
Lucio de la Vega
Mariano Velasco
Manuel Wong
Petronilo Abenoju
Reynaldo Agullar
Jorge Andasan
Ciralo Bala
Nicholas Bautista
Procopio Benitez

Marimo Cero
Jose de la Cruz
Francisco de la Cruz
Ernesto Domingo
Felomino Estipular
Virgilio Grass
Serafin de Guzman
Jacinto Lacuesta
Pedro Lieris
Oscar Maniacop
Rodolfo Mari
Bartolome Oanes
Leopoldo Odonio
Apolinario Perez
Eliseo Peralta
Aurelio Pungan
Arcadio Princesa
Jose Rafel
Anselmo Ramos
Domingo Ramos
Eugenio Reyes
Felix de la Rosa
Feliciano Sulayao
Rosendo Turay
Olympio Aliman
Corlito Fallerina
Francisco Gamboa
Gaudencio Nicolas
Norciso Patricio
Esteban Galleto
Agripino Nague
Sebastian Corpuz
Claudio Domingo
Jose Laquesta I
Jose Laquesta II
Cornelio Tolentino
Feliciano Ora
Feleciano Rexas

Alvaro Domingo
Pfo Palara
Honerio Domingo
Erobe Constancio
Jose Pascual
Francisco Sandino
Felipe Martin
Evaristo Diaz
Bienvenido Cayanga
Marcelino Mendoza
Catalino Aroja
Battolone de los Santos
Ruperto Mucal
Alejo Pagaling
Ernesto Ferrer
Ricardo Cristobal
Cornelio Mariano
Vincente Leogardo, Sr.
Domingo Mercado
Cornolio Diomania
Isidfo Jose
Wenceslao Rivera
Ambrocio Espino
Maximo Galisoje
Jose Lapina
Herminio Agustin
Alfredo Gadiano
Anastacio Mendez
Angel Vicotio
Arsenio Acosta
Valentin Magaway
Mecario Esguerra
Macario Rodriquez
Buenaventura Ventura

GLOSSARY

Bamboo telegraph A name given by the GIs to the communications system employed by Filipinos. Effected by "runners" spreading verbal news from one village to the next.

Banzai (literally 10,000 years) A shout used by Japanese to wish themselves or someone else good luck and long life. In World War II, usually associated with "banzai charge," because imperial troops used it as a war cry when entering battle.

BAR Browning Automatic Rifle. Used by the 6th Rangers instead of the machine gun because it can be carried and fired by one man.

Barrio A small community village.

Bazooka Officially "Launcher, Rocket, Shoulder Type," also called a "stove pipe." A 2.36-inch rocket launcher with a smoothbore steel tube about five feet long, open at both ends. The bazooka gained its name from its resemblance to the crude musical horn of the same name used by a radio comedian of the time, Mr. Bob Burns.

Bolo A narrow blade knife eighteen to twenty-four inches long with a handle made of wood or carabao horn. Used as both a tool and a weapon. Single edge with only a slight curve to the blade.

Buri hat A wide-brimmed round hat, handmade from straw.

Carabao Filipino name for a water buffalo, beast of burden used throughout Asia.

Carabao cart A small wooden two-wheeled cart pulled by a carabao.

Constabulary Similar to our "state police."

DWAKS A large amphibious tank commonly called "Ducks!"

Ganap Slang for the former "Sacdalista" headed by Benigno Ramos, who took refuge in Japan before the war but continued to send instructions for his followers to cooperate with the Japanese Imperial Army (collaborators).

Huks Hukbo Ng Boyan Labon Sa Hapon (Literally People's Army to Fight the Japanese). Also, Hukbalahap. Socialist-communist group lead by Luis Taruc from 1938 to about 1955. Today, known as the NPA (New Peoples Army).

Ilocano A "tribe" or group of people found mostly in the northwestern or central part of Luzon, the Philippines. The Ilocano language is different from Tagalog.

Kamikaze (literally "Divine Wind" or "Holy Wind") A name taken by the imperial air units whose pilots committed suicide by crashing their planes, loaded with explosives, into enemy targets.

Leyte A major island in the center of the Philippine islands.

Mabuhay A Filipino word meaning "long life." It is used as a greeting, goodbye, or a war cry.

Makapili (literally "For the Philippines") Slang for Filipinos who collaborated with the Japanese. The Makapili acted individually. The Ganaps were somewhat organized as a group.

Narra Wood from the narra tree, which is extremely hard. Often used in the Philippines for flooring, doors, and "wood carvings."

NCO Noncommissioned officer.

Nipa Grass and bamboo or bamboo strips handwoven together. A nipa hut, for example, would be a small house made from these materials.

Pajota's machine guns At the battle of Cabu bridge, Pajota's army had four .30-caliber water-cooled machine guns—two from the early days of the war, and two they captured during an engagement with Huks in December 1944.

PT boat Patrol torpedo boat. High-speed sixty- to one-hundred-foot boats usually equipped with torpedoes, machine guns, and depth charge explosives.

Small arms Hand-held firearms: rifles, pistols, carbines, and so forth.

Sucking chest wound   A wound in which the chest and lungs are punctured. The lungs continue to suck in air through the puncture wound.

Tagalog   One of over eighty-five Filipino languages. Now the "official" language of the Philippines. Also used to identify a group of people whose language is Tagalog. Before World War II, the Tagalogs were located mostly around the Manila Bay area of Luzon, the Philippines.

Tommygun   Thompson submachine gun, which fires a .45-caliber bullet. The military model is fed from a magazine-type clip rather than a drum.

USAFFE   United States Army Forces Far East. The combined American and Filipino army when the Filipinos were officially inducted into the U.S. Army in 1941, under the command of General MacArthur.

Very Pistol   (also Verey) A pistol used to fire a colored signal flare into the air.

BIBLIOGRAPHY

BOOKS

Abraham, Abie, *Ghost of Bataan Speaks*. New York: Vantage Press, 1971.

Agoncillo, Teodoro A., *The Fateful Years: Japan's Adventure in the Philippines*. Quezon City, the Philippines: Garcia, 1965.

Apple, Benjamin, *We Were There At The Battle of Bataan*. New York: Grosset & Dunlap, 1957.

Archer, Jules, *The Philippines Fight for Freedom*. London: Crowell-Collier-Macmillan Ltd., 1970.

Asprey, Robert B., *War in the Shadows*. New York: Doubleday & Co., 1975.

Belote, J. H., and W. N. Belote, *Corregidor: The Saga of a Fortress*. New York: Harper & Row, 1967.

Calvocoressi, Peter, and Guy Wint, *Total War*. New York: Pantheon Books, 1972.

Conroy, Robert, *The Battle of Bataan*. London: Macmillan, 1969.

Falk, Stanley, *Liberation of the Philippines*. New York: Ballantine Books, 1971.

Falk, Stanley, *Bataan, The March of Death*. New York: W. W. Norton, 1962.

Hartendorp, A. V. H., *The Japanese Occupation of the Philippines*. Manila: Bookmark, 1967.

Hartendorp, A. V. H., *The Santo Tomas Story*. New York: McGraw-Hill, 1964.

Hersey, John, *Men on Bataan*. New York: Alfred A. Knopf, 1942.

Ind, Lt. Col. Allison, *Bataan, The Judgement Seat*. New York: Macmillan, 1944.

Keats, John, *They Fought Alone*. New York: J. B. Lippincott, 1963.

Keith, Billy, *Days of Anguish, Days of Hope*. New York: Doubleday, 1972.

Krueger, General Walter, *From Down Under to Nippon*. Washington, D.C.: Combat Forces Press, 1953.

MacArthur, General Douglas, *Reminiscences*. New York: McGraw-Hill, 1946.

Mellnik, General Steve, *Philippine Diary, 1939–1945*. New York: Van Nostrand-Reinhold, 1969.

Morton, Louis, *The Fall of the Philippines*. Washington, D.C.: U.S. Government Printing Office, 1953.

Poweleit, Major Alvin C., M.D., *U.S.A.F.F.E.* 1975.

Redmond, Juanita, *I Served on Bataan*. Philadelphia: J. B. Lippincott, 1943.

Reyes, Pedrito, and Grau-Santamaria Mercedes, *Pictorial History of the Philippines*. Quezon City: Capitol Publishing House, 1953.

Romulo, Colonel Carlos P., *I Saw the Fall of the Philippines*. New York: Doubleday-Daron, 1943.

Rutherford, Ward, *Fall of the Philippines*. Washington, D.C.: U.S. Government Printing Office, 1963.

Smith, Robert Ross, *Triumph in the Philippines*. Washington, D.C.: U.S. Government Printing Office, 1963.

Stewart, Sidney, *Give Us This Day*. New York: W. W. Norton, 1957.

Taruc, Luis, *He Who Rides the Tiger*. New York: Fredrick A. Praeger, 1967.

Toland, John, *But Not in Shame*. New York: Random House, 1961.

Volckmann, Colonel R. W., *We Remained*. New York: W. W. Norton, 1954.

Wainwright, General Jonathan M., *General Wainwright's Story*. New York: Doubleday, 1946.

Watari, Gasei, *Philippine Expeditionary Force*. Japan: Group Information Dept., 1943.

Weinstein, Alfred A., *Barbed-Wire-Surgeon*. New York: Macmillan, 1961.

White, W. L., *They Were Expendable*. New York: Harcourt, Brace and World, 1942.

MANUSCRIPTS, DOCUMENTS, OFFICIAL PAPERS,
AND MILITARY STUDIES

Hockstrasser, Lt. Lewis B., *They Were First—The True Story of the Alamo Scouts,* 1944.

"Exposure Under Fire—An Official History of Signal Corps Photography in the Luzon Operations," prepared by U.S. Army Signal Corps, Southwest Pacific Area, 1945.

"Narrative History, 547th Night Fighter Squadron," Albert F. Simpson Historical Research Center, USAF. Maxwell AFB, Alabama, USA.

"Ranger in Review," Luzon, the Philippines: Sixth U.S. Army, 1945.

"War History #6," Defense Training Institute, The Japanese Defense Agency, War History Dept., Tokyo, Japan.

"Guide to Japanese Monographs," Office of the Chief of Military History, Dept. of U.S. Army, Washington, D.C., 1945–60.

"Japanese Monograph #2—Philippine 1941–42 Operations Record, Phase 1," Office of the Chief of Military History, Dept. of U.S. Army, Washington, D.C.

"Japanese Studies in World War II, 14th Army Operations," Office of the Chief of Military History, Dept. of U.S. Army, Washington, D.C.

"Ranger Mission at the Pangatian Prison Camp," Headquarters, 6th Ranger Infantry Battalion, AGO File. U.S. Government Archives, Washington, D.C., 1945.

"The 6th Rangers—Narrative of the 6th Ranger Battalion from January 2, 1945, to July 1, 1945," U.S. Government Archives, Washington, D.C.

"The 6th U.S. Army Report of the Luzon Campaign, January 9, 1945–June 30, 1945," U.S. Government Archives, Washington, D.C.

Wainwright, General Jonathan M., "Report of Operations, U.S. Army Forces, Far East and U.S. Forces in the Philippines; 1941–1942," U.S. Government Archives, Washington, D.C., August 10, 1946.

Pajota, Major Juan, *We Kept the Torch Burning,* 1977.

SELECTED ARTICLES

Bersola, Colonel Pedro C., "We Witnessed General King's Surrender," *Philippine Free Press,* April 1972.

Hibbs, Ralph E., M.D., "Beriberi in Japanese Prison Camps," *Annals of Internal Medicine,* August 1946.

Mucci, Henry A., Lt. Col., "Rescue at Cabanatuan," *Infantry Journal,* April 1945.

Mucci, Henry A., Lt. Col., "We Swore We'd Die or Do It!" *The Saturday Evening Post,* April 1945.

Mydans, Carl, "The Rescue at Cabanatuan," *Life,* February 26, 1945.

St. George, Ozzie, Sgt., "Three Years on Luzon," *Yank,* March 1945.

Stroupe, Ray M., Captain, "Rescue by the Rangers," *Military Review,* December 1945.

GOVERNMENTAL AND PRIVATE AGENCIES THAT CONTRIBUTED

Office of the Chief of Military History, Department of the Army, Washington, D.C.

Office of the Chief of Military History, Department of National Defense, Quezon City, Philippines.

The Defense Agency, War History Department, Tokyo, Japan.

Department of the Navy, Headquarters, U.S. Marine Corps, History and Museum Division, Washington, D.C.

Department of the U.S. Air Force, Office of Information, Washington, D.C.

Department of the U.S. Navy, Photographic Center, Washington, D.C.

National Archives and Records Service, General Archives Division, G.S.A., Washington, D.C.

National Archives and Records Service, Modern Military Branch, Military Archives Division, G.S.A., Washington, D.C.

Department of the U.S. Army, Army Audio-Visual Agency, Washington, D.C.

Department of the U.S. Army, Military History Research Collection, Carlisle Barracks, Pa.

United States Coast Guard, Department of Transportation, Public Affairs Division, Washington, D.C.

Albert F. Simpson Historical Research Center, U.S. Air Force, Maxwell Air Force Base, Ala.

Philippine Consulate General's Office, Chicago, Ill.

British Consulate General's Office, Chicago, Ill.

Royal Norwegian Consulate General's Office, Chicago, Ill.

Consulate General's Office of Japan, Chicago, Ill.

Philippine Department of Public Information, Quezon City, Manila, the Philippines.

Department of the U.S. Army, Office of the Adjutant General, Reserve Components Personnel and Administration Center, St. Louis, Mo.

Department of the U.S. Air Force, Chief Depository Service Section, 1361
Photo Sq. Aerospace Audio-Visual Service (MAC), Arlington, Va.

American Aviation Historical Society, Warren E. Thompson, German-
town, Tenn.

P.T. Boats Inc.—P.T. Boat All-Hands Museum and Library "Boats" New-
berry, Memphis, Tenn.

General Douglas MacArthur Memorial Library and Archives, Norfolk, Va.

Chieko Johnson

ABOUT THE AUTHOR

Forrest Bryant Johnson, born in Louisville, Kentucky, graduated from the University of Louisville. He served nine years with the U.S. Army, rising from the rank of private to captain. The author is a former executive for a division of Mobil Corporation who has lived in the Chicago area for fifteen years and now resides in Nevada. More than six years was devoted to research for the Cabanatuan story. Mr. Johnson is also the author of *Basenji-Dog from the Past, The Strange Case of Big Harry,* and *Tektite.*